MODERN PIRACY

Selected Titles in ABC-CLIO's
**CONTEMPORARY
WORLD ISSUES**
Series

For a complete list of titles in this series, please visit
www.abc-clio.com.

Books in the Contemporary World Issues series address vital issues in today's society, such as genetic engineering, pollution, and biodiversity. Written by professional writers, scholars, and nonacademic experts, these books are authoritative, clearly written, up-to-date, and objective. They provide a good starting point for research by high school and college students, scholars, and general readers as well as by legislators, businesspeople, activists, and others.

Each book, carefully organized and easy to use, contains an overview of the subject, a detailed chronology, biographical sketches, facts and data and/or documents and other primary-source material, a directory of organizations and agencies, annotated lists of print and nonprint resources, and an index.

Readers of books in the Contemporary World Issues series will find the information they need to have a better understanding of the social, political, environmental, and economic issues facing the world today.

MODERN PIRACY

A Reference Handbook

David F. Marley

CONTEMPORARY WORLD ISSUES

ABC-CLIO

Santa Barbara, California • Denver, Colorado • Oxford, England

Copyright 2011 by ABC-CLIO, LLC

Library of Congress Cataloging-in-Publication Data

Marley, David, 1950–
  Modern piracy : a reference handbook / David F. Marley.
    p. cm. — (Contemporary world issues)
  Includes bibliographical references and index.
  ISBN 978–1–59884–433–7 (hard copy : alk. paper) — ISBN 978–1–59884–434–4 (ebook)
1. Piracy—History—21st century. 2. Terrorism—History—21st century. I. Title.
G535.M327   2011
364.16′4—dc22   2010027190

ISBN: 978–1–59884–433–7
EISBN: 978–1–59884–434–4

15 14 13 12 11   1 2 3 4 5

This book is also available on the World Wide Web as an eBook.
Visit www.abc-clio.com for details.

ABC-CLIO, LLC
130 Cremona Drive, P.O. Box 1911
Santa Barbara, California 93116-1911

This book is printed on acid-free paper (∞)

Manufactured in the United States of America

To the memory of another dear departed friend,
Adolfo Langenscheidt Field,
lost too soon.

Contents

Preface

Who are the real pirates? It's not these young boys on the boats.
It's the people behind them, with the money to buy the boats, and
the motors and the guns and the GPS devices.

—Andrew Mwangura, Secretary-General of the East African
Seafarers Association in Mombasa, Kenya, May 2009

Lit only by a blazing sunrise in early May 2009, nine poor young
men—each armed with a Kalashnikov rifle and a grenade—got into
a bare, wooden boat and pushed out into the Gulf of Aden from a
shabby village near Bosaso, the largest city and seaport in the
Puntland region of Somalia. Some time previously, they had been
contacted by a fellow Somali living abroad, who had provided
money for this primitive expedition. Over the next couple of days,
the youthful and inexperienced gunmen would wend their way
250 miles westward, hugging the coastline, before veering north
into the busy sea-lanes which funnel an unending stream of
merchantmen into the Red Sea. Amid gigantic supertankers and
container ships, these modern-day pirates had come to hunt a prize.

It seems impossible to believe that in our twenty-first-century
world of ultramodern vessels gliding peacefully across the oceans,
guided by satellite imagery and steered by such sophisticated com-
puterized systems that only a handful of crewmen are required to
work even the largest ships, that such a throwback to earlier times
could somehow reemerge. Piracy had all but vanished from the
Seven Seas, a historical anachronism remembered mostly in
movies or novels, before inexplicably thrusting itself back into the
world's headlines in our present day, as boatloads of rovers began
reappearing like phantoms, making high-profile seizures and
wresting multimillion dollar ransoms from global corporations.

Our particular band of would-be pirates was intercepted at sea by a patrol boat from neighboring Somaliland, one of the new republics formed from the disintegration of greater Somalia, which clubbed these nine novices into submission and carried them into the port of Berbera to stand trial for piracy. A terse verdict was quickly returned by May 10, 2009, all nine being sentenced to 20 years imprisonment—yet hundreds more still remained prowling the nearby waves, with thousands more willing to take their place, despite all the perils of venturing out to sea off the sun-baked Horn of Africa (Baldauf).

This book constitutes a description of the surprising resurgence of modern piracy, preceded by some explanation of various historical factors which have helped to pave the way for its return. Early-eighteenth-century cutthroats such as Blackbeard and Captain Kidd are fleetingly mentioned, while late-twentieth century trouble-spots such as the South China Sea and Nigerian waters are discussed at greater length—but the most comprehensive analysis is saved for the two most pirate-plagued passageways of the twenty-first century: The Strait of Malacca and Horn of Africa. Both are transited today by the largest volumes of commercial traffic in mankind's recorded history, attracting criminal elements from near and far.

And although the main focus of this book is the current state of piracy, specifically between the victory achieved over Southeast Asian rovers in 2005–2006 and the recent boom in Somali ransom seekers, its broader scope departs from the end of World War II. Chapter 1 opens with an account of the startling capture of the Saudi supertanker *Sirius Star* in 2008, so revealing as to the vulnerable state of modern commercial-shipping that a huge, $350 million behemoth could fall easy prey to eight teenage gunmen in a pair of tiny boats. After a brief "Historical Perspective" recalling highlights from the by-gone Golden Age of Piracy, a detailed recitation follows of seven modern trends which have contributed toward transforming all the world's shipping-industries since 1945 into a highly profitable, yet perplexingly-intertwined global enterprise, strong yet surprisingly exposed to insignificant predators.

Chapter 2 reviews the "Problems, Controversies, and Solutions" associated with modern piracy, opening with two additional factors which are required for any repeat piratical forays: chokepoint hunting-grounds—for easily locating victims—plus land sanctuaries to plunder or exploit any prizes at leisure. This section is followed by detailed accounts of events defining piracy's "Four Recent Hot Spots" between the 1990s to 2005: the South China Sea, Nigeria, Strait of Malacca, and Horn of Africa. Each suffered from a different set of circumstances, though, affecting attempted solutions in each. "Controversies" include strategic differences between U.S. and allied policies; doubts occasioned by underreporting of pirate attacks by the shipping industry, out of concern of exacerbating their insurance-premiums; a nagging international indecisiveness about where and how to hold piracy trials; etc. "Solutions" begin with a description of the remarkably swift elimination of piracy in the Strait of Malacca, principally motivated by a sudden spike in regional insurance premiums during the summer of 2005. Lessons learned are bundled together into the "Six Basic Elements for Success" against modern piracy, a list of general requirements for dealing with this issue.

Chapter 3 offers the "U.S. Perspective" on the global fight against piracy, especially in its present-day incarnation off Somalia. The prior commitment of U.S. forces—as well as some auxiliary allied squadrons—into this region as part of the post-9/11 offensive against terror and invasion of Iraq in early 2003, are described under "U.S. Naval Focus," which clearly established a distinct American agenda before the unexpected surge of piracy off Somalia. A detailed account is provided of the evolution of determined new raiding-tactics out of this sole remaining hot-spot, the last piratical holdouts remaining in the world today, whose lawless strongholds will prove stubbornly hard to stamp out. The number of such seizures escalated so rapidly as of 2007, that it prompted a split away from America's anti-extremist strategy in favor of a new round of "NATO, EU, and UN Commitments" by nations more deeply concerned about this threat to their commercial lifelines. Both the U.S. Navy and Washington were relieved to relinquish the lead in this new struggle. The extremely rare case of the assault on the American-flagged container ship *Maersk Alabama* in April 2009 is studied in considerable detail, before this chapter concludes with a summary of the latest solutions being attempted off Somalia by U.S. and allied forces.

Chapter 4 provides a "Chronology" of events as general background to the rebirth of piracy, starting with the adoption of the United Nations "Convention on the Law of the Sea" in December 1982. Chapter 5 offers "Biographical Sketches" of major and minor participants, some of the latter chosen for their particular insight into this issue, such as teenage gunmen interviewed in port or in captivity. Chapter 6 includes a variety of tables under "Data," the first few describing the radical changes in world shipping since World War II, the latter summarizing the best statistical evidence available from the International Maritime Bureau's Piracy Reporting Center in Kuala Lumpur, on recent pirate attacks—although true figures are difficult to determine, and may actually be considerably higher. The "Documents" section reproduces only official documents related to piracy, rather than sensationalized media reports, so as to offer a more sober perspective on the complications and expenses entailed in any large-scale antipiracy campaigns.

Chapter 7 contains descriptive listings of numerous "Organizations" involved in current anti-piracy efforts, such as "Naval Forces," "Regional Coordinating Hubs," "International Monitoring Agencies," and so on. Chapter 8 provides a select bibliographic listing of some of the "Resources" consulted or quoted in this book, while the brief Glossary explains the many acronyms and colorful terms associated with modern piracy. Hopefully, this entire work shall prove useful to students interested in such a volatile and constantly shifting topic.

David F. Marley
April 2010
Windsor, Ontario, Canada

1

Background and History

There came into Calais five ships from New England full of stores of masts, oak, timber and plank for that King's service. I hope it will be enquired into, and wicked men punished.

—the merchant sailor William Cowes, December 1718

Textbook Case: Piratical Seizure of a Supertanker (2008)

Early on a beautiful Saturday morning, November 15, 2008, the brand-new supertanker *Sirius Star* was running along easily, 520 miles southeast of the Kenyan coast. Launched only that previous March from the Daewoo shipyards at Okpo, South Korea, this double-hulled behemoth measured 1,080 feet in length, was almost 200 feet wide, and weighed 162,250 tons when empty—but was furthermore carrying almost a full cargo of 300,000 additional tons of Saudi Arabian crude oil destined for the U.S. market, valued at $100 million. *Sirius Star*'s route had been prudently planned so as to avoid the troubled waters off the Horn of Africa, instead circling wide out to sea to head directly down around South Africa's Cape of Good Hope, and eventually deliver its consignment into the Caribbean. Despite the vessel's colossal size, its sophisticated automation and computerized systems allowed it to be sailed by only a tiny crew of six officers of diverse nationalities, plus 19 Filipino deckhands. Satellite communications provided instant access to the latest navigational and weather updates, as well as maintaining contact with the owners and other authorities on land.

Yet in the growing light of that sunny Saturday morning, two tiny dots could be seen closing in from astern. Sensing danger, *Sirius Star*'s Polish Captain Marek Niski called for more speed and ordered his deckhands to break out the fire hoses, so as to contest any possible boarding attempt. Yet the ponderous supertanker could not accelerate fast enough before two crude fiberglass speedboats caught up, bearing a total of eight men armed with AK-47 assault rifles and rocket-propelled grenade launchers. They fired a few rounds into the air, and rather than mount a futile and possibly bloody resistance, Niski instructed his deckhands to retire below to safety, allowing the pursuers to toss a homemade rope ladder with a grappling hook over the stern guardrail. The heavy-ladened tanker's freeboard rode only 12 feet above the waves along this section of hull, so that the pirates were able to clamber across this churning gap, and gain its deck by 8:55 a.m.

They seemed like apparitions from a bygone age. Lanky and gaunt, these teenage gunmen wore a motley array of "trousers and cheap shirts and sandals," according to one eyewitness, "while others were barefoot in sarongs" (Jamieson). The first thing that they demanded in broken English, were shoes for walking on the tanker's steel decks, as well as cigarettes, before proceeding up the several decks to secure the bridge some seven minutes later.

After bringing *Sirius Star* to a complete halt, the pirates had both their speedboats hoisted inboard, then veered around to rejoin their "mother ship"—a slightly larger vessel waiting over the horizon, manned by 10 more colleagues—by 3:00 p.m. that same Saturday afternoon. The reunited pirate band then pillaged the huge supertanker of small items while steaming toward the Somali coast, where they would be reinforced two days later near shore by 25 more armed pirates. The prize was eventually ordered to drop anchor a few miles offshore, inside El Gaan anchorage, the seaport for Harardheere (a shabby, sun-baked town some 12 miles inland from the ocean, also variously spelled as Harardera, Xarardheere, etc.). The captive tanker crew noticed how all the pirates frequently chewed on bright-green leaves of the addictive plant *khat*, growing agitated whenever their supply ran low, and would also have goats brought from shore to be slaughtered on deck for their meals (Cramb, Jamieson).

Yet these teenage gunmen were merely frontmen for a much larger, shadowy organization with enough resources to relieve these guards on a regular basis, ample supplies to endure a long wait, plus familiarity with international affairs. By Tuesday, November 18, 2008, this mysterious group's backers had made their first contact with the supertanker's worried proprietors— Vela International Marine, a subsidiary based in the United Arab Emirates of the Saudi Arabian state oil company Aramco—to demand a hefty ransom for the ship's release. Next day, an alleged pirate leader named Farah Abd Jameh even provided an audio tape to Al-Jazeera network, declaring that this cash was to be delivered aboard *Sirius Star* itself, where it could be counted by machines capable of detecting any counterfeits. And the pirates remained so cooly confident of their invulnerability to arrest, either by local authorities or from any sudden strike by foreign navies, that still another spokesman—Mohamed Said—boldly announced during an Agence France-Presse interview on November 20, 2008, that a ransom of $25 million had been demanded, adding:

> We do not want long-term discussions to resolve the matter. The Saudis have ten days to comply, otherwise we will take action that could be disastrous. (Leach)

Within Somalia itself, the beleaguered Transitional Federal Government was powerless to intervene, controlling a mere strip of the national capital Mogadishu.

Only the militant fundamentalist Islamic movement known as Al-Shabaab or "The Youth," headquartered yet farther to the south, spoke out publicly against this seizure—piracy having long been declared *haram* or "religiously forbidden" according to Islamic teachings, most especially of a coreligionist vessel. "Saudi is a Muslim country, and it is a very big crime to hold Muslim property," an Al-Shabaab commander named Sheik Abdullahi Osman told the Bloomberg News Service in a telephone interview from Harardheere:

> I warned again and again, those who hold the ship must free it unconditionally, or armed conflict should be the solution. If they don't free the ship, we will rescue it by force. (Karon)

Yet despite allegedly sending five armored vehicles loaded with fighters into Harardheere, the militants could effect nothing more.

Abroad, Western observers were both surprised by this sudden extension of Somalia's piratical forays—having successfully struck so far away from their coast—as well as concerned by the lucrative prize which had been deliberately targeted. "It does suggest that they are increasing their capacity to stay out at sea for a much longer period of time," commented Cyrus Mody, a manager at the International Maritime Bureau's global piracy-monitoring agency. "They can just sit and wait until a vessel comes along" (Wadhams). Only a few days earlier, a force of British Royal Marines had stormed a captive Yemeni-flagged fishing dhow much nearer to Somalia, which another group of pirates had been using as their covert "mother-ship" in an unsuccessful bid to attack a passing Danish container ship. Eight of these pirates had been arrested and turned over to the authorities in neighboring Kenya to stand trial, yet—despite this naval success—other bands were evidently becoming capable of venturing ever farther out from Somalia, exponentially increasing the expanse of Indian Ocean, which would have to be patrolled by a relatively few American and allied warships.

"Our presence in the region is helping deter and disrupt criminal attacks off the Somali coast," noted Vice Admiral William E. Gortney, commander of the U.S. Fifth Fleet and the Combined Maritime Forces from various allied nations, "but the situation with the *Sirius Star* clearly indicates the pirates' ability to adapt their tactics and methods of attack" (ibid.). The American Admiral wished for greater cooperation from international shipping-firms in adopting more self-defense measures, but who because of their huge volumes of global merchant traffic, remained seemingly unfazed by the insignificant losses due to isolated pirate attacks thus far—a complacency which Gortney felt would encourage better-organized Somali syndicates to begin hunting more lucrative tankers and larger cargo-vessels, in hopes of bagging even heftier ransoms. Other commentators lamented the restrictive "rules of engagement" imposed on patrolling warships, as well as the legal indecision prevailing among diverse Western governments, who often differed as to exactly how to dispose of any captive pirates.

Unwilling to countenance a rescue-attempt so close to the Somali mainland, it would take more than five weeks of clandestine negotiations between the Saudis and *Sirius Star*'s pirate captors, before a bargain was finally struck to ransom the supertanker, and details for actual delivery of this payment could be worked out. At 6:30 a.m. on January 9, 2009, its captive crew were paraded on deck, for a small twin-engine plane to fly overhead an hour-and-a-half later, verifying that all were unharmed. Half the estimated $3 million ransom was then dropped by parachute into the adjacent waters, for the pirates to retrieve. The second half of this total amount was subsequently dropped when the plane returned at 2:10 p.m. that same afternoon, so that after one last round of thefts throughout the tanker, 17 pirates quit the vessel by 4:30 p.m.—although one of their boats capsized near shore and five of them drowned. (The body of one pirate was said to have washed ashore later, reputedly still with $153,000 in cash in a plastic bag.) The remaining eighteen captors finally quit *Sirius Star* at 5:34 a.m. next morning, at which point the relieved crew quickly got up steam and hurried out to sea an hour later, speeding away toward Fujairah in the United Arab Emirates to recuperate from their 57-day ordeal.

Historical Perspective

The motivation and tactics of this ragtag band of Somali marauders were little changed from those of their piratical forebearers, who had roamed the high seas centuries earlier. Ignoring all peacetime conventions or accepted custom, they had attacked a vulnerable civilian vessel in international waters for personal gain, with minimal risk of meeting any serious opposition. Their crude vessels and weaponry—30-foot fiberglass speedboats and handheld light arms, insignificant when arrayed against those of even a tiny modern warship—had nonetheless been handled with sufficient menace to surprise and intimidate the unarmed tanker crew, after which eagerness for booty had galvanized the gunmen into clambering across the dangerous gap to board this huge ship while it was still moving rapidly across the ocean swells. The captors had then retreated to an unpoliced safe haven near shore, where pliant local officials had allowed their covert backers to extort as much profit as possible from their high-value prize, before all melted back into civilian life. Such a brazen high-seas seizure and its subsequent exploitation would have seemed quite familiar to the likes of Captain Kidd or Blackbeard.

Yet for all the familiarity of such actions, the modern world into which these rovers had intruded was supposedly far different from that long-lost era. Twenty-first century maritime traffic is much more highly evolved—technologically sophisticated, globally monitored, to say nothing of vastly larger in volume and scope than ever before in human history—all factors which would seem to have relegated piracy to a historical anachronism. And indeed, criminality on the high seas had in fact been declining steadily, almost to the vanishing point during this past century, except for a few isolated pockets of sporadic violence.

Cradle of Piracy: The Caribbean (1500–1650)

What is today remembered as the "Golden Age of Piracy" of the late seventeenth and early eighteenth centuries, had like today's personfication, also grown out of a period of great maritime expansion. Spain's desire to monopolize its chance discovery of the Americas, had soon been contested by other West European seafarers trailing across the Atlantic in the Spaniards' wake. The desire by these latecomers to at least be allowed to tap some exotic New World produce, which commanded fantastic prices back in Europe, had been denied by the Spanish authorities, who steadfastly refused to grant any licenses to foreigners and regarded any such unauthorized visitors as lawless poachers, subject to dire punishments.

But the vastness of the West Indies and its sparse Spanish population had provided many open anchorages to receive such interlopers, who were furthermore often discreetly welcomed by local residents, starved for European imports. Temporary shore camps therefore began to spring up, usually occupied for only a season or two by crews from resting ships or squadrons—although as such repeat visits multiplied, more permanent bases came to be created along remote stretches of coastline, where commercially minded traders then began to barter for native goods, and even harvest their own cash crops, such as tobacco or sugar.

As the volume of this unauthorized traffic to the New World boomed, Madrid could only dispute such trespassing with occasional naval sweeps, so that these foreign settlements grew in number, spread inland, and became more firmly entrenched. Official hostility against their very presence hardened into Spanish Crown policy, yet the waning economic and military power of Spain meant that its leaders could no longer successfully contest such violations. By the mid-seventeenth century, most private West Indian settlements could resist the enfeebled Spanish assaults, and colonists routinely retaliated with local counteroffensives of their own.

Rise and Fall of the "Golden Age" (1650–1720)

The best means available to such pioneer settlers to combat Spanish-American rivals was the ancient European expedient of commissioning private vessels to act as unpaid privateers, their crews reinforced from mixed groups of local mercenaries—unemployed Dutch, English, or French men-at-arms, runaway slaves, sometimes even a few Spaniards—who were willing to serve for booty alone, under almost any flag. The prizes which these rovers brought back into port furthermore provided a welcome boon to the economies of these fledgling outposts.

During the second half of the seventeenth century, such freebooters grew so powerful and bold that even well after any European-sanctioned hostilities had ceased, they continued to gather at remote tropical anchorages and launch their own renegade raids. Exhausting most rich targets in the Caribbean within the next few decades, they eventually struck across the Isthmus of Panama during the 1680s to prey upon hapless Spaniards in the Pacific. When King William's War ensued from 1689 to 1697, some ventured even further, sliding across the Atlantic to then prowl down beyond the slave stations of West Africa, rounding the Cape of Good Hope to Madagascar, then on to terrorize neutral merchant shipping in the Red Sea and off the coasts of India.

This lawless privateer heyday was at last checked during the early eighteenth century, when the gradual emergence of plantation-based economies throughout the West Indies—vast Crown-backed enterprises, on whose transatlantic exports many home countries would increasingly come to depend—required stable maritime traffic in order to continue flourishing, undisturbed by any renegade elements. Huge sums were already being invested into transporting such produce to market, as well as importing ever more slaves to plant and harvest new crops, all of which required safe sea lanes and no unauthorized hostilities. Random depredations by rogue Captains had therefore become unwelcome, as they created needless losses and uncertainty. Privateers were furthermore no longer necessary to help defend Caribbean colonies against foreign attacks during wartime, having been supplanted by permanent colonial squadrons and fortified royal garrisons throughout the islands.

As a result, those die-hard renegades who refused to give up roving once general peace was restored in 1713, soon became outlawed as pirates and were hunted down by the Royal Navy or licensed bounty-hunters. And unlike previous such crackdowns, the broadening Crown rule overseas meant that freebooters now found fewer and fewer sanctuaries open to them to lay low for a spell, or foreign flags under which they might serve. English courts had long since dismissed all such fugitive felons as *hostis humani generis*—"enemies of all mankind"—thus unprotected as the King's subjects, and so liable to summary execution by any nation which chanced to apprehend them upon the high seas (*The King v. Marsh*, 81 Eng. Rep. 23, 23, K.B. 1615). Even the fearsome and brutish Blackbeard, who at the peak of his powers in 1717 had commanded a flotilla of several hundred cutthroats, was reduced within a year to slipping into North Carolina's ramshackle frontier capital of Bath—under cover of darkness, accompanied by only 20 followers—to buy a pardon from its obliging Governor Charles Eden, and vainly try to blend back into civilian life.

Recent Development (1945–Present)

Two-and-a-quarter centuries later, the conclusion to World War II would usher in yet another era of unprecedented maritime expansion. The enormous losses inflicted on global merchant-fleets by six years of unrestricted naval warfare would be followed by a period of massive reconstruction and incredible expansion, during which traffic volumes rebounded on a much vaster scale than ever before dreamed of—with new generations of huge vessels steaming the oceans, ultra-efficient cargo-handling capacities emptying and reloading them with relentless speed in purpose-designed seaports, and other refinements which were to exponentially augment and streamline the global transportation of goods and produce.

Modern Trends Contributing toward a Rebirth of Piracy

Yet ironically, several of these very innovations that were to so significantly improve human commerce, also unwittingly led to an unexpected resurgence of criminality at sea. And while certain steps in this evolutionary process might have been better directed, most simply lay beyond the control of either the developers themselves, or any leading world governments. The seven recent trends that have jointly abetted a revival of piracy today, are:

1. the virtual disappearance of the United States and Western merchant fleets;
2. the launching of much larger ships, to be manned by much smaller crews;
3. the expansion of many national jurisdictions into adjacent territorial waters;
4. a continuing irresolution over pirate trials under international law;
5. a shift of large-scale commercial traffic into Asian waters;
6. the widespread resort to "flags of convenience" by global shipping firms;
7. and the proliferation of potent military light arms in civilian hands.

The end result of this evolution would be much larger and wealthier vessels, yet thinly manned with mixed foreign crews, moving steadily under a variety of flags through ever more crowded chokepoints, temptingly exposed to capture by a few heavily armed teenage gunmen from among the poorest peoples on Earth. The numbers of such felons, whom by chance, are caught by overstretched naval patrols, are too few to deter imitators, and must furthermore be passed along for prosecution elsewhere.

The seizure of the *Sirius Star*, described at the beginning of this chapter, is an example of the thicket of legal complications which can accompany any such incident, even involving only a single vessel: for it was a supertanker flying a Liberian flag, registered as operated by a company based in the United Arab Emirates, yet actually owned (along with its cargo) by a Saudi corporation. *Sirius Star*'s Captain and one officer were Polish, two others British— both of these being member nations of the European Union—while the remaining pair of officers were a Croat and a Saudi, plus 19 deckhands from the Phillipines. After its capture by a handful of pirates, this huge prize had then been sailed through Kenyan waters to a lawless stretch of Somali coastline, well beyond the jurisdiction of its hapless national government beleaguered in Mogadishu—yet who would nonetheless have to give at least nominal authorization for any foreign naval pursuit or intervention close to shore. Finally, its ransom had been negotiated through middlemen suspected of criminal ties extending as far throughout the Middle East as Cairo and Beirut.

Decline of the U.S. Merchant Marine

International maritime commerce had been far different when World War II had erupted back in September 1939, most of the then-small oceangoing freighter fleets—almost 30 percent—being owned by either Great Britain or one of its imperial partners, such as Canada or Australia, and plied largely in Atlantic waters. The United States had owned slightly less than half this total amount, yet a combination of enormous American wartime output and its relative safety from the catastrophic losses endured by other nations more directly embroiled in the six years of fighting, meant that the United States would emerge as the leading merchant-shipping power once peace was restored in August 1945.

When movement back toward a peacetime footing resumed, Washington wished to shed the expense of so many extra vessels that it had acquired as part of its war effort. Further spurred by a sincere desire to assist the recovery of war-ravaged economies all around the globe, the U.S. government generously offered to make such surplus vessels available on very easy terms to American and allied citizens alike, through the Merchant Ship Sales Act of March 1946 (Marx). This proved to be a very successful plan, as many as 5,000 vessels of all types eventually being disposed of— Liberty and Victory cargo ships, tankers, coastal or other specialized vessels, even passenger liners—whose acquisition laid the foundation for a notable revival and explosive growth in many other countries' merchant fleets (Greenman).

Already by the end of 1948, the U.S. Maritime Commission had disposed of more than 2,000 surplus ships, and placed many of the rest into the National Defense Reserve Fleet against future need. Although American merchant-fleet records for that year would still list 3,644 ships as remaining active, this number would continue to plummet as owners also increasingly turned to the expedient of "re-flagging" their freighters to other countries as a means of achieving significant tax-breaks, freedom to employ less costly non-unionized foreign crewmen, plus less restrictive operational regulations. Between 1946 and 1950 alone, about one million tons of American shipping were transferred to foreign flags, and the number of merchantmen flying the Stars and Stripes at sea dwindled away (Greenwald).

Furthermore, as this first generation of wartime freighters and tankers—many hastily assembled and mass-produced, unintended for long-term service—began to wear out, they would be replaced by foreign-built and -operated vessels. Today, the actual number of American oceangoing merchantmen (not including Great Lake carriers) is believed to be 46 or less in total and consist mainly of older ships, with little life left in them. America in the twenty-first century carries little of its own commerce, relying instead on foreign carriers. Consequently, when the first outbursts of global piracy began to reappear, there were virtually no U.S.-flagged ships left traveling through those distant waters, and thus little initial urgency for Washington to become involved.

Table 6.1 in the Data and Documents chapter highlights the impact of World War II on global shipping trends, while Table 6.2 examines the steady disappearance of the U.S. merchant fleet from the mid-1950s onward.

Bigger Vessels, Smaller Crews

Not only have American merchantmen been supplanted on the high seas, but the new generations of oceangoing vessels being launched in modern yards are much larger, yet manned by greatly reduced crews—rendering such richly ladened behemoths easy prey for even tiny boatloads of armed gunmen. Typically, cargo ships at the end of World War II displaced between 9,000–15,000 tons, and were equipped with a maze of booms and other mechanized gear to hoist goods in and out of their holds. Crews consisted of a few dozen skilled seamen, not merely to work the vessel at sea, but more importantly to operate the motorized winches, derricks, and lines necessary in harbor to swing in and out an endless stream of piecemeal items—known as "break-bulk" cargo, where each piece had to be loaded and unloaded individually.

In major seaports, stevedores along these piers also used forklifts, cranes, trucks, even conveyor belts to speed up this process, as any lengthy layover could prove costly to the shipper. Yet since the standard wooden pallets of that time measured only four-by-four feet, any loading or unloading procedure was bound to be protracted. Merchantmen would continue to grow modestly in size during the immediate postwar decade, into the mid-1950s, yet the antiquated cargo-handling limitations in every port made any further escalation in size pointless. It therefore remained for a few innovators to resolve the problem caused by such bottlenecks, their efforts eventually producing a radical overhaul of the entire process, so as to more efficiently streamline deliveries.

Container Ships

Ironically, it was to be a North Carolina trucking entrepreneur named Malcolm P. McLean, unfamiliar with the sea, who was to be in the very forefront of the development of a more practicable scheme. Impressed by a concept that he had first seen used during the 1930s by Seatrain Lines out of New Jersey—in which as many as 100 fully-loaded railway cars would be shunted onto their four-decker ships, sailed to another port, then shunted off again upon arrival—McLean in 1955 bought the Pan-Atlantic Steamship Company of Mobile, Alabama, with the idea of creating his own "trailer-ships": vessels which instead of carrying railway cars, could receive trailers detached from semitrucks, so as to be driven out of their holds by different truck cabs once they reached their destination. This method of transporting goods directly atop rolling stock would soon become dubbed as "roll-on/roll-off" or RO/RO.

When his original idea was deemed too wasteful of cargo space, though, McLean refined his concept further—to instead include the hoisting of specially reinforced, 35-foot long, stackable containers off a truck's trailer and onto a ship's deck, so that only these piled boxes need be transported at sea, and lifted off onto other trailers once they arrived—such vessels consequently becoming known as *container ships* or "box" ships. By January 1956, McLean had purchased two or three World War II-vintage tankers and begun transforming them into his envisioned design by the erection of wooden spar-decking several feet above their actual weather decks (a technique known as "Mechano" decking, a common wartime practice for carrying oversized cargos, such as aircraft).

His first extemporized container ship—the 10,500-ton SS *Ideal X*—would set sail from Port Newark in New Jersey on April 26, 1956, bearing 58 trailer boxes in addition to its regular liquid-tank cargo for a six-day run to Houston, Texas. The savings gained through adopting this method were immediately obvious: at that time, hand-loading a ship cost $5.86 a ton, compared to only 16 cents a ton per container. Other shipping firms soon began experimenting with McLean's concept, some by merely lashing a few extra containers atop their freighters' decks for a particular passage. Loading and unloading nonetheless remained quite difficult and slow in most harbors, especially because of a lack of standardized containers throughout the industry. It would not be until 1961 that 20- and 40-foot metal shipping units would be widely agreed upon—chosen to conform with most existing highway limits, as well as rail, bridge, and tunnel dimensions—and being designated as TEUs or "Trailer Equivalent Units." By then, McLean's container ship operation had become quite profitable, so that he kept adding routes and buying bigger vessels.

But it was to be during the Vietnam War of the late 1960s and early 1970s that his methods truly came to excel. In order to deliver the vast amounts of supplies needed to sustain a large-scale U.S. expedition in distant Asia, the Military Sea Transportation Service (today known as the Military Sealift Command) signed an agreement on March 29, 1967 with McLean's company, Sea-Land Service, Inc. This lucrative contract contained provisions not only for the transportation of containers into Vietnamese ports, but deep inland as well, to the forwardmost American depots—an arrangement which allowed Sea-Land complete control and limitless support in its efforts to move this vital stream of supplies. Shipments would be made through new, custom-built harbor facilities and transport-hubs, while Sea-Land's oversight of its containers meant that boxes could be more effectively employed, in repeat usage both ways. Over the next half-dozen years, using only seven container ships (plus another four, feeding replenishments into way stations on Okinawa and the Philippines), McLean's company accounted for 10 percent of all cargo shipped into Vietnam during the U.S. involvement, reaping bountiful profits. And by the end of America's commitment to that campaign in 1973, 80 percent of all material entering Southeast Asia was being brought in by container ship.

McLean had profited personally from this success by selling his company in May 1969 to the R. J. Reynolds Tobacco Company for $530 million in cash and stocks, receiving $160 million as his own share, plus a seat on Reynolds's board. Inspired by his good fortune, other global shipping firms began fully embracing his concepts. For example, the United States Lines of New York had placed its first orders for purpose-built container ships in 1968, the first pair of its new so-called *American Lancer* series still retaining the old onboard combination of cargo- and container-handling apparatus—yet the last eight would be built totally devoid of any traditional hoists, booms, or winches, intended to rely solely on shore-side cranes. This sparse design allowed for the maximum deck-space to be made available for transportation of 1,178 TEUs apiece, and with a sea speed of 22 knots, the eight ships of this stripped-down class allowed United States Lines to replace 24 of its older ships yet still turn a handsome profit.

More competitors began emulating McLean's practices, so that container ships boomed in numbers, size, and capacity. This third-generation of vessels primarily sought to maximize the amount of containers that each could carry, soon growing to the very size-limits of the Panama Canal itself, a set of dimensions known as "Panama maximum" or "Panamax." Late in 1978, McLean—who had resigned from Reynolds' board to buy up his old rival, United States Lines—further accelerated this size escalation by placing an order with the Daewoo Shipyards in South Korea for a dozen massive 57,000-ton container ships, each measuring almost 1,000 feet in length and 106 feet in width, and capable of bearing more than 4,250 TEUs apiece. These 12 giant "Econships" were to be propelled by slower-speed diesel engines at a fuel-saving 16–18 knots, and manned by only 21 crewmen. They entered into service one after another, departing eastward from New York at one-week intervals, each taking 84 days to circle the globe before returning into their home-port to initiate another circumnavigation (Cudahy, pp. 152–153).

However, competition from other container ship firms had by now grown so intense, that McLean's globe-circling fleet proved to be a commercial failure. Fuel-efficient, but slow and unreliable, United States Lines went bankrupt by 1987, and McLean was driven almost entirely out of the business which he had helped revolutionize. His trend was now firmly entrenched, though: Rival companies continued launching ships that even went beyond many physical and geographic limitations, such as when American President Lines began construction during the late 1980s of their C-10 and C-11 classes, massive vessels whose beam exceeded the width of the Panama Canal locks, thus introducing the first "post-Panamax" generation of container ships to the world. These were soon eclipsed by even bigger megaships: Maersk Lines launching its 6,000-TEU *Regina Maersk* in 1994, quickly followed by its the new G-class—exemplified by the 7,000-TEU *Gudrun Maersk*—then the 8,000-TEU *Sorø Maersk* by 1999, with plans for future ships capable of carrying up to 10,000 TEUs or more.

McLean's pioneering efforts at containerization and intermodalism had radically altered the worldwide movement of cargo. By 2008, global merchant fleets included 3,375 container ships, with a total carrying-capacity of 7.2 million TEUs. They had multiplied to such an extent, as to be subdivided into four specialized categories:

- "feeder" ships, those carrying less than 1,000 TEUs apiece, designed to shuttle containers to and from smaller ports into major seaports;
- "handy-size" medium vessels, carriers capable of bearing 1,000-3,000 TEUs apiece on regional runs;
- "Panamax" ships, long-range seagoing vessels capable of bearing up to 4,000 TEUs per voyage;
- and "post-Panamax" giants, running the major ocean routes with many thousands of TEUs at a time.

The growth of world trade thanks to container ships has been undeniable. For example:

— in 1983, total U.S. foreign ocean-born commerce was measured at 694.4 million metric tons;
— 10 years later, this figure had increased to 884.4 million metric tons;
— 10 years after that, it had magnified to 1,167.9 million metric tons, nearly doubling in volume in just two decades (Mercogliano, p. 11).

Escalation of this magnitude could only have been achieved through containerization.

During the 1950s, a typical freighter could handle some 10,000 tons of cargo, taking nearly two weeks to load or unload— yet by 2004, the port of Los Angeles-Long Beach alone was receiving 8.6 million containers annually, a figure representing over 23,000 containers a day, each TEU being capable of holding up to 20 tons of cargo (ibid.). And world container traffic still continues to rise today, augmenting by another 13.4 percent during 2006 to reach 440 million TEUs. Early the following year, it was further noted that while the average age of all merchantmen in service had fallen slightly to 12 years old, the youngest class of shipping still remained container ships, at an average of only nine years (*Jane's Overview*, 2008).

Most unexpectedly, though, one of the downsides of this emergence and domination of commercial traffic by superefficient, minimally manned merchantmen, would be the numerous rich targets roaming the world's sea lanes, relatively easy prey for even tiny bands of armed pirates.

Supertankers

Just as freighters have evolved over the past few decades into much larger, yet more vulnerable vessels, the same would occur with the development of tankers into modern supertankers. The average oil tanker at the end of World War II measured some 525–550 feet in length, and displaced between 10,000–16,000 tons. Like freighters, their upper works were also clustered with pumps, booms, winches, and other equipment for loading and discharging their bulk cargoes, and their crews included numerous specialized workers. The first new tankers built during the immediate postwar era would retain these features, and most continued to be designed so as to pass through the narrow waterways of the Suez Canal—which was already becoming a busy and important route. By 1955, tankers loaded with Mideastern petroleum products constituted fully half of its annual traffic, and their cargoes represented two-thirds of Europe's total consumption.

Yet ironically, when the Canal was temporarily closed for six months as a result of fighting during the Suez Crisis of late October 1956, tankers had to be diverted the long way around South Africa's Cape of Good Hope—and notwithstanding the greater distance involved, owners soon discovered the economical benefits of transporting large volumes of crude on a few big vessels, rather than the numerous small ones which had previously been their practice. The American shipping magnate Daniel K. Ludwig had already begun building larger bulk carriers, having leased the enormous Japanese naval shipyard at Kure as long ago as 1950 to lay down bigger hulls. Less than two years after the Suez Crisis, his corporation—National Bulk Carriers, Inc.—would launch the huge *Universe Apollo* in 1958, a tanker measuring 950 feet in length and 135 feet in width, displacing almost 105,000 tons when fully loaded. It was to be followed two years later by its sister ship *Universe Daphne*, both vessels barely meeting the maximum dimensions of what the 90-year-old Suez Canal could accommodate: ships 151 feet in width, and running 62 feet deep when fully loaded at 150,000 tons (figures commonly referred to throughout the industry as "Suezmax").

Over the next couple of decades, Ludwig would compete in a building-race with Greek rivals such as Aristotle Onassis, launching six mammoth 335,000-ton ultra-large crude carriers, or ULCCs, to transport oil from the Persian Gulf to Ireland. By the mid-1970s, he owned 5–6 million in deadweight tonnage, spread among 50-odd tankers and bulk carriers operated by his Universe Tankships subsidiary. As a further cost-saving measure, most of these modern new vessels—devoid of any deck equipment and manned by only minimal crews—were registered under Liberian or Panamanian flags of convenience. The success of his enterprises not only provided Ludwig with huge amounts of collateral and cash for other giant ventures, it had made him one of the richest men in America, and spawned a host of commercial imitators. Indeed by 1980, Ludwig ranked only third in global tonnage, having been overtaken by the Chinese shipowners Y. K. Pao and C. Y. Tung (Shields).

The boom in supertanker construction proved irreversible. The largest one ever built had been launched at Sumitomo's Oppama shipyard in Japan in 1979, being named the *Seawise Giant*: It measured over 1,500 feet in length, drew almost 81 feet of water, and had a maximum capacity of 565,000 deadweight tons, being too large to pass through the English Channel. Because of their immense size, such vessels could not even enter most ports fully loaded. Instead, they had to take on loads from offshore platforms and single-point moorings, then pumping them off at the other end of their journey onto smaller feeder tankers at designated lightering points. In order to maximize profitability, these bulk-carriers' ocean routes were generally very long, requiring them to stay at sea for 70 days at a time or beyond. Even so, transportation costs on such huge volumes worked out to only two or three cents per gallon. Smaller tankers in the 10,000–80,000 ton-range were used to carry the more expensive and volatile products, such as gasoline, from refineries directly to regional markets, and became known as "product carriers."

As of 2007, the Central Intelligence Agency estimated that there were 4,295 oil tankers operating worldwide, Panama having the largest number listed in its registry, at 528—most being foreign-owned vessels merely flying its flag. Liberia also listed 464 such vessels; Singapore had 355; the Marshall Islands, 234; and the Bahamas, 209. By comparison, major powers such as China only listed 252; Russia had 250; the United States, 59; and the United Kingdom, a mere 27, despite tapping major oilfields in its adjacent North Sea waters. These huge, rich, yet scantily manned vessels would prove tempting targets for a new generation of seaborne criminals.

Expansion of Territorial Waters

A third twentieth-century trend that would unwittingly abet a resurgence of piracy during our modern day would be a manifold expansion of territorial-water claims by most world governments. Since the early eighteenth century, European nations had generally recognized a jurisdiction of only one league or three nautical miles—the farthest distance that any artillery piece of that era could fire a shot, as in a theory first propounded by the Dutch jurist Cornelius van Bijnkershoek in his 1703 treatise *De Dominio Maris* or "On the Sovereignty of the Sea." This so-called "cannon-shot rule" meant that only that expanse of ocean which lay within three miles of a nation's shores could be considered as falling within its jurisdiction, allowing its government the right to police, regulate, and adjudicate all activities thereon, as well as proprietary rights to any natural resources beneath its waves. Foreigners could be excluded from their exploitation, so that trawlers wishing to cull fish or sea mammals near shore would have to secure permission from the host nation, as would warships conducting nearby military exercises. Peaceful visiting vessels—such as merchantmen approaching to trade—were entitled to "innocent passage" through this three-mile zone, but naturally had to abide by any local laws and customs once within territorial waters. The remaining vast expanses of open ocean, known collectively as "the high seas," were regarded as being common to all nations, freely available for navigation, fishing, or any other lawful pursuit.

The newly-independent United States officially established its own three-mile territorial limit as of 1793, but during the great technological and industrial innovations of the twentieth century, many nations began disputing such a small ancient measure, and some unilaterally extended their claims to as much as 12 nautical miles—a distance not initially recognized by most maritime powers. Then at the end of World War II, the victorious U.S. government—at least partly at the behest of its domestic oil company interests—introduced a new variant: Wishing to retain control over the valuable offshore resources lying just beyond its three-mile limit in the shallow Gulf of Mexico and other adjacent waters, President Harry S. Truman issued a proclamation in late September 1945 which declared that his administration regarded "the subsoil and seabed of the continental shelf beneath the high seas, but contiguous to the coasts of the United States, as appertaining to the United States, subject to its jurisdiction and control" (U.S. Presidential Proclamation 2667, September 28, 1945).

While theoretically still recognizing only a three-mile limit as the international standard, this claim by the American government to an additional 750,000 square miles of territorial waters, was promptly imitated by other nations. Argentina asserted a similar claim in October 1946 to its own stretch of continental shelf, while the following year Chile and Peru both extended their sovereignty claims 200 nautical miles out to sea—followed by Ecuador in 1950—so as to restrict access by foreign trawlers into their traditional Humboldt Current fishing grounds, whose stocks were becoming depleted by modern fishing fleets. In 1958, the government of Guatemala—angered by repeated poaching in its territorial waters by Mexican fishing boats—threatened to fire upon any such trespassers from its military aircraft, declaring that such violations constituted outright "piracy."

With ever more nations emerging during the aftermath of World War II, many being impoverished Third-World governments anxious to tap or protect their natural resources as a source of income, more than 40 countries had expanded their territorial claims by the 1970s to at least 12 nautical miles. Many would go well beyond this distance, often in incremental cycles: for example, the African nation of Gabon first claimed a jurisdiction of 25 miles nautical miles, then 30, then 100, before finally settling on 170 nautical miles; Somalia went from six to 12 nautical miles, before finally adopting 200 nautical miles; etc. (Rembe, p. 92).

As claims, counterclaims, and conflicting interests mounted, the United Nations convened its third Conference on the Law of the Sea in 1982, attempting to find common ground on several key issues. Eventually, over the next half-dozen years, 130 member-states would ratify the resultant "Convention on the Law of the Sea" or UNCLOS, which—among many other things—included a recognition of a 12-mile limit as a generally acceptable standard, although only 104 countries actually claimed such a distance by 1988. The United States even voted against this convention, because of a variety of other complaints, but President Ronald Reagan tacitly recognized the suggested limit by issuing Executive Proclamation 5928 that same year, which officially increased American territorial waters from three to 12 nautical miles—a figure which also applied to Puerto Rico, Guam, American Samoa, the U.S. Virgin Islands, and the Northern Mariana Islands (54 Fed. Reg. 777).

The Reagan administration nonetheless refused to accept many of the economic arguments advanced by other nations in favor of their expansions, instead justifying America's extension on grounds of national security, specifically to hinder Soviet spy vessels from operating so close to the U.S. coastline. Piracy was a minimal concern for all parties involved in this UN conference during the 1980s, having faded to historic lows. But when piratical attacks were to resurge two decades later, the few warships assigned to patrol international waters would find their boundaries significantly restricted, especially near the busiest traffic channels. The concept of "the high seas" had contracted significantly in scope.

Sea Robbery

Expanding national boundaries further entailed another specific complication, the blurring of distinctions between piracy and sea robbery, a long-used legal charge to prosecute attacks against commercial vessels in ports or near shore. According to international law, such attacks did not constitute true acts of piracy, but rather criminal assaults in territorial waters, similar to armed robberies suffered by truck drivers moving about a port area, and so should be dealt with by the local police. Modern variants of such attacks have also included deception, in which criminals have identified themselves to anchored vessels over VHF radio as official visitors, such as customs-inspectors or the national coast guard.

One clearcut example of a sea robbery occurred to the car ferry *Mexico I*, as it was returning from the Caribbean resort island of Cozumel toward Playa del Carmen on the mainland, with 253 passengers on the night of May 31, 1999. Suddenly, a half-dozen hooded men began brandishing a grenade and firing assault rifles into the air, their intent being to rob an armored car that was traveling aboard the vessel. Two of its security guards were thrown overboard, one of whom subsequently drowned, before the robbers sped off in a small boat. Given this lurid encounter on the waves, local newspapers branded it an "act of piracy" yet it was merely a felony and so delegated to the police.

But as national boundaries were extended far beyond the historical three-mile limit, it would prove impossible for police jurisdictions to keep pace. A legal no-man's-land would develop, with many larger vessels being anchored too far from shore to receive protection, yet not far enough out to receive assistance from any Coast Guard patrols. Container ships visiting such crime-prone ports as Santos in Brazil or Lagos in Nigeria, would often anchor 20 miles out while awaiting a berth, yet nonetheless be boarded at night by boatloads of thieves.

Irresolution in International Law

Piracy was still considered a relatively minor issue when hundreds of national delegations had attended the first United Nations Conference on the Law of the Sea in 1958 at Geneva, Switzerland, their primary interest being focused instead on economic matters such as ownership of offshore resources or fishing banks. Even Western nations had not been unduly concerned by the few instances of piracy occurring at that time, historically dismissing it as a crime which fell under what was then known as "universal jurisdiction"—meaning that any such outlaws, whatever their nationality, could be summarily tried and punished by any government that captured them, because of the indiscriminate nature of their depredations on the high seas. Even a precise definition of the crime itself had never been clearly codified: for example, whether an intent to rob (in Latin, *animus furandi*) was a necessary element for leveling such a charge. Even such an abbreviated definition of piracy as "any armed violence at sea which is not a lawful act of war," would be questioned by partisans of insurgent privateers or revolutionary fighters—pointing out that personal gain was not their objective, rather a national cause.

Legal distinctions such as these had never really been at issue in past centuries, when only Britain's Royal Navy and a handful of other Western sea powers had been in a position to detain suspected pirates on the open ocean. But the post-World War II era not only saw an end to the last vestiges of colonial rule and a reduction in blue-water navies, but many of the newly emergent nations would begin staking claims to their own expanding territorial waters, and patrolling them with small warships or police-craft. The legal status of merchantmen transiting through ever more crowded sea lanes would also become increasingly complex, as ownership of many of these vessels and their cargoes were divided among several different nationalities, while the freighters and tankers themselves would soon be operated under a shifting array of flags of convenience, manned by hired crews drawn from diverse countries.

The resultant "Convention on the High Seas" issued by this first 1958 conference in Geneva, contained only eight brief articles related to piracy, further leaving their actual interpretation and application to legal experts in each signatory nation. Basic tenets still remained undefined, moreover, such as:

- How was the issue of universal jurisdiction to be understood?

- Could piracy only be committed on the high seas, or could piratical acts also be perpetrated in territorial waters or in ports?
- Was piracy limited to private motivations, such as personal gain or revenge, thus exempting politically driven renegades targeting civilians for a public cause?

With almost no pirates troubling the world's sea lanes at that time, and more pressing national concerns demanding each delegate's attention, such issues were not addressed. And when a high-profile case was to occur less than three years afterward, it was to be decided by political rather than legal arguments.

Santa Maria *Hijacking (1961)*

At 1:45 a.m. on the morning of January 22, 1961, the bridge of the 20,900-ton, 609-foot Portuguese luxury liner *Santa Maria* was stormed by a party of armed men, a few hours after it had cleared the Dutch-West Indian island of Curaçao on a Caribbean cruise. Two-dozen of the 600 passengers were not actually innocent civilians, but rebel gunmen who had come aboard in disguise under ex-Portuguese Army Captain Henrique Carlos Malta Galvão, an escapee from the repressive 35-year-old regime of the dictator, Dr. António de Oliveira Salazar. A decade earlier, while serving as the elected Angolan Deputy to the Portuguese National Assembly, Galvão had presented a confidential report on the terrible labor practices in that impoverished African colony. Its recommendations had been ignored, though, and he himself arrested and sentenced to a lengthy prison term as a dissident when he persisted.

Having escaped in January 1959 into the Argentine Embassy in Lisbon, Galvão made his way to Venezuela, where he planned this hijacking—grandly codenamed Operation "Dulcinea"—as a call for Portugal's insurrection. *Santa Maria*'s Third Mate having been killed and several crewmen wounded during this assault, Galvão paused that following evening of January 23, 1961 off Castries, the capital of the British West Indian island of Saint Lucia, to allow a lifeboat to be rowed inshore by loyal hands, while his captive liner then sped away over the horizon. Informed by these survivors of the violent seizure of *Santa Maria*, the British authorities immediately dispatched the frigate HMS *Rothesay* in pursuit from Barbados, while the American destroyers *Wilson* and *Damato* and a pair of aircraft also sortied from Puerto Rico (Zeiger).

Upon learning of this rebel outrage, the Salazar regime in Lisbon had in turn immediately contacted Washington and London, requesting help as a NATO ally in the hunt and retrieval of the liner from Galvão's criminal "act of piracy." But on Tuesday, January 24, 1961, the rebel commander began a series of radio interviews with news organizations, explaining that he and his followers—who consisted of 13 Portuguese citizens, ten Spaniards, and a Venezuelan—were acting on behalf of "the international junta of liberals" presided over by General Humberto da Silva Delgado, exiled in Brazil after being fraudulently defeated in Portugal's recent presidential election. No passengers had or would be harmed, Galvão informed the reporters, and many (including 36 Americans) were allowed to radio reassurances to their families.

Then on Wednesday, January 25, 1961, the Danish freighter *Viveke Gulwa* spotted the fleeing liner far out in the Atlantic, running in bad weather 900 miles east of Trinidad. A U.S. Neptune P2V search plane arrived overhead by that same evening, establishing radio contact with Galvão. He declared that he was steering for Angola, with the apparent intent of pausing off Fernando Pó island to raise a host of native volunteers, then press on to topple the Portuguese colonial administration in the capital of Luanda, replacing it with Delgado's "National Independence Movement." *Santa Maria*'s passengers were being well-treated, Galvão reiterated, and could be freely discharged in a neutral harbor at the earliest possible convenience. He furthermore agreed to meet with any American or Western naval officers (ibid.).

Because of these circumstances, world opinion began to swing behind the rebel leader. Officials in both Washington and London no longer viewed his seizure as a piratical act, and the British withdrew altogether from the pursuit, unwilling to help the fascistic regime in Portugal. The U.S. Navy was directed by the adminstration of President John F. Kennedy to discreetly facilitate a peaceful resolution to the crisis, rather than an interception at sea, a decision which sparked angry protests from Lisbon against both Washington and London, for having failed to live up to their NATO obligations. Pro-Salazar newspapers in Portugal attempted to win back global support by writing that the hijacking was a crime against "the moral and judicial rules of the civilized world," carried out by "criminals who publish pamphlets showing Communist intentions" (ibid.).

Yet it was nonetheless agreed to allow Galvão to divert into a neutral Brazilian port, and discharge his captive passengers.

American Rear Admiral Allen Smith, Commander of the Caribbean Sea Frontier, had the unenviable task of flying into Recife to arrange the actual handover, plus the surrender of the liner. A welter of complications ensued. Brazil's outgoing conservative administration was hostile to the notion of a rebel visit, although it was about to be succeeded in office within the next few days by the more liberal President-elect, Janio Quadros. Dozens of diplomats pressed conflicting demands upon Smith on behalf of their home governments; swarms of eager reporters hastened out in flimsy boats to greet *Santa Maria* as it entered territorial waters; and living conditions deteriorated aboard the liner as the final surrender terms were slowly negotiated (ibid.).

Eventually, the new administration of Janio Quadros assumed office, and in a chaotic scene at Recife's dockside on February 2, 1961, *Santa Maria*'s unhappy passengers and 350 captive crewmen were disgorged in a tumultous throng, after which Galvão surrendered to the Brazilian authorities and was granted political asylum. In its aftermath, Western legal scholars were to remain troubled by the evident ineffectiveness of international law in handling such a blatant case of piracy.

Achille Lauro *Hijacking (1985)*

Two-dozen years later, yet another high-profile incident would once more reveal the weak influence of international antipiracy statutes. On October 7, 1985, a crewman aboard the Italian liner *Achille Lauro*—while steaming peacefully from Alexandria toward Port Said in Egypt on a cruise—surprised four members of a faction of the Palestinian Liberation Organization known as the Palestinian Liberation Front, or PLF, who had boarded in Genoa by posing as tourists. This premature discovery meant that the heavily-armed quartet moved immediately to hijack the vessel, separating out 100 passengers to act as hostages. The gunmen then ordered *Achille Lauro* to sail for Tartus in Syria, while threatening by radio to start killing captives unless Israel released 50 Palestinian prisoners.

Rebuffed by the Israeli authorities and refused entry into Tartus, the gunmen next afternoon shot 69-year-old Leon Klinghoffer—an American Jew who was partly paralyzed and confined to a wheelchair—then threw his body overboard, before reversing course for Port Said. Unaware of this murder, the Egyptian government sought to resolve the standoff next day by granting the hijackers safe passage to Tunisia, in exchange for freeing the liner and its passengers. Once Klinghoffer's death was revealed, though, the administration of U.S. President Ronald Reagan characterized the gunmen's seizure of the *Achille Lauro* and murder of an American citizen as wanton criminal acts, with the Department of Justice securing arrest warrants which charged the hijackers with hostage-taking, conspiracy, and "piracy on the high seas" (Halberstam, p. 270).

U.S. F-14 naval fighters intercepted the Egyptian airliner which was transporting the gunmen toward safety, along with a regular complement of civilian passengers, as it was flying over the Mediterranean on October 10, 1985, forcing it to land at NATO's "Sigonella" Naval Air Station in Sicily. Over American objections, however, the four hijackers were then taken into custody by the Italian authorities, eventually being tried in that country, two receiving lengthy prison terms. The Egypt Air plane had meanwhile been cleared to resume its interrupted flight to Tunisia, with some of the hijackers' suspected accomplices still on board, and Cairo demanded a formal apology from Washington for this mid-air interception. A great deal of public opinion, especially in the Arab and non-aligned world, refused to regard the hijacking as a piratical act.

Continuing Confusion

The intervening quarter-century would see no real progress on clearly defining piracy, much less of devising a universally-recognized legal mechanism for trying such perpetrators. Many emergent nations would oscillate between a reluctance to lay piracy charges against their own citizens for seaborne crimes, while seeking heavy-handed remedies against regional rivals, such as trespassing fishermen. Many new national courts were also unauthorized or lacked the body of law to apply international statutes during their proceedings. Governments nonetheless jealously upheld all prerogatives within their territorial waters, while describing any coastal opponents or subversives as "pirates," as a means of stigmatizing and pursuing them as criminals.

One such variant occurred when officials in Manila announced on May 1, 1986 that during the previous 16 months, "pirates and Moslem rebels" had hijacked as many as 530 motorboats in the Southern Philippines, mostly small craft used to carry passengers and light cargo in interisland traffic—although doubts would linger as to the actual identity of all these perpetrators, some believed to have been rogue elements of the military. And during the violent separatist insurgency which troubled Sri Lanka in the late 1990s, its majority government often charged fighters of the Liberation Tigers of Tamil Eeelam or LTTE as pirates.

The end result would be that when a wave of true global piracy revived during the early part of the twenty-first century, no internationally recognized set of legal standards existed among the many nations drawn into this crisis, so as to deal easily and uniformly with the problem. Even the dozen or so navies actively pursuing pirates, were fragmented by a variety of legal limitations.

Traffic-Shift into Asian Waters

A fifth factor unwittingly contributing toward the rebirth of piracy, was the spectacular boom in trade out of Asia. While a positive development in and of itself, this economic upsurge since World War II would also funnel huge volumes of rich traffic through remote and unpatrolled waterways, past once-lawless shorelines still blighted by poverty. By the late 1990s, more than half the world's merchant-tonnage was already streaming every year through the Straits of Malacca, Sunda, or Lombok—a tremendous and vulnerable flow of shipping whose losses could affect the economic well-being of Southeast Asia, the Far East, Europe, even the United States. (For example, seaports along America's West Coast had accounted for only 24 percent of this country's total seaborne trade in 1980, compared to 42 percent by 1997; during this same interlude, East Coast ports had seen their volumes decline slightly from 41 to 38 percent, while Gulf Coast ports had dropped most precipitously of all, from 33 to 18 percent. The longer Pacific routes into the West Coast were also proving to be the most cost-efficient.)

As a result of such unbridled growth, four of world's five busiest seaports by 1998—in terms of "through-put" tonnage, as it is known—were all in Asia: Rotterdam still being the biggest at 315 million metric tons a year, yet followed by Singapore at 241 million; Shanghai at 164 million; Nagoya at 134 million; and Hong Kong at 128 million. In terms of modern container traffic, Singapore was already handling 15.1 million TEUs a year, followed closely by Hong Kong at 14.9 million, while Taiwan's Kaohsiung was processing 6.3 million. Although only 25 percent of China's traffic was containerized at that time, it was nonetheless already the world's largest manufacturer of dry-freight containers, and its port facilities were being rapidly upgraded.

Such immense trade volumes had naturally fueled a commensurate rise in Asian merchant fleets as well, which by 1995 constituted 34 percent of total world tonnage—and 72 percent of all new construction that following year was to be built in Asia, with Japanese yards receiving 35 percent of world orders for new ships in 1996, followed by South Korea at 30 percent, and seven percent distributed among several lesser builders. Insatiable demand for raw materials in Japan and the rapidly expanding industries of Hong Kong, Singapore, Taiwan, and South Korea, meant that vast amounts had to be continuously imported through the narrow and perilous Strait of Malacca, crude oil being the single largest cargo in terms of sheer bulk tonnage. By the mid-1990s, tanker traffic through the Strait was already more than three times that of the Suez Canal, and well over five times that of the Panama Canal. Over 1,100 fully laden supertankers were passing through it eastbound every year, many so huge as to have only a few scant feet of clearance, and bearing an average of 9.5 million barrels of oil every day, worth in the tens of millions of dollars.

Manufactured goods were also being exported through the Strait of Malacca in the opposite direction, smaller in volume yet higher in value, a stream of tempting consumer products that still continues to escalate today. Such a parade of wealthy prizes would provide easy pickings for tiny gangs of renegades, without even a token defense by the home-bound Japanese and Chinese Navies.

Widespread Resort to "Flags of Convenience"

Another trend unexpectedly facilitating a resurgence of modern piracy, was the cost-cutting expedient adopted by many ship owners, of registering their vessels under cheap "flags of convenience." Simply put, this meant listing or transferring a ship's title to another willing country, which—being only interested in collecting some easy money as registration fees—would accept most any application, while requiring minimal operational standards. Annual tonnage fees would be far lower, taxes on any company profits or dividends virtually nonexistent, so that savings could amount to millions of dollars a year, even for a single large merchantman. Ownership did not necessarily even have to be disclosed, as shares could be held in "bearer form" without revealing the true identity of an owner.

The first nation to offer such an "open registry" for international shippers was Panama, whose laws had been amended immediately after World War I to permit foreign-vessel registrations starting in 1919, with no taxes and nonexistent labor standards being offered as inducements for applicants. Relatively few ships had been reflagged at first, until Standard Oil of New Jersey (ESSO) transferred several tankers to the Panamanian flag in 1935, achieving such quick savings and improved profit margins that other multinational firms soon began to follow suit. U.S. authorities remained unconcerned by these first few instances of reflagging, though, erroneously assuming that such vessels still remained under the legal control of their American owners, and thus could be recalled for service during times of war.

Abuses and other deficiencies in the Panamanian registry had then led former U.S. Secretary of State Edward R. Stennius, Jr.—in his capacity as America's United Nations representative, spearheading post-World War II relief-efforts in Africa—to suggest that Liberia open its own competing registry in 1948, as a means of gaining some foreign revenue. Its regulating "Liberian Maritime Code" was actually drafted by tanker owners and approved by all major oil-shipping concerns—in particular ESSO officials—so that it naturally favored corporate interests. Provisions proved so enticing that by 1967, Liberia had surpassed the United Kingdom as the world's largest merchant-ship register. (Today, paperwork for most Liberian listings is still handled by a private company based in Virginia.)

Already by 1998, more than half—51.3 percent—of the world's total merchant tonnage was registered under flags of convenience (Alderton and Winchester), a figure which grew to over 53 percent within the next three years and continues to rise today. In recent times, even less-demanding registries have been opened by at least a dozen other money-strapped countries. The initial pioneers in this field, Panama and Liberia, had at least required that ship owners maintain some kind of office or presence in their chosen flag-state; these new registers have proven even more perfunctory in their requirements. For example, Cambodia's registry (actually based in the seaport of Singapore) will accept applications on a 24-hour-a-day basis from any person or company claiming to own a ship, and—based solely upon faxed or e-mailed documentation—can process a request within one hour. Such lax and hasty oversight has naturally lent itself to abuses.

For example, on November 17, 2002 the Malaysian-owned, Panamanian-flagged cargo vessel *Natris* was hijacked while departing a shipyard on Batam, and disappeared. Next year, it was reregistered with the Merchant Marine Registry of Belize as the *Paulijing*, being granted a provisional registration based on falsified records stating that its previous name had been the *"Victoria."* According to notarized documents which accompanied this application, the ship had been deleted from the Sierra Leone registry and sold to its new owner for a mere $10,000. *Paulijing* went on to trade under its new identity for more than two years, before the Malaysian Marine Police finally identified and detained it in August 2005. The International Maritime Bureau or IMB chastised the Belize register for failing to run even the most rudimentary background check on this stolen vessel, to little avail. Organized pirate gangs still continue to benefit today from such laxity, especially in Asia, where it is easy for them to reregister hijacked vessels—merely by repainting a few features and presenting false documentation. The renamed vessel can then either be sold to a third party, or used by the crime-syndicate as a "phantom ship" (Tanter, "Roots").

The flag-of-convenience system also entailed serious shortcomings for crewmen. Management is, of course, exempt from paying the higher wages customary in industrialized nations. Canada's Prime Minister Paul Martin, who had been owner of the Canada Steamship Lines in his private capacity before entering politics, was embarrassed when a television exposé revealed how the Canadian crew aboard one his vessels had been replaced by a Filipino crew, after it was reflagged in 1988: The Canadian crew had earned $11.68 an hour, while the Filipino workers were to be paid only $1.74 an hour. Like many other owners, Martin argued that shipping firms had no choice but to resort to such measures, in order to remain competitive in the international market.

The most recently-created registers are even less concerned about seafarers' welfare, training, or pay. Since some of these flag states have not ratified international agreements regarding minimum wages, their registers will obviously not intercede on behalf of any employees. As a result, seamen from Third-World countries are sometimes paid substandard wages and may even experience difficulty in collecting their meager due. In 2004, for example, the International Transport-Workers' Federation, or ITF, was asked to help two Burmese seafarers working aboard the Panamanian-flagged *Lung Yuin*, who had received a mere $300 for two years' work. It is feared that such low wages among seafarers, port officials, and dock workers might also lead some individuals into accepting bribes from criminal organizations, in exchange for information about a vessel's cargo, departure-time, route, etc.

Lax scrutiny of important professional documents, such as training certificates, can also pose safety problems. Excessive cost-cutting by ship owners and managers can moreover reduce crew numbers aboard some merchant vessels to such low levels, that the few overworked seamen become worn out by fatigue and stress. One such junior officer blearily recorded:

12–15 hour days, never had six hours continuous sleep, 87-hour week for three months. Regularly made errors in passage-planning and execution. Did not dare to sit down on watch. (Tantner, "Roots")

Lastly, poor pay also attracts less well-trained and more unreliable seafarers, with no allegiance to an employer. One such irresponsible crew was manning the freighter *Clown* in 2000, when they decided to make an unauthorized stop one evening on an island near Batam, notorious for its inexpensive prostitutes, drugs, and gambling. Unfortunately for the carousing crew, their anchored vessel was hijacked that same night by pirates. While it was later established that they had not colluded with these thieves, all crew members nonetheless lost their jobs because of making this unscheduled stopover.

See Table 6.3 in the Data and Documents chapter for detailed statistical information regarding the number of vessels registered under flags of convenience.

Proliferation of Military Light-Weaponry

The seventh and final factor spurring a resurgence of piracy in its modern guise, would be the proliferation of military light weaponry into virtually every troubled corner of the world. Technical innovations achieved during and since World War II had resulted in mass production of new generations of formidable small arms, originally intended for use by trained soldiers on a battlefield. Such weapons augmented individual firepower several times over, and within a few decades would pass beyond the control of any recognizable military establishment. Starting during the covert rivalry of the Cold War, both Eastern Bloc nations and their Western foes had begun funneling such armaments to their supporters in Third-World nations, a traffic which has only flourished further since the end of this competition with the collapse of the old Soviet Union.

AK-47 Assault Rifles

Doubtless the most famous of these formidable new firearms would be the AK-47. The idea for such an assault-rifle had been conceived in October 1941 by a 21-year-old Soviet tank commander, Sergeant Mikhail Timofeyevich Kalashnikov, while he lay recuperating in hospital after being wounded in his left shoulder during the Battle of Bryansk, southwest of Moscow. While retiring rearward to seek medical aid, most of his injured companions had been murdered by German troops armed with machine guns, so that even before being discharged from the hospital as an invalid, Kalashnikov had already begun dreaming of designing a weapon which would help turn the tide and throw back these cruel invaders.

He had started by tinkering with existing submachine guns, and two years later entered a competition, whose specific requirement was to create a firearm capable of functioning in the muddy, wet, and frozen conditions of the Soviet frontline. Kalashnikov submitted a carbine design that lost, yet when the Red Army held another similar competition for assault rifles in 1946, a revamped gas-operated model of his carbine was selected as one of three finalists.

After each of these guns had undergone its initial round of tests, one of Kalashnikov's assigned assistants—Aleksandr Zaytsev— suggested a major redesign late that same year of 1946, to further improve their entry's reliability. Kalashnikov reluctantly agreed, and their improved model was chosen as the winning design next year, proving to be a weapon of brilliant promise, economical yet simple. Designated the *Avtomat Kalashnikova obraztsa 1947 goda,* or "Kalashnikov's automatic rifle model year 1947," the AK-47—after more than another 100 further modifications—was finally adopted as the Soviet Army's new assault rifle as of 1949. However, production difficulties and a shroud of secrecy prevented the issue of any large numbers until 1956, after which a refined version known as the AKM, or "AK Modernized," was introduced three years later, which went on to be manufactured in mass quantities and remains the most common variant known today. (Technically, only very early models were true AK-47s, while the many later derivatives of the AKM are usually referred to simply as "Kalashnikovs.")

The main advantages of this powerful new assault-rifle were:

- its straightforward design, having only sixteen moving parts;
- its inexpensive manufacture;

- its easy operation and maintenance;
- and a ruggedness which would become truly legendary.

The Soviet government granted licenses to its Warsaw Pact allies to manufacture this weapon in their own factories, as well as to the People's Republic of China, so that all Communist forces would enjoy the same standard armament. Eventually, its use would spread to over 55 national armies, as well as dozens of paramilitary groups.

Tens of thousands were furthermore sent clandestinely to bolster leftist regimes in the Third World, as well as to arm guerrilla factions fighting to topple non-Communist governments. It was in many of these latter arenas—the steamy jungles of Southeast Asia or Latin America, the stark dusty plains of Africa—that the Kalashnikov truly came into its own. Tales were told of its fearsome firepower, toughness, and reliability, all seemingly based on fact. The Kalashnikov's large gas piston, ample clearances between moving parts, and tapered cartridge-case allowed the weapon to be fired, even with large amounts of extraneous matter fouling its interior. For example: "American Gis in Vietnam reported that AKs buried in rice paddies for six months or more, unearthed filthy and rusted shut, fired perfectly after kicking the action-bolt with the heel of a boot" (Kahaner, p. 3).

During the 1980s, the Soviet Union became the principal arms-dealer to countries embargoed by the United States, including many Middle Eastern nations such as Syria, Libya, and Iran. After the fall of the Soviet Union, AK-47s were sold both openly and on the black market to any group with cash, including drug cartels and dictatorial states, and became abundantly available in strife-torn areas of the Third World. Today, after six decades in use, the AK-47 and its numerous variants are still the most widely-used assault rifles in the world; in fact, more have been produced than all other assault rifles combined, while nearly one million unlicensed copies are manufactured every year.

Chinese versions are prevalent among the pirate-gangs of Asia, and Kalashnikovs have also made widespread inroads throughout Africa, proving so robust that they have even become relatively cheap—used models selling in Somalia, Rwanda, Mozambique, Congo, and Ethiopia for between $30–$125 or even lower. Moisés Naím observed that in a small town in Kenya in 1986, an AK-47 cost fifteen cows—but that by 2005, its price was down to four cows, because the local supply was so saturated.

(Nyuydine) In many places on the continent, the AK-47 is jokingly referred to as the "African credit card," in the advertised sense of "don't leave home without it" (Choong).

Rocket-Propelled Grenades

Another similar Soviet-era battlefield weapon—intended for a single operator, yet awesomely destructive—whose use would spread throughout the world's hot spots, is the slender, shoulder-fired, Rocket-Propelled Grenade launcher, abbreviated as an RPG-7. Originally introduced into the Red Army in 1961 as an infantryman's handheld anti-tank weapon, it too was soon being licensed and mass-produced abroad in Warsaw Pact nations, as well as in Communist China. Its relatively compact size, economical manufacture, and potent punch meant that the RPG-7 would transcend its original military purpose of penetrating heavily-armored tanks, and instead become another popular choice among civilian guerrilla movements such as the Irish Republican Army and Palestinian Liberation Organization.

Like the AK-47 assault-rifle, the rocket-propelled grenade-launcher would provide pirates with sufficient handheld fire-power to threaten even large merchantmen with serious damage, especially if any combustible materials were aboard. Simple to use and abundantly available, such weapons would allow even tiny boatloads of teenage gunmen to overawe and capture gigantic supertankers.

Summary

There is no question that the world's seaborne trade has never been so vast, so extensive, and so successful. Twenty-first century maritime traffic constitutes a highly evolved and ultra-efficient delivery system, both technologically sophisticated and globally monitored—all factors which would seem to have relegated piracy to a historical anachronism. And indeed, criminality on the high seas had already been declining almost to the vanishing point, before this recent resurgence of violence. Yet ironically, some of the very innovations and improvements that have contributed so significantly to this exponential growth in our seaborne commerce, have also contained a few inbuilt seeds of future trouble. For today's lengthy sea lanes are teeming with:

— rich prizes, yet manned by the fewest possible number of
— low-paid, hired hands from diverse nationalities,

— sailing under an impotent flag of convenience,
— beholden to economic interests split among different countries,
— unprotected by any home navies,
— expensively vulnerable to light weapons' fire, and
— beyond rescue if carried into any nation's territorial waters.

Sources

Alderton, Tony, and Winchester, Nik J. "Regulation, Representation, and the Flag Market." *Journal for Maritime Research* [UK], September 2002.

Choong, William. "Today's WMD of Choice—the AK-47." *The Straits Times* [Singapore], December 25, 2008.

Cramb, Auslan. "Sailor Tells of the Moment Pirates Captured the *Sirius Star.*" *The Daily Telegraph* [UK], January 29, 2009, Telegraph.co.uk

Cudahy, Brian J. *Box Boats: How Container Ships Changed the World.* New York: Fordham University Press, 2006.

Dubner, Barry H. *The Law of International Sea Piracy.* The Hague: Martinus Nijhoff, 1980.

Fenwick, C. G. "Piracy in the Caribbean." *American Journal of International Law* 55, Number 4 (October 1961), pp. 426–428.

Greenman, David. "Freedom Freighters." *Ships Monthly* [UK], June 1976.

Greenwald, Richard A.; Gibson, Andrew; and Donovan, Arthur. *The Abandoned Ocean: A History of United States Maritime Policy.* Columbia: University of South Carolina Press, 2000.

Halberstam, Malvina. "Terrorism on the High Seas: The *Achille Lauro,* Piracy, and the IMO Convention on Maritime Safety." *The American Journal of International Law* 82, Number 2 (April 1988), pp. 269–310.

Jamieson, Alastair. "Briton Captured by Somali Pirates on *Sirius Star* Tells of Fears." *The Sunday Telegraph [UK]* January 25, 2009, Telegraph.co.uk

Jane's Overview 2008: Growth of Merchant Shipping. London: Jane's Information Group, 2008.

Kahaner, Larry. *AK-47: The Weapon That Changed the Face of War.* Hoboken, New Jersey: John Wiley & Sons, 2007.

Karon, Tony. "Battling the Somali Pirates: The Return of the Islamists." *Time Magazine,* November 25, 2008.

Killicoat, Phillip. *Weaponomics: The Global Market for Assault Rifles.* Washington, D.C.: World Bank Policy Research Working Paper 4202, published in April 2007 as "Post-Conflict Transitions Working Paper No. 10."

"Lawless Tradition of Piracy off the Coast of Somalia." *The Guardian* [UK], November 18, 2008.

Leach, Ben. "Somali Pirates Who Hijacked Supertanker *Sirius Star* 'Demand Ransom of $25 Million.'" *The Daily Telegraph* [UK], November 20, 2008, Telegraph.co.uk.

Marx, Daniel, Jr. "The Merchant Ship Sales Act of 1946." *The Journal of Business of the University of Chicago* 21, Number 1 (January 1948), pp. 12–28.

McKesson, Chris B. *Alternative Powering for Merchant Ships: Task 1—Current and Forecast Powering Needs.* Long Beach: California State University "Center for the Commercial Deployment of Transportation Technologies," 2000.

Mercogliano, Salvatore R. "The Container Revolution." *Sea History* 114 (Spring 2006), pp. 8–11.

Nyuydine, Ngalim E. "Outdated Laws as Impetus for Illicit Proliferation of Small Arms and Light Weapons in Cameroon."

Raby, David. "Transatlantic Intrigues: Humberto Delgado, Henrique Galvão, and the Portuguese Exiles in Brazil and Morocco, 1961–62." *Portuguese Journal of Social Science* 3, Number 3 (December 2004).

Rembe, Nasila S. *Africa and the International Law of the Sea: A Study of the Contribution of the African States to the Third United Nations Conference on the Law of the Sea.* Germantown, Maryland: Sijthoff & Noordhoof, 1980.

Roberts, Lesley. "Hostage's Secret Pictures of £2 Million Ransom-Drop on Ship Hijacked by Pirates." *Sunday Mail* [UK], February 1, 2009, dailyrecord.co.uk.

Shields, Jerry. *The Invisible Billionaire: Daniel Ludwig.* Boston: Houghton Mifflin, 1986.

Stanley, William R. "Serving Aboard the World's Largest Flag-of-Convenience Fleet: Some Geographical Implications Concerning Crew's Nationality." *GeoJournal* [The Netherlands] 7, Number 3 (May 1983), pp. 261–269.

Tanter, Richard. "The Roots of Piracy in Southeast Asia." *Nautilus Institute: Austral Peace and Security Network [Australia]*, Austral Policy Forum Paper Number 07–18A, October 22, 2007.

Wadhams, Nick. "As Somali Pirates Get Bolder, Policing Them Gets Tougher." *Time Magazine*, November 19, 2008.

West's Encyclopedia of American Law. Farmington Hills, Michigan: The Gale Group, second edition, 2008.

Zeiger, Henry A. *The Seizing of the Santa Maria.* New York: Popular Library, 1961.

2

Problems, Controversies, and Solutions

I saw the flash of five to ten shots. Straight away, I knew it must be pirates.

—Captain Sellathurai Mahalingam of the UN-chartered aid ship *Semlow*, off Somalia in June 2005

Problems

Maritime traffic today is at an all-time high. Historically, cargo has always been easier to move by water than over land, and the volume of global commerce has soared exponentially since the end of World War II. Even during this—our modern age—90 percent of all commercial goods and raw materials are still conveyed aboard ships, at some stage during their progression toward market.

Yet ironically, the centuries-old problem of piracy—which had virtually ceased to exist everywhere on our planet as recently as 1990—has also rebounded during these past two decades, while peaceful seaborne trade was attaining such unprecedented expansion and growth. And in a curious sidelight, some of the very innovations which have contributed so significantly to the evolution of this ultra-efficient new delivery system, also contained certain inbuilt seeds for future trouble—flaws which, when combined together, have inadvertently facilitated a reappearance of predators amid today's busy sea lanes. As has been noted elsewhere, "the problems and loopholes in the regulation and control of the maritime industry are conducive to the operations of pirates" (Tanter, "Roots").

Seven Underlying Preconditions

The seven undercurrents and trends in the world's shipping industry, which have unexpectedly contributed to a resurgence of our uniquely modern brand of piracy, can be summarized as follows:

1. The almost *total disappearance of U.S. and Western merchant fleets* from the high seas as a result of severe cost-cutting measures embraced by most shipping firms. In order to reduce taxes, salaries, and operating expenses as much as possible, owners long ago began transferring their ships on paper to more accommodating regimes, so that very few large merchantmen still fly the American or West European flags today. Their absence from the world's oceans has also diminished any interest which major sea powers might have had in maintaining far-flung patrols, to help defend their nation's vessels against piracy.

2. The *construction of much larger merchantmen, manned by much smaller crews*—another economizing strategy adopted by most company directors and managers, yet which has also filled the oceans with rich and thinly manned behemoths, easy to be captured by even the tiniest band of armed pirates.

3. A vast *expansion of territorial waters claimed by most governments*, as well as additional outlying stretches recognized as "contiguous zones" or "exclusive economic zones." This practice was vigorously pursued by most nations during a worldwide drive in the mid-twentieth century, to secure as much as possible of their offshore natural resources—yet which also contracted the parts of open sea where naval warships might intervene against pirates. Such limitations today are specially enforced near the most heavily transited international waterways, where marauders frequently lie in wait in small shore boats to prey upon passing ocean vessels.

4. A persistent *irresolution in framing a suitable piracy charge under international law*, with the few general guidelines

once observed by Western maritime-powers now codified by the United Nations—yet still subject to interpretation and application by every signatory government. Not even all allied navies participating in the current antipiracy efforts off the Horn of Africa, can agree upon a single common legal standard. This issue is further clouded by the multiple nationalities involved in virtually every major piratical incident, from ship owners scattered in diverse capitals overseas; the role played by a particular flag state; actions taken by management subcontractors, who actually operate most vessels; the polyglot mixture of crewmembers and their diplomatic representation; the interests of various multinational insurance brokerages; etc.

5. The *shift of large-scale commercial traffic to Asian waters*, resulting in ever more supertankers, container ships, and trawlers crowding through narrow chokepoints beside impoverished and often lawless shorelines, with no naval support from their home governments. The swelling number of Asian fishing boats poaching in Somalia's unguarded fishing banks has also provided the motivation for that nation's piratical forays.

6. A *widespread adoption of flags of convenience by global shipping firms*, which—among several other drawbacks—have left many large ocean-going vessels staffed by only the lowest-paid seamen available, who cannot be expected to help defend their ship during a time of emergency. Indeed, a few ill-paid seafarers have even been suspected of colluding with criminal gangs ashore, helping arrange robberies.

7. The *proliferation of potent military light weaponry in civilian hands*, furnishing enough firepower for even a handful of ragtag teenage gunmen in a flimsy speedboat to halt and overawe resistance aboard the largest oceangoing ships.

An unforeseen result of all these combined shortcomings, has been a parade of rich, scantly manned prizes moving through tight chokepoints, temptingly within reach of seafarers from some of the poorest and most lawless nations on Earth. In such places, there is no government for foreign representatives to mount an appeal, while the few foreign naval patrols must remain far out at sea. Prizes can be detained offshore almost indefinitely, with little hope of rescue.

Special Piratical Needs

In addition to the seven factors listed above, all pirates—whether ancient or modern—required two additional elements in order to truly flourish: chokepoint hunting-grounds and sanctuaries ashore. Given the profit-driven motivation behind most of their criminal activities, rovers typically venture out to sea only on hit-and-run raids, choosing busy nearby sea lanes so as to increase their chances of locating a victim, after which they require a safe haven into which to return, so as to plunder or exploit their prize without being disturbed. Today's pirates are little different from their forbearers in these regards.

Chokepoint Hunting Grounds

Almost all narrow waterways have experienced periods of piracy during their history. The Strait of Messina and other Mediterranean chokepoints were prowled by marauders since the earliest days of the Roman Republic, while the English Channel was scoured by lawless brigands throughout medieval times. Sixteenth-century Elizabethan sea dogs hovered in Caribbean narrows such as the Windward Passage and Straits of Florida, which were still being hunted 150 years later by renegade freebooters such as Blackbeard. The dread Barbary corsairs preyed upon ships transiting through the Strait of Gibraltar for several centuries, plundering cargoes and enslaving crews, before finally being subdued by a military conquest during the early decades of the nineteenth century. And modern piracy has revived in a very similar fashion, by resurging around two vulnerable passages: the Strait of Malacca and Horn of Africa.

Strait of Malacca

This strategic waterway is some 500 miles long, yet relatively narrow: scarcely more than a mile-and-a-half wide at its narrowest point, in the Phillips Channel of the Singapore Strait. The only sea route through an extensive geographic barrier comprised of the Malay Peninsula and a sprawling mass of islands, it is lined by countless inlets and bays, ideally suited for piracy. And since this strait has served for many centuries as the sole link between the Indian Ocean and South China Sea, commercially connecting the Far East to the Arabian Peninsula and Africa, it has never lacked for merchant traffic funneling through its waters.

A treatise recorded as long ago as the fourteenth century by the Chinese writer Long Ya Men, described the dangers lurking within this "Dragon Teeth Strait." Junks carrying bulk-cargos from east to west, he noted, would be allowed to pass through peacefully, exiting into the Indian Ocean to trade on its far shores. Yet upon their return passage, rich and heavy with their accrued profits and bartered goods:

> some two or three hundred pirate *praus* will put out to attack them. Sometimes [the junks] are fortunate enough to escape with a favorable wind; otherwise the crews are butchered, and the merchandise made off with in quick time. (Freeman, p. 175)

And even today, there are still attacks being made against modern merchantmen passing through these same waters, an eternal hunting-ground for pirates.

Horn of Africa

For as many centuries, coastal traffic from India, Arabia, and Africa has likewise had to funnel into the Gulf of Aden, so as to gain the Red Sea and tap into the distant Mediterranean trade. At the bottom of this Gulf, a twenty-mile-wide entrance into the Red Sea is still known today as *Bab el-Mandeb* or the "Gate of Tears," because of its difficult navigation. Its strong currents and countercurrents had often frustrated seafarers during the days of sail, the narrow strait itself being bisected by an island into a shallow, two-mile eastern channel characterized by a surface current flowing into the Red Sea, while a deeper and 16-mile western channel has a strong undercurrent outwards.

In addition to its marine difficulties, this chokepoint bound by the Horn of Africa has often been a haunt for pirates as well. During the late-seventeenth century, its rich and vulnerable merchant traffic even attracted rogue privateers from as far away as New England. Among the first to lay in wait was Thomas Tew of Newport, Rhode Island, who in the autumn of 1693 intercepted a wealthy Indian prize and returned home next spring—having logged more than 22,000 miles on an epic 15-month cruise—with an exotic plunder of gold, silver, jewelry, elephants' tusks, ivory, spices, and silk valued at more than £100,000. This dazzling success spawned a host of eager imitators known as the "Red-Sea men," including Captain William Kidd of New York City, who all hunted much the same waters in the Gulf of Aden frequented by today's Somali pirates.

Land Sanctuaries

Once having secured a valuable prize, all pirates—both ancient and modern—need a safe harbor to plunder or exploit its contents, as well as a welcoming haven ashore to enjoy its proceeds and melt back into civilian life, without fear of arrest. Thomas Tew first carried his rich Indian prize more than 3,000 miles south into the lawless anchorage on St. Mary's, a slender island off the Madagascar coast, arriving there by October 19, 1693 (O.S.) to begin dividing the spoils with his crew, far from the scene of their crime and careening his own brigantine *Amity*. He subsequently burned the Indian hulk and sailed *Amity* home to Rhode Island next spring, rejoining civilian existence as a newly-rich man a half-world away.

Still earlier, Caribbean pirates had rested in Samaná Bay on Hispaniola, or amid the maze of sparsely populated islands off Southern Cuba, to dispose of their most blatantly ill-acquired goods before returning into the Crown-administered ports of French Tortuga or English Jamaica. Later renegades such as Blackbeard and Captain Benjamin Hornigold briefly converted unclaimed Nassau in the Bahamas into a veritable pirate-base, before London sent out a tough new governor to restore royal rule. Even during the early nineteenth century, the Lafitte brothers were still carrying prizes into Barataria, it being a open secret that they pillaged and auctioned off stolen cargoes there, just beyond the immediate gaze of pliant nearby authorities.

In today's world, with all its modern satellite surveillance, it is much more difficult to hide a large ship. Some pirates in the South China Sea occasionally do so by re-registering a hijacked vessel under a false name, a temporary expedient. But the only places where contemporary pirates can openly anchor a huge prize offshore, for weeks and months on end, are certain stretches of stark coastline off central Somalia.

Four Recent Hot Spots

Although isolated piratical incidents can erupt almost anywhere, most recent occurrences have been reported as being concentrated in four main zones:

1. the South China Sea,
2. Nigeria,

3. the Strait of Malacca,
4. and the Horn of Africa.

All four have experienced a manifold increase in ship traffic during these past few decades, as well as extended their maritime jurisdictions, yet struggled to provide adequate security in a timely fashion.

Perilous South China Sea

The ancient and closed society of seafarers plying the south coast of China and neighboring Indochina is difficult for outsiders to penetrate. Even the central Communist authorities in distant Beijing could exert only a limited control over these waters, and reliable information on piratical activities in this shadowy world was almost impossible to obtain until recently. An occasional report might emerge, such as the account of the *Petchompoo*, which after reporting its position on August 26, 1991 as being 180 miles east of the Vietnamese capital of Ho Chi Minh City, went silent and never reappeared, the fate of its crew and $4 million onboard remaining a mystery to this day.

As the Cold War drew to a close and China began its gradual tilt toward capitalism during the 1990s, piratical depredations apparently multiplied as well in the triangular area that borders Hong Kong, China's Hainan Island, and Luzon in the Philippines, expanding beyond the outer fringes of these boundaries to become more widely known. A series of very brazen attacks even occurred, either carried out by rogue elements of the Chinese Navy or pirate masqueraders:

> **May 15, 1995:** Twenty uniformed men from a Chinese naval patrol vessel, armed with AK-47s, board a Taiwanese ship off Subic Bay in the Philippines, steering this prize outside territorial waters to plunder its cargo.
>
> **June 23, 1995:** North of Redang Island, off the east coast of Malaysia, twelve men wearing Chinese Army uniforms board the Panamanian-flagged cargo ship *Hye Mieko*, which has departed Singapore two days previously with $2 million worth of cigarettes and photographic equipment as its cargo. By June 25th, the ship is sighted under escort by a Chinese patrol boat, 140 nautical miles southeast of Ho Chi Minh City. Its captors sail it on into the Chinese port of

Shanwei, where it is eventually released—empty—along with its crew members by July 23rd.

January 22, 1996: Early this morning, a Philippine Navy gunboat spots two suspicious vessels twelve miles off Capones Island, so fires a warning shot for them to heave to. One craft flees, but the other tries to ram the gunboat, so that a chase and 90-minute gun battle ensues off Luzon Island, until the Philippine vessel's guns jam and its fuel runs low.

The intruder vessel is described as a People's Republic of China patrol-vessel with the bow number 04420, flying a Red Star flag and with military men onboard. However, the Philippine Navy Chief, Vice Admiral Pio Carranza, believes that the intruders are most likely Chinese pirates in disguise.

January 27, 1996: At daybreak about 40 miles southwest of Maobitou in the Taiwan Strait, the 5,000-ton, Panamanian-flagged, Taiwanese container-ship *Hangjung No. 9*—bound from Indonesia toward Kaohsiung with a cargo of low flash-point ethanol—is followed for three hours by a green-colored, iron-hulled boat bearing a mainland Chinese flag and bow number F-4404.

Around 9:30 a.m., this pursuer closes to within 20–30 yards and opens fire, striking the freighter several times with machine-gun and automatic-rifle rounds. The Taiwanese Captain reports seeing at least four men in military uniforms onboard his assailant, who send across men armed with handguns to ransack the Master's and Radio Officer's safes, stealing about $10,000 in cash and property. The two ships accidentally collide after about 10 minutes, prompting the boarders to depart and their boat to leave the scene.

February 10, 1996: A Philippine naval patrol spots a Chinese vessel about five miles from the entrance into Subic Bay, trying to warn it off with shots fired into the air and radio-contact. The intruder responds by trying to ram the patrol-craft and firing rifles back in its attempts to escape, before being cornered by three Philippine Navy ships. The twenty surrendered pirates prove to be Chinese, although General Arturo T. Enrile—Chief of the Philippine Armed Forces—is convinced that the Beijing government has no knowledge of their activities.

The evident lack of official oversight and resultant lawlessness in the South China Sea, would result in a unique regional phenomenon associated only with Asian piracy: phantom ships. Criminal gangs such as the secretive triads especially favored this tactic, which involved arranging for the hijacking of a small-to-medium-sized merchantman, which could then be repainted and given a new identity, by reregistering it under a false name so as to use it in further felonies, such as smuggling. No other part of the world experienced the rash of such incidents as the South China Sea, the following being but a few examples:

September 13, 1995: The Cypriot-flagged cargo ship *Anna Sierra* is stormed 70 nautical miles southeast of Bangkok, by 25–30 pirates armed with machine guns and wearing masks. Its Master and 22 crewmembers are handcuffed in pairs in the engine room for two days, before being set adrift in dinghies, later being rescued by a Vietnamese fishing boat. Upon quitting their freighter, the crew notice that their captors are altering its name, as well as repainting hatch covers and other visible points. It is sailed into the southern Chinese port of Beihai by September 20th as the Honduran-flagged *Artic Sea*.

November 22, 1996: Near Horsburgh Lighthouse east of Singapore, the Malaysian gas oil tanker *Suci* is boarded by six armed pirates, 15 of its seventeen crewmen being blindfolded and set adrift in a lifeboat, to be rescued later by a fishing vessel. The two crewmembers retained aboard the hijacked *Suci* are released unharmed by January 14, 1997, reporting that their tanker still has approximately 3,000 metric tons of gas oil onboard, its name having been painted over and replaced with *Glory II*, registered in San Lorenzo, Honduras—allowing the pirated tanker to continue operating with a new complement of 19 crewmen.

December 26, 1998: The 3,113-ton cargo ship *Hong Peng* disappears after departing from Hong Kong toward Taichung on the island of Taiwan, with a cargo of clay and a crew of twenty on board. When it fails to arrive, the International Maritime Bureau or IMB offers a reward of $50,000 for information leading to the location and recovery of this vessel. In view of the hijacking and murder of the crew of the *Cheung Son*, this disappearance of another small ship with a similarly low-value cargo raises fears that yet another crew may have been murdered, and their vessel retained as a phantom ship.

May 25, 1999: After sailing from Tuticorin in India on May 25th with a cargo of bagged salt, the 2,818-ton Malaysian-flagged cargo ship *Sik Yang* fails to arrive at its destination of Malacca six days later as scheduled. It is initially feared that it has been hijacked by pirates and retained as a phantom vessel, the fate of its 15 crewmen being unknown. However, it is subsequently reported on June 30, 1999 that the *Sik Yang* may have been captured by guerrillas from the Sri Lankan rebel group, the Tamil Tigers.

June 8, 1999: While steaming from Singapore toward Songkhla with a cargo of 2,060 tons of gas oil, the 1,247-ton Thai-flagged tanker *Siam Xanxai* is boarded near midnight by pirates off the Malaysian island of Pulau Tioman. Fifteen of 16 crewmen are held in their cabins for two days, then cast adrift in a faulty motorboat. Only a Thai oiler is kept aboard, allegedly because he knows how to operate the ship's valves.

After drifting for 14 hours, the castaways are rescued by a passing ship, and subsequently learn that *Siam Xanxai* has been renamed *Auo Me 2*, before being detained for smuggling on July 18th in southern China's Guangdong Province.

July 22, 1999: The 2,581-ton, Panamanian-registered cargo ship *Kenduri* is reported as missing, having sailed from Bangkok via Ko Sichang on June 16th with 3,200 tons of steel destined for Vietnam. Having failed to reach its discharge port, and with a transit route that runs through waters known as hunting-grounds for several Chinese pirate gangs, the *Kenduri* is feared hijacked and retained as a phantom ship.

Although such dire perils have apparently receded during more recent times, as China continues to open up to the outside world and drive toward modernization, reliable information on the actual degree of current piratical and criminal activities still remains fitful and spotty. Nevertheless, it has been noted how the revival of global piracy "reached a peak between 1999 and 2003, because of the activity of pirates in the South China Sea and Malacca Strait" (*Piracy Off the Coast of Somalia*, p. 13).

Nigeria's Beleaguered Oil Route

Violent incidents off Nigeria are regularly featured among the world's leading piracy statistics, yet since virtually all occur well within its territorial waters or inland rivers, they do not constitute true piratical acts but rather felonious assaults and robberies. No foreign naval patrols will ever redress this problem, but rather local prosecutions and social intervention by Nigeria's government itself.

Since the discovery of oil in the Niger Delta during the late 1950s, the refining and export of petroleum has become the biggest industry, employer, and moneymaker for this large West African country—the most populous nation on the entire African continent, with an estimated 155 million inhabitants. Originally, what is today Nigeria consisted of dozens of disperse semi-autonomous states and ethnic communities, which became amalgamated into a single colony by its British administrators in 1914. As a result, at least 40 distinct ethnic groups still reside today within the Niger Delta alone, speaking about 250 individual dialects.

Shortly after gaining its independence from Great Britain in October 1960, Nigeria became a republic, but regional and ethnic tensions soon erupted into conflict, plunging the nation into a cruel civil war. The Ibo or Igbo peoples of its oil-rich Delta region attempted to secede from the federal state, only to be crushed by 1970, many survivors being left marginalized and harboring bitter animosity against the victorious central government in the distant capital of Lagos, dominated by Yorubas. Such resentment simmered and began to deepen further after the Nigerian oil industry was nationalized next year, while a simultaneous boom in international petroleum prices that same decade meant that huge amounts of money were soon flowing into the nation—much being misspent on patronage and other corrupt practices. By 1979, the Delta was producing 82 percent of all of Nigeria's federal government revenues, yet few benefits accrued among its impoverished inhabitants.

Demands for greater local shares soon began to be heard, which were eventually joined by a growing concern over the environmental damage being caused to the Delta's rivers and lands by the ever-sprawling and spewing oil installations. National exports of such traditional cash crops as cocoa, rubber, and cotton meanwhile declined, to the point where Nigeria was reduced to importing foodstuffs, leaving many of its inhabitants struggling against poverty and want, amid official indifference. Unrest therefore escalated in the Delta, until vessels traveling in and out of its oil-fields began to be targeted, as in the following typical examples:

April 24, 1996: Seven Nigerians armed with guns and long knives board a vessel which is heading downriver toward the open sea from the inland port of Warri. Its Master sounds an emergency-alarm, and all external doors are locked. After stealing six mooring-ropes, a winch-drum, and six life-rings, the thieves jump into the water and are picked up by an accomplice in a speedboat.

August 27, 1997: While outward bound from Warri, the 2,514-ton, Liberian-flagged cargo ship *Frischland* is attacked in Chanomi Creek at 12:10 p.m. by seven armed men in a speedboat. They pursue until the ship is near Bedford Point, then use hooked poles to clamber aboard. Brandishing guns, clubs, and knives, they subdue the crew and force the Master to open his safe, emptying it of cash while other thieves ransack the crew's cabins, taking whatever valuables they can find. The pilot and two bridge hands are beaten by a pair of pirates, who remain there throughout this incident, so that the ship sails for about 20 minutes with its helm unattended. Eventually, the looters spot a nearby police boat and flee at 12:30 p.m., with this patrol in hot pursuit.

March 28, 1999: As it nears the pilot station at Escravos Bar off Saples at 2:00 a.m., the Panamanian-registered cargo ship *Fione* is boarded in the darkness from a speedboat by six masked men armed with axes, hammers, and machine guns. Master and crew are gathered on the bridge, and when these attackers learn that no money is aboard, they beat their prisoners, as well as smashing navigation and radio equipment. One crewman suffers a skull fracture, the Captain injuries to an arm, by being hit with a hammer while trying to protect the instruments.

Armed guards are subsequently hired to escort *Fione* to its berth, and are also aboard during its outward transit.

April 22, 1999: A standby tug at the Forcado Oil Terminal is attacked by an armed gang but rescued by Nigerian military forces. Nevertheless, all loading is temporarily suspended out of fear of reprisal, as Nigeria's oil terminals and production fields "have experienced significant violence during the past year from local tribes and townspeople seeking greater share in proceeds."

April 29, 1999: After running aground off Madangho in the Escravos River, the 497-ton Nigerian-flagged tanker *Stronghand* is boarded and stripped by local youths, while three captive crewmembers are not released until a ransom is paid by the vessel's owners.

July 11, 1999: While navigating the Escravos River, the 3,172-ton Lithuanian-flagged reefer ship *Vega* is approached at 9:30 a.m. by a speedboat, whose occupants—clad in military uniforms—order it to halt. On advice from his onboard pilot, *Vega*'s Master refuses to comply, but his vessel is then pursued and raked by more than fifty rounds of heavy-caliber machine-gun fire, before these aggressors give up their chase.

July 28, 1999: The fishing boat *Dolphine 4* is stormed by youths off Pennington Island, its Captain and crew assaulted while the boat is looted of sundry goods and communication equipment, being left so vandalized that it has to be towed into port next day. At least six other fishing boats have recently endured similar attacks, echoing tribal unrest ashore.

October 14, 1999: The St. Vincent-flagged tug-supply boat *Damas Victory* is seized on the Bonny River, for failing to display the "permit sticker" demanded by local youth gangs.

October 23, 1999: As part of a series of tribal protests, a Belize-flagged vessel with an all-Nigerian crew owned by the Tidewater Oil Company is briefly detained in the Bonny River by an armed youth gang, along with the *Explorer Seahorse* several days later.

Then on November 1st, another Tidewater merchant vessel is seized and a U.S. citizen kidnapped, along with a Polish engineer, and 12 Nigerians. This ship and its hostages are released two days later, after a court injunction has been obtained.

November 15, 1999: The Shell Petroleum Development Company boat *MM22*, while transporting guards up the Bonny River toward the Cawthorne Channel Float Station, is intercepted by six armed youths in a speedboat, members of a tribal group seeking to compel Shell to hire 200 more local workers. *MM22*'s passengers and crew are held for "interrogation" before being released.

As foreign complaints mounted, the central government in Lagos responded by deploying Nigerian Army units into the region, as well as Mobile Police or "MoPol" paramilitary units— so quick to resort to their weaponry, that they were nicknamed the "Kill-and-Go" Police. Yet the presence of these outside forces merely aggravated the problem, breeding more resistance from increasingly better-armed groups such as the "Movement for the Emancipation of the Niger Delta." And the fact that the Nigerian Navy was wholly unprepared for any significant deployment meant that river-dangers would continue.

The Strait of Malacca Gauntlet
As with most other major sea passages around the world, piracy had declined dramatically by the early-twentieth century in this long and narrow channel, although occasional threats to transiting ships were never entirely eradicated. A few attacks were organized by secretive Chinese crime syndicates known as the triads during the 1930s, oftentimes targeting specific vessels as they steamed between Shanghai and Singapore.

A few more depredations recurred after World War II, but the scholar Carolin Liss has argued that it was to be the postwar modernization of Asia's fishing industries which unwittingly revived the problem of piracy. Sophisticated new technologies and equipment became widely available as of the 1950s, allowing fishermen to net much larger catches and tap stocks that had previously lain beyond their reach—but such large-scale sweeps also depleted many traditional fishing grounds, reducing the volume of catches within a decade. And overfishing was not the only problem: The destruction of many shoreline estuaries, wetlands, and reefs through industrialization and urban sprawl, as well as spreading ill effects from pollution, also diminished stocks further.

Consequently, some coastal communities were plunged into poverty, especially those whose fishermen only owned small boats, incapable of seeking out more distant banks. And even those trawlers which could go in search of less-exploited waters, often encountered complications brought on by expanding national claims. Formerly open ocean stretches might now be deemed part of another country's jurisdiction, with exclusive rights over its natural resources, however tenuous the legitimacy of such a claim. Fishermen driven by a decline of their own stocks into a nearby, yet ill-defined jurisdiction, might be subjected to violence as trespassers by local fishermen, or arrest as criminals by disputatious regional authorities. A study has estimated that between 1970 and 2000, fisheries depreciated by over 40 percent within the Strait of Malacca, its northern portion being particularly affected; some Malaysian fishermen therefore began illegally working adjacent Indonesian waters, which were believed to be better fishing grounds (Tanter, "Roots").

If caught by an Indonesian patrol, such Malaysian poachers might have their boat towed into port and detained for months, until a substantial fine was paid for its release along with the crew. Many therefore began offering to pay the "fine" directly to pliant members of the Navy or Marine Police at sea, after which they could continue fishing. But when trawlers then began routinely carrying extra cash to bribe such corrupt officials, they proved even more tempting targets for other types of attack. Malaysian politicians openly worried about the potential harm from such poaching in foreign waters, as when Deputy Home Minister Datuk Chor Chee Heung stated in 2002: "We are asking our fishermen not to encroach into Indonesian waters, as they will not only face pirates, but also cause misunderstandings with the Indonesian Navy" (ibid.).

Less well-positioned fishermen, desperate to supplement their meager and dwindling livelihoods, resorted to even more criminal acts. As an example, Liss mentioned the impoverished fishermen from Kampung Hitam, on Pulau Babi Island in the Riau Archipelago. The waters around their island had become so polluted and overfished that catches could no longer sustain their families, while their boats were too small to reach and work more distant banks. As a result, some turned to outright piracy, launching opportunistic strikes against any passing trawlers, yachts, or even small-to-medium-sized merchantmen. Similar loosely organized pirate bands also began stealing out from other indigent islands such as Belakang Padang and the Jemaja group, while even unemployed taxi-boat drivers were known to have become involved occasionally in nocturnal raids, when they could not find sufficient passengers during the day to make a living.

Most of these assaults were nervous hit-and-run affairs, taking whatever could immediately be grabbed, then fleeing. Soon, a rash of such low-grade raids began to be reported:

January 29, 1985: Near Singapore, six men clamber aboard the American tanker *Falcon Countess*, despite the fact that it is running along at 13.5 knots. Its Master is forced at knifepoint to open his safe, $19,471 in cash being stolen, plus several personal items.

October 25, 1985: Without warning near the island of Noord Natuna Eil or Kepulauan Natuna Besar, pirates open fire at 8:00 a.m. with automatic rifles on the Greek tanker *Marianna*, while it inbound toward Singapore. Its Master increases speed to 17 knots and so prevents these attackers from boarding, but a subsequent inspection reveals the tanker has been riddled by over 100 bullet holes.

January 7, 1986: At 3:20 a.m., a small craft stops a mile ahead of the approaching *President Johnson*, turning its searchlight onto the ship's bridge. Its watch officer alters course, yet the unknown boat deliberately runs into *Johnson*'s path again, shining its searchlight along the port side while attempting to close. Returning onto his original heading, the officer then sights another boat without lights, trying to approach *Johnson* on its starboard side. Neither craft can match the ship's speed of 23 knots, so soon fall behind.

June 15, 1986: While steaming 13 miles off Horsburgh Lighthouse, at the eastern entrance into Singapore Bay, the Australian container ship*Anro Australia* is boarded by pirates, its Master being robbed of $3,000 and personal items.

February 1987: The Soviet vessel *Slutsk* is boarded off Singapore by pirates using rope ladders, yet who are beaten back and flee aboard a motorboat, having seriously stabbed one crewman in a shoulder.

April 1, 1987: Five pirates armed with knives board the *Igloo Moss* from a small fast boat, while this liquid propane-gas carrier is passing Horsburgh Lighthouse, inward bound from Thailand. Some crewmembers are robbed.

Late April 1987: The Yugoslav vessel *Durmitor* is robbed by pirates off the coast of Singapore.

May 1, 1987: In the Phillips Channel, six pirates armed with knives and a pistol board the 24,090-ton, Panamanian-registered chemical carrier *Molley Laura*, manned by

23 South Koreans. The Chief Mate is seized, the safe opened, and crew quarters ransacked—$16,000 in cash and other valuables being stolen, although no injuries inflicted.

The Yugoslav vessel *Krk* is also boarded this same day near Singapore by pirates armed with knives and machetes, who likewise steal money and valuables.

May 3, 1987: Early on this Sunday morning near Singapore, a band of pirates in high-powered canoes come alongside the Philippine bulk carrier *Lydia 5*, using ropes with grappling hooks to swarm aboard. Brandishing guns and knives, they steal $7,000 in cash, plus other personal valuables.

August 6, 1987: The Panamanian-registered tanker *Orion Trader* is boarded by pirates armed with swords. Cash and valuables worth $2,000 are stolen, but no injuries reported, before the pirates flee in a small boat.

August 30, 1987: While steaming at 16 knots this night with its decks well lit, *President Madison* is stealthily boarded 15 miles east of Singapore's pilot boarding station by five pirates armed with machetes. They come aboard over the stern, binding and gagging the Chief Engineer in his stateroom, then robbing him of money and personal effects. He eventually frees himself and notifies the Master, but the pirates have by then disappeared.

April 27, 1988: At dawn between Bangka Island and Sumatra, the 5,300-ton, Bahamian-registered container ship *Klang Reefer* is boarded by four pirates. The Master's cabin is looted of personal belongings, electrical equipment, and a flare pistol, totaling about $15,000 in value.

May 13, 1988: Once again in the Bangka Strait, four pirates board the container ship *Swan Reefer*, robbing it of electrical equipment, as well as ransacking several commercial containers on deck.

July 2, 1988: While steaming past Horsburgh Lighthouse at 15 knots, *Iver Chaser* is boarded stealthily at night by four pirates from a fast boat, who have tossed a line undetected over its stern railings. They surprise the Master in his stateroom, leaving him bound and gagged when they depart with some valuables and drugs.

As the volume and value of commercial traffic through the Strait began to escalate most dramatically during the 1990s, more professional crimes would also begin to occur on its waters, some even being organized by syndicates from distant parts of Asia, such as the Japanese Yakuza or mainland Chinese triads. The economic, political, and social changes injected into the entire region with the end of the Cold War were to be accompanied by a resurgence in organized crime. In particular, the opening of China and its gradual tilt towards capitalism; the 1997 Asian financial crisis; plus the emergence of major financial centers at Singapore and Hong Kong, all contributed toward a covert spread of renewed criminality.

Given their involvement elsewhere in Asia in illegal activities such as smuggling, it is believed that Chinese triads soon began introducing their own methods into the busy Strait region. An individual triad might contact a local crime-associate or gang, arranging for low-ranking members or other recruits to carry out a designated attack. Medium-sized vessels were most often targeted, being retained for use as "phantom-ships" in further criminal enterprises. Such seizures were well-organized, with advance planning and ample funding for expenses. In August 1999, a certain "Mr. Wong"—believed to be head of operations in Indonesia for a triad operating out of Hong Kong, Malaysia, and the Philippines— was arrested and tried for allegedly having masterminded more than twenty such hijackings in the Strait.

The tanker *Selayang* almost shared this same fate, when it was seized by 19 pirates on June 20, 2001. However, since it had a tracking device onboard, the Indonesian authorities were able to free this vessel and arrest some of its captors a week later near Balikpapan—yet the plot had been so carefully devised, that the perpetrators could only say they had been hired to make the attack by a certain "Mr. Ching," whom they had never met and therefore could not identify (ibid.).

Unemployed and desperate fishermen continued to furnish easy recruits for such organized crime strikes. A buoy-tender ship was assaulted that same June 2001 near Indonesia's Karimun Island, part of Riau Province southeast of Singapore, although this attack was beaten back and crewmembers managed to capture one of the pirates, as his colleagues fled. This prisoner revealed that eight out of the 13 assailants involved were fishermen from Karimun, whose banks had been almost totally destroyed by illegal bomb and cyanide fishing, while other sources of income were impossible to find on their island. The shadowy masterminds behind this attack were apparently based on Indonesia's Batam Island, having merely hired some of these struggling fishermen to carry out the attack.

In addition to such criminal enterprises, rebels of the *Gerakan Aceh Merdeka* (GAM) or "Free Aceh Movement" are also believed to have conducted some piratical attacks in the northern stretches of the Malacca Straits, in order to finance their struggle against the Indonesian government. For example, GAM has been blamed for seizures of the Malaysian *Penrider* in August 2003 and Indonesian *Tri Samudra* in March 2005, during which hostages were seized and ransoms extorted. GAM is furthermore believed responsible for assaults against fishing boats, specifically targeting Indonesian trawlers, thereby amassing a fleet of stolen fishing vessels, which—being slimmer and faster than Malaysian boats—are ideally suited for more strikes. GAM's leadership, until recently exiled in Sweden, has vehemently denied these charges and accused the Indonesian military of attempting to smear their group.

The Horn of Africa and Disintegration of Somalia

Compared to other troubled waters, such as the South China Sea or Strait of Malacca, the Gulf of Aden did not suffer from ingrained piracy as the twentieth century drew to a close—only sporadic incidents off poor and fragmented Somalia, the country whose eastern tip represents the "Horn of Africa." Prior to its colonization by Great Britain and Italy during the latter part of the nineteenth century, Somalia had never been a single unified nation. Rather, because of its arid landscape, only a few scattered concentrations of inhabitants had ever developed along its shoreline, most residents preferring to live in tribal groupings around fertile pockets in its interior.

In ancient times, its ports had served as lonely way stations for traders importing Indian spices, which were then transported up the Red Sea by Arab merchants for resale. Somalia's modern pirates hail from this long tradition of seafaring clans, who in addition to fishing and trading, were also known to occasionally prey on passing ships from their small towns, concealed all up and down the country's long and flat coastline. They often supplemented their meagre living through smuggling, or trade in stolen goods, and even taking hostages—who were sometimes sold into slavery. In the recent past, most piracy was centered on the coastal towns of Harardheere and Hobyo in Central Somalia, targeting the Mogadishu port area farther to the southwest ("Lawless Tradition").

The opening of the Suez Canal during the latter half of nineteenth century led to a great new flow in the world's maritime traffic, so that major European powers soon began claiming coaling stations and other strategic facilities along the Horn of Africa. As only a few thousand impoverished inhabitants actually lived there in scattered tribal pockets, under the nominal rule of distant sultans, British interests acquired concessions from these absentee rulers to a stretch along the inner span of Red Sea shoreline—known today as "Somaliland"—while Italy, eager to establish its own colonial empire in Africa, gained title over various parts of southeastern Somalia during the 1880s. Rome encouraged its citizens to emigrate out to this territory, and on April 5, 1908, formally united its patchwork of diverse private concessions into a single colony, called *Somalia Italiana*. When the Dervish state furthermore collapsed during the 1920s, Mussolini's Fascist government took over Somalia's north-eastern sultanates as well.

Colonial rule was ended during the aftermath of World War II, and Mohamed Siad Barre seized power in 1969 as Somalia's autocratic President. By late 1990, his repressive regime was in serious trouble, controlling little more than a few pockets of the increasingly fractured nation. Rebel factions led by the warlord Mohamed Farrah Aidid attacked the outskirts of its capital Mogadishu, driving Barre from office by the evening of January 26, 1991, who then fled to his power base among the Marehan clan in the southwestern Gedo region to continue fighting. Ali Mahdi Muhammad, a prominent businessman of the Hawiye Abgaal clan, succeeded as president, but could not exert any political or military authority in the country, so that Somalia disintegrated into hostile clan enclaves, frequently realigning as they clashed repeatedly against one another.

Unnoticed amid this power vacuum of the early 1990s, lowly fisheries along the coastline became wholly neglected. Foreign trawlers therefore began edging ever closer inshore to make their catches, soon depleting the traditional grounds worked by local fishermen. Regional Somali authorities proved either indifferent or powerless to help, so that confrontations ensued at sea. Boatloads of poorly armed Somali fishermen began seizing a few trawlers, confiscating their catches and imposing hefty "fines" as self-proclaimed coast guards. However, the Chinese, Taiwanese, and South Korean trawler fleets were not easily deterred, instead contacting warlords ashore so as to hire their gunmen for protection, and better arming their own fishing-vessels. Confrontations became more aggressive, yet the poor Somalis were no match against these interlopers, therefore began turning indiscriminately upon any vessel which chanced to pass (Report S/2006/229, p. 25).

A series of assaults began to be reported out of this low-grade "war zone" in Somalia's waters:

April 5, 1995: A small vessel fires a mortar round at the racing yacht *Longo Barda*, and some pirates prepare to come board. They flee when the frigate *Fredericton* and a container vessel approach to the rescue.

April 22, 1995: East of Suqutra Island, the vessel *Radnor* is approached by two motorboats, whose occupants open fire with machine guns and light artillery. The ship increases speed to 12 knots and is able to evade its attackers.

April 28, 1995: Near Cape Guardafui, the vessel *Ming Bright* comes under light artillery fire from a motorboat, outrunning its attackers.

May 3, 1995: At 1:10 p.m., about 100 nautical miles west of Suqutra Island, a small boat fires upon the vessel *Liliana Dimitrova*, one crewman being wounded during this attack.

October 23, 1995: During this night, a speedboat mounting a heavy machine gun fires upon a vessel anchored at El-Maan port, about 20 miles northeast of Mogadishu, compelling it to retreat out to sea.

February 1, 1996: Near Mogadishu, eight gunmen in speedboats seize the Kenyan-registered ship *Clove*, reputedly demanding as much as $100 million in ransom for its release. They allegedly identify themselves as "Coast Guard" personnel upon boarding the ship, and contact the vessel's owner, who was shipping consumer goods from Mombassa toward Kismaayo with a crew of 20.

March 7, 1997: The 3,016-ton tanker *Helena* is approached by two fishing vessels, one of which fires a rifle grenade that falls short. They signal the tanker to stop, but *Helena* increases speed and outruns their pursuit.

May 20, 1996: While on standby sixteen nautical miles off the Arab Bank Sandbar, in international waters near

Djibouti, the 2,050-ton Russian salvage tug *SB-408* is approached by two patrol boats manned by Somali militiamen in civilian dress, toting automatic weapons. The tug's Master and Third Officer are forced at gunpoint onto one of these launches, while the twenty crewmembers aboard the tug are escorted toward the Horn of Africa. En route, the captors pillage *SB-408* of money and supplies for their boats, this 12-hour ordeal finally ending when the Master agrees to surrender about $8,000 in cash, ten tons of diesel fuel, two drums of lubrication oil, and about $2,000 worth of stores and provisions.

September 27, 1998: The 299-ton, Djibouti-flagged freighter *Nourstar* is hijacked from the port of Bosaso by seven men, who shoot a crewman while forcing their way aboard. Half the crew is then released at Ras Hafoon near Socotra, reporting that heavy guns have been installed aboard their freighter to prey upon smaller ships and dhows, both off Somalia and in the Gulf of Aden. Eventually, *Nourstar* is released, and arrives back at Djibouti by December 14th.

December 24, 1998: The Belize-flagged coastal trader *Sea Johanna* is hijacked off southern Somalia, being held about 70 miles northeast of Lamu Island, near the border with Kenya, while 15 members of its predominantly Pakistani crew are kept ashore as hostages. The owners report that this attack has been carried out by the Jaamatul Ihtizam group, which is demanding a large ransom. The abandoned vessel is recovered adrift by the Kenyan Navy on March 27–28, 1999, its owner still trying to raise $60,000 to free the crew—who are eventually released on May 11th by their captors, having apparently grown tired of awaiting payment.

March 14, 1999: At 2:00 p.m., while passing within 25 miles of Somalia's eastern coast, the 5,916-ton, Belize-flagged cargo ship *Salwah* sights four approaching craft, so alters course. They nonetheless close in and open fire by 2:43 p.m., compelling *Salwah* to heave-to by 3:10 p.m., now 33 miles offshore. Seventeen armed pirates come aboard, soon followed by another 10, who secure *Salwah*'s 19 Ukrainian crewmembers and demand an undisclosed ransom for their release.

Next day, a Taiwanese trawler is also seized near Eli Town.

March 16, 1999: The Greek-flagged tanker *World Kinship* is approached by three vessels while steaming past eastern Somalia, being hailed by radio to halt and prepare to be boarded. Gunmen at the same time open fire on the ship, which increases speed and escapes with only a few bullet holes.

April 5, 1999: At 9:00 a.m., pirates pretending to be fishermen approach a ship running 20–25 miles off the Somali coast, opening fire with machine guns and attempting to board, although impeded by its high freeboard. After a pursuit of 30 minutes, they give up their chase.

April 11, 1999: The Antigua-flagged container ship *Karin S* is intercepted off Somalia's east coast by two boats, six or seven armed men waving their weapons as a signal for it to stop. When the ship's Master alters course farther out to seaward, they open fire with light weaponry and pursue, yet give up their chase only three minutes later.

Such recklessness by armed bands of rovers—some claiming that they were acting as "coast guards," charged by regional chieftains with protecting dwindling local resources—led to a reputation for lawlessness in Somalia's territorial waters, where the strong simply preyed upon the weak.

Yet attacks were mostly confined to within 50 nautical miles of its coast, because the basic means available for pirates to venture out to sea were 20- to 30-foot skiffs, open and merely powered by outboard motors, whose range was limited by the small amount of fuel that they could carry. Such craft were usually manufactured of fiberglass in Yemeni boatyards, and sold to coastal traders or fishermen for $2,500–$3,500 apiece. They typically have high freeboards, and were usually powered by an 85-horsepower Yamaha outboard motor, although skiffs with twin 150-horsepower models could speed in short bursts of 30 knots across relatively calm seas, with four people aboard. Given that these craft were so light and exposed, though, no one dared sortie out onto the ocean waves during the summer monsoon seasons, which occur between late April and early September, interrupting or at least diminishing all maritime activities off Somalia— including piracy.

These seagoing gunmen also obtained most of their hand-held weaponry out of Yemen, or from around Somalia's national capital of Mogadishu. Typically, a weapons-dealer or middleman would receive a deposit from a *hawala* broker on behalf of a distant group of pirates, and the weapons would then be delivered by vehicle, at which point the balance would be paid.

Worst-Case Scenario: Piracy in a Void

Statistically, present-day piracy hit its peak worldwide between 1999 and 2003, because of a rash of criminality in the busy sea lanes of the South China Sea and Strait of Malacca. However, thanks to coordinated efforts by local and regional governments, plus timely international assistance, this brief upsurge would virtually disappear within a single year in the Strait of Malacca and around Singapore, while being greatly decreased by a general crackdown in the South China Sea (*Piracy Off the Coast of Somalia*, p. 13).

Somali piracy, by way of contrast, was seemingly insignificant during that same period, because its lawless rovers only had small boats with which to opportunistically strike close inshore, so that transiting merchantmen simply remained in the safer traffic-lanes farther out at sea—giving the false impression that such unbridled outbursts in its lonely coastal stretches only posed a minor threat to commercial shipping. But criminality would take such deep root in that uncontrolled environment, that it would then turn into a much more intractable problem, "because Somalia is a failed state where anarchy has prevailed for most of the past two decades" (Karon).

Extortion as Business

Specifically, the desperate poverty and utter lack of any secure prospects would lead a penniless ex-civil servant named Mohamed Abdi Hassan Hayir, more commonly known as *Afweyne* or "Big Mouth," to deliberately try to organize these random attacks against chance targets offshore, into a moneymaking business venture. In 2003, he would raise some capital and travel northeast into Puntland, to recruit veteran pirates to act as instructors. Notorious rovers such as Garad Mohamed, Farah Hirsi Kulan "Boya", and Farah Abdullahi would be lured south by Hassan's inducements, to serve both as active commanders offshore, as well as indoctrinating his local followers.

Afweyne would soon manage to create a structured pirate organization, whose sole purpose was to waylay foreign vessels and hold them for ransom. The very remoteness of his base at Harardheere—a forlorn and sun-bleached port in the Mudug region, on the Central Somali coast—proved ideal as a base of operations, being scarcely accessible to the rest of the fragmented country by road and so completely beyond any hint of governmental authority. In such a neglected backwater, Hassan's ill-gotten profits could more effectively influence its few unpaid officials to ignore prizes anchored offshore, plus constitute a dominant portion of the local economy, through generous payments to his suppliers.

These organizational practices would spread northeastward when his hired mercenaries, hardened marauders such as Garad Mohamed and Boya, returned to their own lawless home port of Eyl and began applying them there. Soon, other imitators would also appear, especially as ransoms grew in size and volume, producing tempting streams of cash in such poor and backward regions. The number of reported captures off Somalia would consequently jump from two in 2004, to 35 by 2005, prompting worried foreign shipping firms to begin shifting their routes a couple of hundred miles farther out to sea, in the vain hope of moving beyond range of ever more avaricious pirates.

By April 2008, even the conservative British weekly *The Economist* would be editorializing about the palpable shift in piratical activities on the high seas:

> Somalia's coastal waters are proving increasingly perilous for mariners. Some 31 attacks on ships were reported in 2007, compared with just two in 2004, according to the International Maritime Bureau. Pirates operating around the lawless African country are more likely to use weapons than in the past; a Spanish fishing vessel was attacked at the weekend using grenade-launchers. It is now considered so risky, that this week France and America announced a draft UN Security Council resolution, allowing foreign governments to pursue and arrest pirates in territorial waters. Nigeria's oil wealth is also attracting more brigands to its seas. Ships navigating through traditional piracy hot spots, such as the Malacca Strait and the vast coastal waters of Indonesia, have suffered fewer attacks since 2004.

Corruption and Dependence

Bribery and lavish spending by pirates and their financial backers would come to entrench the business among otherwise hopeless communities. Underemployed fishermen who agreed to pilot gunmen out to sea in pirate skiffs, would be paid far more than they could ever earn from their depleted fishing stocks. One convicted pirate would declare that a teenage gunman could earn anywhere from $6,000 to $10,000 from a million-dollar ship ransom, roughly equivalent to two or three years' salary from working as an armed guard at a Western humanitarian agency, and much better than any local business could ever pay. He would also explain that the normal division of ransom payments was 20 percent to the bosses of the pirate enterprise; 20 percent invested in guns, fuel, provisions, and other materials for future missions; 30 percent split up among the gunmen themselves; and 30 percent distributed as bribes among local government officials.

This blood money would ooze into the economy in many innocuous ways. "We give them supplies, medicines, food, fuel, and clothes when they go to sea to stalk ships, and they pay us after they obtain the ransom," one trader in Puntland's main seaport of Bosaso would declare in October 2008 ("Somali Piracy"). Residents in the inland city of Garowe would report a boom in lavish wedding parties. A resident of Bossaso, a woman named Asha Elmi, would describe with a mixture of envy and amusement the transformation that her neighbor had undergone:

> He used to be a poor fisherman a year ago, but now he is rich. He bought three beautiful houses in the same neighborhood. He had a wife, but married a second one recently. There were maybe 150 cars in the wedding [procession].

Proceeds from ransom payments would also finance an extensive network of coastal watchers and port informants, many in neighboring countries, who would pass along information about ship departures and routes.

Entrenchment

Somali piracy, like that in the Strait of Malacca, originated from a disputatious depletion of its fishing industry, and came to be dominated by money-seeking criminal syndicates. But whereas government rule in Singapore, Malaysia, and Indonesia would remain strong and intact, needing only the spur of economic necessity to mount an effective antipiracy campaign which stamped out their problem within a year, Somalia remains divided and ungovernable to this day, its pirate organizations functioning and covertly influential in its political life. A March 2009 report by UN Secretary-General Ban Ki-moon would identify the two primary networks still operating freely out of their bases around Eyl and Harardheere, with smaller bands slipping out of the ports of Bossaso, Qandala, Caluula, Bargaal, Hobyo, Mogadishu, and Garad. The Secretary-General would further note that some of these larger pirate groups "rival established Somali authorities in terms of their military capabilities and resource bases" (Ploch, p. 7).

The millions of dollars pumped into the depressed economies of these remote regions from extorted ransom payments would make any outside dictates banning piracy meaningless, unless accompanied by a significant inducement. An American reporter would note in November 2008:

> Establishing order on shore, however, remains the key to stamping out the problem, for the simple reason that keeping a dozen or more vessels from the navies of the United States and its allies engaged in escort missions for all commercial shipping in the area, is too costly to sustain over the long term. As long as the pirates remain unmolested on shore and flush with cash—Kenya last week suggested that the pirates have extorted as much as $150 million in ransom payments over the past year— they will find ways around the protection offered by sophisticated warships. (Karon)

Except for a brief six-month interlude between June to December 2006, when the fundamentalist Islamic Courts Union or ICU would crack down on piracy in areas under their control, including Harardheere, no government in Mogadishu would be able to challenge the grip of piracy. Some analysts would come to believe that the Islamists represented the best hope for restraining future depredations, although both they and the Transitional Federal Government remain riven by internal power struggles, complicating the task of forging a remedy, either internally or internationally.

Controversies

Although it has long been accepted as a general duty of all nations to cooperate in the repression of piracy, not every country sees the issue in exactly the same way or even applies the charge in a universal manner. One contentious difference in recent decades has been the view that to commit an act of piracy, it must be done for private ends—such as seizing a civilian ship for plunder on the high seas—while the same act committed for purely political motives, as in the case of insurgents not recognized as belligerents by their home governments, is not deemed piratical.

And although technically by committing such an act, pirates may lose the protection of the nation whose flag they are otherwise entitled to fly, many governments are still loathe to surrender their jurisdiction to another. Pirates may be captured on the high seas, or outside the territory of any state, under international law; yet they are to be tried and punished under the criminal law of the state holding them, in local courts, not under international law in an international tribunal. Pirates therefore constitute somewhat unique defendants in a courtroom, in that they are arguably a hybrid between a criminal and a combatant—neither true civilians, nor true belligerents. It is not even entirely clear whether they are protected by international humanitarian law—such as the Geneva Convention—or by country-specific protections for the criminally accused, such as the U.S. Bill of Rights.

Such discrepancies are only a few of the issues which hamper the prosecution of modern pirates. Moreover, while the handful of major Western maritime powers have a long history and have developed their own bodies of law for this crime, numerous Third-World nations—many of whom were former European colonies—are loathe to apply these same standards in their courts.

Differing U.S. and European Goals

One underlying distraction in the world's struggle against piracy, has been the larger strategic objective being pursued by the U.S. government, which does not entirely coincide with those of other nations. After September 11, 2001, the administration of Pres. George W. Bush moved to take its "war on terror" overseas, being seconded by a host of allied nations. Some hesitated to support the invasion of Iraq in March 2003, yet still remained committed to assisting with counterterrorist operations.

After almost five years of this single-minded drive, a Somali religious faction known as the Islamic Courts Union or ICU defeated various bickering warlords and fought its way into the battered capital of Mogadishu by June 5, 2006. Officials in Washington were concerned by reputed links between certain fundamentalist elements within the ICU and the international pariah network of al-Qaeda, it being asserted that some ICU extremists were even sheltering three leaders involved in past terrorist attacks, including the bombings of the U.S. Embassies in Kenya and Tanzania in 1998.

Covert American support was therefore directed to fund a counterinsurgency against Somalia's new Islamist rulers, led by a group of displaced Mogadishu warlords, who banded into the so-called "Alliance for the Restoration of Peace and Counter-Terrorism." With the assistance of Ethiopian troops, they defeated and drove the ICU from office by late December 2006, and a U.S. airstrike by an AC-130 gunship was carried out next month against certain al-Qaeda members embedded with ICU forces in southern Somalia, near Ras Kamboni. The aircraft carrier USS *Dwight D. Eisenhower* and other American naval forces were positioned off the coast to provide support, and prevent any al-Qaeda members from escaping by sea.

However, regional and European governments had noted how during its brief term in office, the ICU had effectively curtailed Somali piracy: within a few weeks of seizing the capital, their militiamen had pushed 300 miles northeastward, sweeping uncontested into the major pirate-lairs of Hobyo and Harardhere by mid-August 2006, proclaiming and enforcing a halt to all future sorties—the Islamists abhorring piracy on religious grounds, especially condemning the allure of its ill-gotten material wealth. True followers were even told not to participate in or support such criminality, some leaders going so far as to say that any marriage to a pirate was null and void in the eyes of strict Sharia law (*Piracy Off the Somali Coast*, pp. 15–18).

The ICU had also succeeded in reopening Mogadishu's airport and seaport to international traffic, for the first time in more than a decade, and may well have intended to repress piracy so as to help nurture Somalia's maritime trade back to life, and revive its prostrate national economy. With only ten pirate attacks reported during the ICU's six months in office, some European and regional analysts believed—and still insist—that the Islamists remain the best bet for restraining Somali piracy, which has since soared back into a dizzying wave of attacks. The Transitional Federal Government installed at Mogadishu with American support remains powerless and disinterested in even addressing the problem.

Consequently, what for Washington had been simply the removal of a remote government with extremist sympathizers, constituted a lost opportunity for European and regional allies to reduce the spreading plague of Somali piracy, which more directly threatened their own commercial sea traffic, insurance rates, oil supplies, etc. Eventually, they would organize their own independent campaign to tackle this problem, in which America collaborated.

Underreporting

Another difficulty hampering any study of piracy, is the well-known propensity among maritime companies to under-report attacks. For example, Young and Valencia have pointed out that for a commercial shipper to officially report an incident of suspected piracy, "the ship may be idled for days, and at operational costs of about $25,000 per day," this constitutes a powerful disincentive—especially if the object is to merely record a failed pursuit or otherwise insignificant act. Both authors furthermore add that too-frequent reporting of attacks "may damage the owners' reputation as a commercial shipper," leading to increased insurance premiums and thus heightened costs which have to be passed on to customers, when weighed against those of rival firms who only report the most egregious offenses. And thirdly, the very broad definition of piracy as applied by monitoring-agencies such as the International Maritime Bureau (IMB)—"everything from petty theft in port to hijacking" by armed gunmen at sea—can also give a false impression of the severity of the situation when converted into tables of dry statistics, where everything is lumped together under a single heading, without being weighted by categories (Young and Valencia).

The British Defense Intelligence Service (DIS) has estimated that the actual number of piracy cases world-wide could be as much as 2,000 percent higher, on an annual basis, while the Australian Defence Intelligence Organization or DIO places the figure at around a minimum of 20 to 70 percent. Incidents involving fishermen and recreational boaters seem to be especially under-counted, while if losses from an assault do not cross a certain monetary threshold for insurance action, most will go unreported, except in cases of damage to a foreign interest. And in his excellent study on Somali piracy, Hansen has also pointed out how few of the international trawlers would report on attacks they had endured in Somalia's waters, for fear of embarrassing or exposing their owners to liability, by revealing how often they had poached illegally among that prostrate country's unprotected banks (Hansen, p. 10).

Thus for a variety of reasons, large international shipping firms who suffered the capture of a single vessel, might often prefer to simply and discreetly:

> pay a ransom. Yet the threat of falling prey to pirates has not deterred shipping companies. Though some have changed their routes to avoid the Gulf of Aden, with the global economic downturn threatening to drive down demand for their services, they appear willing to risk the occasional ransom-payment in order to stay in business. Nor are they transferring the cost to customers. Tony Mason, secretary-general of the London-based International Chamber of Shipping, says the pirate attacks have not pushed shipping rates significantly higher. (Wadhams)

The upshot of this pernicious practice of underreporting, is that any true assessment of the extent of the problem posed by modern piracy remains ill-defined, as does the judgment as whether any real progress is being achieved in any particular zone. For example, the Strait of Malacca was deemed so risky and dangerous a passageway by the Joint War Committee (JWC) of Lloyd's Market Association in June 2005, that it branded the Strait an area "highly prone to piracy, war strikes, terrorism, and related perils for ocean shipping," so that insurance premiums were immediately raised by as much as 30 percent for the thousands of ships transiting through its narrow waters. This enormous economic burden imposed upon one of the busiest waterways in the world, promptly galvanized a concerted policing effort by all three nations adjoining the Strait, resulting in such a dramatic decrease in reported pirate attacks, that the Joint War Committee removed Malacca's name from its danger list that very next August 2006. But it is impossible to know with certainty how much of this improvement was attributable to better security measures, and how much simply to a stricter screening of reports. Inroads had been made, piracy had been reduced, but by how much, and how permanently?

Unwanted Piracy Trials

When five Somali pirates captured by a Dutch naval patrol were flown to The Netherlands to face trial in May 2009, media interviews indicated that "some of the suspects were enjoying their stay in Dutch prison cells, and were considering eventually claiming asylum." When this comment was relayed to Foreign Minister Maxime Verhagen, he groaned that he wished the defendants had been taken elsewhere to be tried—such as Kenya—revealing a common reluctance among many nations, against the expense and unforeseen difficulties involved in prosecuting foreign prisoners over such immense distances, when witnesses and even arresting officers could not be readily summoned (Westcott).

Likewise, the prosecution of Abduwali Abdukhadir Musé— the single surviving Somali pirate brought to New York City to stand trial for the *Maersk Alabama* incident—is certain to prove protracted, with a cost running well into the millions of dollars. And with the number of suspected pirates now being snared by United States and allied naval patrols rising into the hundreds, the cost of flying out all such defendants to face trial overseas would soon prove prohibitive and so is being resisted and circumvented by most governments.

Many detainees intercepted off the Horn of Africa are consequently being handed over to authorities in nearby Bosaso, the biggest seaport and most populous city in Somalia's semi-autonomous northeastern State of Puntland. As long as such prisoners do not hail from that particular region, they are tried without compunction, allowing the Puntland officials to claim an active role in the world's ongoing campaign against piracy. The same is occurring in the neighboring State of Somaliland, which faces out onto the Gulf of Aden. Yet other captives are being handed over to the Kenyan government to stand trial, which receives some financial support for these efforts, under an agreement signed with the European Union on March 6, 2009.

However, European diplomats are expected to be present in Kenyan courts on the trial dates to ensure that any prisoners handed over under this arrangement receive fair treatment—a clause which has caused further unexpected complications, as one Somali suspect delivered up by a German warship has already filed a lawsuit in Berlin, for what he alleges has been inhumane treatment since being handed over to the Kenyan authorities. Moreover, that country's court system is inefficient and overstretched. As of June 2009, it was believed that only 10 of the 111 pirates handed over had actually been fully processed.

Western jurists worry about the legality and long-term consequences of simply "dumping" suspected pirates into a third country, while naval officers sometimes grow discouraged at making so many of these inconsequential yet potentially-frustrating arrests at sea, so instead simply prefer letting some intercepted pirates go, after first confiscating their weapons—known as the "catch-and-release" method. With the campaign against piracy off the Horn of Africa still raging, this unresolved issue will only grow into more of a burden for the nations involved.

Ignored Somali Complaints

"Illegal fishing-ships, they are the real pirates," the veteran chieftain Garad Mohamed angrily rebuked a Canadian reporter in April 2009. He himself had begun his career as a lowly fisherman from the port of Eyl, he insisted, watching as its meager offshore stocks were stripped bare by foreign trawlers during the mid-1990s, and so had become a teenage gunman—with the sole objective of defending his livelihood and that of his fellow fishermen against poachers, he concluded rather piously (Bahadur, "Pirate King").

However self-serving, this belief among many Somalis that such illegal sweeps through Somalia's exposed shoreline fishing-grounds by foreign trawlers, can justify retaliatory strikes against any passing foreign vessel—even hundreds of miles farther out at sea—is often quoted in defense of the present-day wave of piratical seizures. "All we do is ask ransoms for the ships we hijack," a pirate named Jama Ahmed tried to explain to another reporter at Harardheere in October 2008, "because we believe a ransom represents a legal tax, that a government may have taken."

While it is obvious that the money being criminally extorted today has nothing to do with defending Somalia's territorial waters, or restoring its lost fishing industry, the matter nonetheless bears on an eventual repression of piracy. Simply put, improvements would offer an alternate source of income to the many jobless or underemployed Somali fishermen, rather than piloting skiffs out to sea for pirate gunmen to use in their assaults and hijackings. The issues of illegal foreign fishing and much more harmful toxic-waste dumping will have to be addressed at some point, however difficult and costly their resolutions may prove to be.

Overfishing

In the years immediately following the collapse of Somalia's central government early in 1991, foreign vessels—notably Chinese, Taiwanese, and South Korean trawlers—began taking advantage of this absence of any national authority, to edge closer into its previously-restricted territorial waters and work the shore-side banks traditionally reserved for small-time local fishermen, often with steel-pronged dragnets and other illegal equipment that stripped these stocks bare. Angry Somali fishermen, their meager livelihoods under threat and without any regional government support, resorted to armed violence by 1994, banding together and capturing several foreign fishing vessels, keeping their catches and ransoming the crews.

But undaunted, the foreign fishing fleets countered by arranging for "protection" from local warlords ashore, so that armed guards and anti-aircraft guns soon became regular fixtures aboard trespassing trawlers. The makeshift bands of Somali fishermen were no match for such formidable targets, therefore began turning upon any passing commercial vessel, which proved much easier prey. Efforts by the regional government of Puntland to create a proper Somali Coast Guard as of 1999, only worsened the fishermen's plight. The few craft ever deployed on patrol duty were often diverted to serve as private guard boats for foreign trawlers who had purchased "fishing licences" and curried other favors from corrupt government officials. More serious confrontations ensued, such as when the local leader Boyah and his followers seized several fishing-vessels in 2001 that had been "licensed" by Pres. Abdullahi Yusuf, and as such were being escorted by the regional coast-guard craft.

The various half-baked official efforts at creating a Coast Guard inevitably ended in dismal failure, anyway, with the dissolution of the contracting company and dismissal of its employees, who not only retained much of their equipment but then ironically—having been left unpaid and unemployed—provided easy recruits for future pirate bands. The issue of defending and restoring Somalia's fishing grounds remains unresolved today, with locals wary of any outside offers of help, and the distant government unable to exert any influence in such piracy hotbeds.

Toxic Dumping

Another pernicious practice, and an often-repeated justification by Somali pirates for their depredations, has been the callous disposal of dangerous wastes in their waters by foreign vessels. Such dumping does seem to have proliferated after the collapse of its central government during the early 1990s, when Somalia's long and vulnerable shoreline became a favorite disposal area for unwanted toxic materials. When a massive tsunami struck the region in December 2004, the huge waves that battered northern Somalia for days on end dredged up tons of nuclear and toxic wastes, which in turn prompted the European Green Party to investigate these allegations. They were soon able to present before the European Parliament in Strasbourg, copies of contracts signed between two companies—the Italian-Swiss firm Achair Partners and the Italian waste brokerage Progresso—and representatives of various pliant Somali warlords who had agreed to accept 10 million tons of toxic waste in exchange for a payment of $80 million.

According to an assessment subsequently compiled by the United Nations Environment Program (UNEP): "European companies found it to be very cheap to get rid of the waste, costing as little as $2.50 a ton, where waste-disposal costs in Europe are something like $1,000 a ton." The exact extent of such illegal seaborne dumping proved difficult to gauge, yet it was established that there were far higher than normal cases of respiratory infections, mouth ulcers and bleeding, abdominal hemorrhages, and unusual skin eruptions among many inhabitants of the coastal areas around the northeastern towns of Hobyo and Benadir, facing out onto the Indian Ocean—diseases consistent with radiation sickness. UNEP concluded that the situation along that particular stretch of coastline posed a serious environmental hazard, not only to Somalia, but to the entire East African region.

Somalis complain that dozens of foreign warships have been deployed into the theater to combat piracy, yet no international efforts have been made to restrict or even acknowledge the problem of toxic dumping, which still continues today and only stokes local resentment and hostility.

Expense

Lastly, a significant yet often-unspoken problem associated with modern antipiracy efforts has to do with their significant cost. Many governments may speak of the need to take action, yet the direct expense associated with deploying a single frigate into the Horn of Africa amounts to about $1.3 million a month. For navies on a peacetime footing, the expense of ramping up and dispatching a warship can be even higher than for those already engaged on active duty. The European Union, for example, in its first-ever overseas commitment, budgeted 450 million euros in 2009 to finance and sustain a year's campaign by its Operation "Atalanta," an amount that is certain to be exceeded.

Even for the U.S. Navy, with its established shore bases and numerous warships already deployed into those same waters as part of its Fifth Fleet, ongoing costs are an important consideration. In particular, the extended tours by such large warships as amphibious-assault ships and guided-missile destroyers in support of the occupation of Iraq will hopefully soon be drawn down. The reluctance by Washington to have these frontline, expensive battle vessels diverted into a protracted antipiracy effort, extending their presence for a mission where they would be excessively oversized and unsuitably overarmed, has resulted in European navies assuming the burden for these operations.

Yet costs of this magnitude will bring into question any sustained naval commitment, especially if there is no discernible decline in pirate attacks.

Solutions

Most of the underlying preconditions that facilitated the resurgence of modern piracy remain without remedy. It would be virtually impossible to turn back the hands of Time and:

— reconstitute the American and Western merchant fleets,
— reduce the size of vessels, while manning them with larger crews,
— roll back the expanded territorial waters of almost 200 nations,
— expect or desire any reduction in the volumes of Asian traffic,

— eliminate the many flaws inherent in the "flag of convenience" system,

— or realistically hope for any contraction in available military weaponry.

It might be possible to devise an internationally-acceptable piracy charge that more nations would recognize and apply, and it certainly should be a reasonable goal to deny land sanctuaries to modern criminals—most especially the brazen practice of anchoring pirate prizes directly off the Somali coast, while extorting their ransoms.

International support and regional cooperation are necessary ingredients for beating piracy, the latter proving most effective when motivated by self-interest and including a voice for disaffected parties. Increased naval patrols can only provide a short-term and impermanent reduction in assaults, as virtually every expert agrees that in the long run, piracy will be—and always has been—defeated on land, not at sea.

Textbook Case: Strait of Malacca, 2005

The world's most recent success in the struggle against piracy was gained in this crowded strategic waterway. Between 2000 and 2005, there were a total of 2,224 attacks reported worldwide, almost half—1,055—taking place in Southeast Asian waters. Many of these occurred among the unending columns of merchantmen patiently moving through this 500-mile-long, 20-mile-wide Strait so narrow along certain stretches that vessels could not even deviate from their heading to avoid clearly visible pirate boats as they approached. And this great volume of commercial traffic still continues to soar today: annual numbers of transiting ships rising from more than 50,000 in 2003 to 70,000-plus only five years later and are projected to double to 141,000 by 2020. This ceaseless stream of shipping is already carrying roughly 40 percent of all world cargo, and more than half of all oil and liquefied natural gas.

In the three years between 2003 and 2006 alone, oil shipments through the Strait increased from 10 million to an estimated 15 million barrels a day, feeding the insatiable demands of China, Japan, and South Korea. Present oil flows through the Strait are three times greater than those of the Suez Canal and 15 times greater than the Panama Canal. Major client nations in the Far

East such as Japan and China had quietly complained in recent times about size restrictions imposed by the Strait's 82-foot shallowest depth so that larger and more economical supertankers cannot be used for transport that exceed these "Malaccamax" dimensions. Consequently, proposals for possibly building a pipeline, or even digging a canal as an alternate route across the Malay Peninsula, have been raised occasionally by these countries as a cost-saving measure. Persistent piratical strikes against transiting ships, some deliberately targeted by criminal gangs operating ashore, had also been a continual source of irritation.

Crisis

Because of the pernicious nature of such attacks, the Joint War Committee or JWC of Lloyd's Market Association suddenly included the Strait of Malacca on its listing of danger zones as of June 20, 2005, branding it a passage "highly prone to piracy, war strikes, terrorism, and related perils for ocean shipping." This declaration quickly shot up insurance premiums by as much as 30 percent for the masses of vessels already heading toward the Strait, so that safer but more distant alternate routes soon began to look more economically attractive. Faced with a potential loss of hundreds of millions of dollars in revenue, the three states that share control over this waterway—Singapore, Malaysia, and Indonesia—were galvanized into addressing and rapidly resolving their problem of piracy.

Singapore had already invested significantly in its naval forces and Coast Guard so that its relatively small expanse of territorial waters retained a reputation for safety, an important consideration for what had become the world's largest transshipment hub (its modern port facilities handling more than 29 million containers by 2008). Malaysia had also substantially upgraded its maritime agencies, although their operations remained riddled with corruption. Local fishermen had complained that Malaysian Marine Police officers regularly harassed them, demanding money or fish while senior officials moreover acknowledged that numerous pirate victims did not even bother reporting attacks, as they were "afraid of acts of revenge because they believe, or know, that law-enforcement agencies are themselves involved in illegal activities" (Tanter, "Roots").

Similar shortcomings existed among the Indonesian Navy and police, which had the world's largest archipelago to patrol. Each government therefore moved quickly to rectify its own problems so as to make any cooperation between all three that much more effective. In November 2005, a new "Malaysian Maritime Enforcement Agency" or MMEA was created, the equivalent of a Coast Guard, while the Indonesian Navy also achieved remarkable improvements, despite limited resources. Its theater of operations was contracted when the Indonesian government struck a peace deal with the rebel group GAM that same year of 2005, helping reduce regional violence and thus freeing up more vessels for policing the Strait. Lingering jurisdictional issues between all three nations were also resolved so that pirates could no longer enjoy the advantage of raiding in neighboring zones, then fleeing back across the boundary into their territorial waters, beyond pursuit. And timely American assistance also provided the necessary technology for this newfound joint resolve to work.

Effective U.S. Assistance

It had always been a long-standing American foreign-policy objective to secure sea-lines of communication in Southeast Asia so as to ensure orderly traffic, commercial freedom of navigation, and stability in the South China Sea. In addition, as part of its "Global War on Terrorism" after the events of September 11, 2001, the administration of President George W. Bush had begun providing financial assistance and training to strengthen the capacities of police and armed forces in various countries. Starting as of 2006, this ongoing "Global Train and Equip" Program would add a further $80 million in funding and equipment, which allowed Indonesia to create 12 new coastal surveillance stations—including five along the Strait of Malacca—plus nine new Malaysian radar stations along the Sabah coast, which together greatly enhanced surveillance and made interdiction swifter and more effective, so that new patrol crafts were soon running down pirate boats wherever they chose to flee.

[See Table 6.5 in Chapter 6, for more detailed statistical information on the reduction of piracy in the Strait of Malacca and Indonesian waters during this period.]

Beyond its obvious efficacy and immediate impact in helping curtail pirate attacks, foreign observers commended this U.S. assistance for having been "implemented in a sensitive, subtle fashion" (Tanter, "Roots"). Japan and India had been involved in providing much of the actual equipment, conducting antipiracy training exercises and other forms of technical assistance to the three frontline states.

Resolution

Within a year, such a dramatic decline was achieved in the number of pirate attacks being reported out of the Strait, that Lloyd's removed Malacca's name from their danger list by August 11, 2006. Yet even with this crisis seemingly resolved, all three nations maintained their energetic new antipiracy policy, reducing assaults still further over the next few years, almost to the vanishing point.

Major client nations in Asia noted this success and acknowledged the expense entailed in sustaining this level of security in the Strait into the future, as well as the necessary navigational aids and pollution-prevention—which together might cost as much as $300 million a year by 2020. Japan's Nippon Foundation has therefore recommended that all ships transiting through the Strait voluntarily contribute one cent per deadweight ton of cargo, a fee which would generate about $40 million annually toward offsetting such expenses. Another option would be to ask shipping companies that to make contributions as a form of corporate social responsibility, but both ideas have been resisted.

Six Basic Elements for Success

The spectacularly swift turnaround achieved during 2005–2006 in the Strait of Malacca demonstrated how effectively modern piracy can be contained by a concerted, multiprong effort. The lessons derived from this success underscore six basic elements required in all such victorious antipiracy campaigns—whether in the past, present, or future:

Accurate Intelligence

No campaign can succeed without first determining the roles of most major parties involved, especially leading groups of perpetrators, financiers, collaborators, sympathizers, etc. Not that every individual need be identified fully for an overall effort to succeed; for example, the shadowy triad organizers who once launched repeated strikes in the Strait still remain anonymous today, although their criminal enterprise has been successfully dismantled. Nevertheless, the general structure and workings of any pirate network should at least be understood, its bases and methods of operation revealed, finances and disposal of booty probed so as to exert pressure upon its weakest points.

In other recent instances, reliable information on piratical activities was difficult to obtain out of the South China Sea during the late 1990s, making any resolution unattainable; yet participants in Nigeria's currently ongoing piracy problem are broadly known throughout the troubled Niger Delta, although the motivations behind their depredations have still not been directly addressed by the national authorities, so that such difficulties will fester. Lairs and tactics employed by pirate bands around the Strait of Malacca quickly became apparent to their police pursuers, accelerating their defeat; but while abundant information is available today on the tactics and methods employed by Somali pirates—who brazenly anchor their prizes within plain sight off its barren coastline for weeks on end, while negotiating multimillion dollar ransoms—there are no local authorities available who are willing to put a stop to this criminality.

International Commitment

Since piracy is by definition a crime which can only be perpetrated in international waters, beyond any country's jurisdiction, it is best solved through a joint international commitment. Nor does such an effort necessarily require a major deployment of naval squadrons; for as has been noted above, America's low-cost financing of a few strategic surveillance bases and coastal outposts proved decisive in defeating piracy in the Strait of Malacca, providing existing patrol forces from neighboring countries with the necessary means to locate and run down their quarry, thus finishing the job themselves without any outside assistance.

International commitment furthermore works best when it is generally welcome in a region; appeals to the self-interest of at least some of the local parties involved; and doesn't drag on too long.

Regional Cooperation

This element is an essential, and in the case of the Strait of Malacca campaign, a crucial factor in the defeat of piracy. Prior to that campaign, local pirates would deliberately strike out of their shore bases across international boundaries so as to escape any pursuit by running back into their territorial waters with their plunder. Patrol boats from the victimized nation would have to break off their pursuit, while police boats in the pirates's nation remained unaware that any crime had even been committed. A reciprocal agreement between Singapore, Malaysia, and Indonesia, which permitted coordinated pursuits by all naval and police units throughout the Strait, proved a decisive factor in ending this practice.

A similar approach is being attempted by European navies in Somalia, as deals have been struck with its autonomous States of Somaliland and Puntland—which face out onto the busy shipping lanes of the Gulf of Aden—to assist in the detention and prosecution of any pirates. A notable decline in attacks has resulted in that waterway, although pirates from distant Central Somalia have instead shifted to operations farther out into the Indian Ocean expanses.

Local Involvement

The last phase of an antipiracy campaign usually includes some element addressing local conditions or grievances as a means of ensuring that such criminality will not return. Yet piracy was defeated in the Strait of Malacca without any significant assistance to the impoverished Malaysian or Indonesian fishermen who turned to this crime, while any relief for their desperately-poor counterparts in Central Somalia is a long way off.

Denial of Prey

Just like robbers on land, pirates primarily seek to profit from their criminality at sea, not engage in pointless armed clashes. The handheld weaponry which they typically brandish during a pursuit is intended to frighten and subdue their victims, not pose a serious military threat.

Naval professionals have long deplored the weakened state of most modern merchantmen, as even huge vessels carrying immensely valuable cargo through known danger zones will often only be lightly manned and lacking in any rudimentary defensive procedures. Such easy prizes can be denied to pirates by such simple and relatively cost-effective measures as organizing into convoys; transiting through high-risk areas in rough weather or darkened at night; refusing to reduce speed for pirate boarders; limiting access-points into a ship's interior; fortifying and provisioning an internal "safe room" so as to await rescue; stringing razor-wire coils along low-freeboard railings; minimize communications; keep fire hoses pressurized for instant discharge; etc.

Legal Recourses

Still an unresolved issue, given that most major maritime powers are reluctant to shoulder the expense and unexpected complications of flying suspected pirates out of a region to stand trial in their own courts, while many Third-World nations are loathe to be involved in such prosecutions on behalf of wealthier governments.

In the case of the antipiracy efforts in the Strait of Malacca, such defendants were arraigned in local courts. As for the more complicated circumstances off Somalia, the European Union temporarily circumvented this issue by signing an agreement with the Kenyan government on March 6, 2009, whereby suspected pirates could be landed in that East African nation to face trial in Kenyan courts under the international statutes of the UN's "Convention on the Law of the Sea." Similar, less-formal deals were also struck with authorities in Somaliland and Puntland, which may not withstand long-term scrutiny.

Sources

Bahadur, Jay. "The Pirate King of Somalia." *Globe & Mail* [Canada], April 26, 2009.

Freeman, Donald B. *The Straits of Malacca: Gateway or Gauntlet?* Montreal: McGill-Queen's University Press, 2003.

Karon, Tony. "Battling the Somali Pirates: The Return of the Islamists." *Time Magazine*, November 25, 2008.

"Lawless Tradition of Piracy Off the Coast of Somalia." *The Guardian* [UK], November 18, 2008.

"Peril on the High Seas." *The Economist: Premium Content Online* [UK], April 23, 2008.

Piracy Off the Somali Coast: Workshop Commissioned by the Special Representative of the Secretary-General of the United Nations to Somalia, Ambassador Ahmedou Ould-Abdallah. Nairobi, Kenya, November 2008.

Ploch, Lauren, et alia. *Piracy Off the Horn of Africa.* Washington, D.C.: "Congressional Research Service" Report for Congress, September 28, 2009.

Report S/2006/229 of the U.N. Monitoring Group on Somalia, Submitted to the Security Council on May 4, 2006. New York: United Nations Security Council, 2006.

"Somali Piracy: 'We're Defending Our Waters.'" *Mail & Guardian Online* [UK], October 14, 2008.

Tanter, Richard. "The Challenges of Piracy in Southeast Asia and the Role of Australia." *Nautilus Institute: Austral Peace and Security Network*

[Australia], Austral Policy Forum Paper Number 07-19A, October 25, 2007.

Tanter, Richard. "The Roots of Piracy in Southeast Asia." *Nautilus Institute: Austral Peace and Security Network [Australia]*, Austral Policy Forum Paper Number 07-18A, October 22, 2007.

Wadhams, Nick. "As Somali Pirates Get Bolder, Policing Them Gets Tougher." *Time Magazine*, November 19, 2008.

Westcott, Kathryn. "Pirates in the Dock." *BBC News* [UK], May 21, 2009.

Young, Adam J., and Valencia, Mark J. "Conflation of Piracy and Terrorism in Southeast Asia: Rectitude and Utility." *Contemporary Southeast Asia* [Singapore] 25, Issue 2 (August 2003), pp. 269–284.

3

Special U.S. Issues

Ultimately, piracy is a problem that starts ashore, and requires an international solution ashore. We made this clear at the offset of our efforts. We cannot guarantee safety in this vast region.

—Vice Admiral William E. Gortney, U.S. Naval Forces
Central Command, before the House Armed Services Committee,
March 5, 2009

No vital aspect of America's overseas trade, nor the nation's broader economic well-being, had been affected by the recent resurgence of piracy in distant Asia or off the Horn of Africa. Few U.S.-flagged merchantmen transited those waters, and the flow of commerce reaching U.S. ports had scarcely registered a flicker. Insurance premiums remained the same, costs unwavering, the importation of goods and oil unimpeded. Humanitarian concern was naturally felt for piratical victims, while Washington was worried about any potential damage to frail economies, which might spiral into bigger regional problems. One timely response had been the targeted assistance extended to Malaysia and Indonesia during 2005–2006, which had allowed their own local forces to reverse piratical gains, crowned by a swift restoration of security to an immense flow of multinational traffic, without any overt U.S. commitment or major expense.

Yet the U.S. government also remained wary of assuming responsibility for more difficult and costly problems created by others, such as the overfishing by Asian trawler fleets or disposal of toxic wastes by European dumpers, which had so devastated Somali fishing grounds as to send hundreds of its despairing fishermen out to sea as pirates. And the administration of President George W. Bush had its own separate, single-minded agenda, which initially did not include any antipiracy component.

U.S. Naval Focus during the War on Terror

In the immediate aftermath to the terrorist strikes of September 11, 2001 which had so shocked New York City, the capital, and the entire nation, U.S. and allied forces quickly launched President Bush's riposte by occupying Afghanistan, decimating the guilty al-Qaeda organization and driving out its Taliban hosts. The second phase of this "Global War on Terror" had then seen a sweeping counteroffensive throughout the Near and Far East, codenamed Operation "Enduring Freedom," before a third phase shifted into the Horn of Africa theater as of early 2002.

Thirty years previously, while the Arab island-emirate or kingdom of Bahrain had still been in the process of gaining its independence from British colonial rule, the U.S. Navy had leased part of a former Royal Navy base on the outskirts of its capital city of Manama. Only a token U.S. "Administrative Support Unit" had ever occupied this outpost until July 1995, when mounting regional tensions had led to its upgrade into the headquarters for the U.S. Naval Forces Central Command and its adjunct squadrons out at sea, the newly-reactivated U.S. Fifth Fleet.

From this strategic vantage-point deep within the Persian Gulf, Central Command would come to direct over the ensuing years regional operations by its warships, which were rotated in and out according to need from the U.S. Pacific and Atlantic Fleets. The mission statement indicated that this presence was intended to "help ensure peace and stability, and protect America's vital interests," on what would eventually become a 7.5-million square-mile theater of operations encompassing the Red Sea, Arabian Sea, Gulf of Oman, parts of the Indian Ocean, as well as the coast of East Africa as far south as Kenya (COMUSNAVCENT "Command," "History," etc.).

Coalition Maritime Contributions

A significant element of this third phase in the global offensive against terror were the warships from more than a dozen allied nations, which soon began reaching the Indian Ocean as well, to bolster the U.S. Fifth Fleet, which was also being ramped up. So many coalition warships had joined by February 2002 that a separate "Combined Maritime Forces" division was created within the structure of Central Command, comprised of vessels from Australia, Canada, France, Germany, The Netherlands, Italy, Pakistan, New Zealand, Spain, Turkey, and the United Kingdom.

Assigned to patrols against suspected terrorist traffic, these coalition vessels—along with a few detached U.S. warships— were formed into a multinational squadron initially dubbed "Combined Task Force-150" or CTF-150, its leadership being exercised by diverse nationalities in turn: German Adm. Gottfried Hoch being appointed CTF-150's first commander as of May 5, 2002, then succeeded a few months later by Spanish Rear Admiral Juan Moreno, etc. Yet the duties of both this new task force and the U.S. Fifth Fleet, did not directly entail pursuit of pirates.

Combined Joint Task Force-Horn of Africa

Toward the end of that same year of 2002, it was decided to establish a new fortified U.S. land base in Djibouti, a strategically-placed former French colony at the mouth of the Red Sea overlooking the Gulf of Aden. From this stronghold, U.S. Marines and Special Forces were to carry the fight inland against Islamic extremists, who were believed to be recruiting and training more followers throughout the desert expanses of northeastern Africa. A lease was signed by October 2002 for an abandoned Foreign Legion compound—long ago named for General Emile-René Lemonnier—which lay just southwest of Djibouti's Ambouli International Airport, and which was to serve as the advance headquarters for the fast-strike Combined Joint Task Force-Horn of Africa to use in their "demining, humanitarian, and counter-terrorism" efforts.

The first Marine staff arrived off the coast of Djibouti next month aboard the USS *Mount Whitney,* finding the remnants of Camp Lemonier so uninhabitable that it had to be cleared first and then entirely rebuilt by U.S. Army Engineers. Work proceeded over the next five months while the invasion of Iraq was going forward. The completed 88-acre compound was turned over to Combined Joint Task Force-Horn of Africa personnel by May 6, 2003, capable of housing up to 2,000 servicemen and eventually expanded into 500 acres to further accommodate Marine helicopters, Navy P-3 reconnaissance planes, U.S. Air Force HC-130, and heavy C-17 transports, U.S. Army Field Artillery units, plus naval Seabees. As part of its overall "Trans-Saharan Counter-Terrorism Initiative," this base also provided training in counterinsurgency tactics for select regional forces, as well as humanitarian assistance in the form of free medical clinics and school constructions.

As of December 2002, this foothold in Djibouti had been reinforced offshore by the allied Combined Task Force-150, which was to act as naval support group for this deployment. Again, the primary mission of these warships was to monitor, inspect, board, and stop "suspected shipments from entering the Horn of Africa region," not conduct antipiracy sweeps.

Invasion of Iraq

While Camp Lemonier was still being constructed in early 2003, the U.S. Fifth Fleet had been built up into a massive force with the addition of five aircraft carriers, a half-dozen huge amphibious assault ships, plus numerous lesser warships in anticipation of the war against Iraq. Aerial bombardment of Baghdad started on March 20, 2003, and twin fast-moving armored columns quickly brought about the downfall of the Saddam Hussein regime by April 9th, with an end to all conventional fighting six days afterward.

Post-War Mission

Soon after the war had concluded, the large extra number of U.S. Navy battle-groups and major warships deployed into the Arabian Sea and Indian Ocean to support this campaign quickly began to be drawn down. Meanwhile, lighter U.S. and allied warships were moved in closer to Iraq so as to protect its offshore oil installations, patrol its porous borders, and escort convoys bringing in the vast amount of supplies required by the occupation forces. But as Iraq's internal security then began to spin out of control, this unexpected shift in circumstances meant that a visible naval presence would have to be sustained in this theater, much longer than anticipated, to help maintain watch against foreign fighters and bomb makers slipping in from hostile neighboring states.

It should be noted that none of these U.S. or coalition warships had been specifically tasked with combating piracy. Occasionally, some might be diverted on a rescue mission for a limited time, and within an adjacent zone, while any would naturally steam to the assistance of any nearby merchantman under attack. But the United States would not formally assign any naval assets—at all—solely to the task of antipiracy operations in the Horn of Africa region, until 2008 (Ploch, p. 4). Not that there was any pressing need for such a commitment during the immediate postwar phase, when such assaults were very few in number in those waters. However, depredations were about to dramatically mushroom hundreds of miles farther south, off the central Somali coast, with a purpose and brazenness that caught many by surprise.

Ominous Piracy Surge Out of Somalia

The lawlessness gripping this prostrate, fragmented, and impoverished nation—wracked by civil wars and strife for the past 15 years—was universally known by 2005. Most regional vessels passed by cautiously, well away from its extensive coastline, and keeping a wary eye for any self-proclaimed "coast guards" or desperadoes who might venture offshore in small boats. Yet coastal traffic was so sparse and low-value in this region that outright pirate attacks had become relatively rare—only three captures being reported out of Somali waters during 2003, and two in 2004.

The Extortionate Business of Ransoms

However, a penniless ex-civil servant named Mohamed Abdi Hassan Hayir, more commonly called *Afweyne* or "Big Mouth," was about to transform the forlorn and sun-bleached town of Harardheere, a neglected port on the central Somali coast, into a major pirate lair. Determined to unify the random attacks being sporadically launched against chance targets offshore into a profitable business, he had raised some capital in 2003 and traveled into Puntland, to recruit veteran pirates as instructors. Notorious rovers such as Garad Mohamed, Farah Hirsi "Boyah" Kulan, and Farah Abdullahi had been lured south by Hassan's inducements to serve him both as active captains offshore, as well as indoctrinating his own local followers.

Afweyne soon managed to create a structured pirate organization, whose sole purpose was to waylay foreign vessels and patiently hold them for ransom with proper logistical support ashore so as to await eventual payment. Harardheere's very remoteness proved ideal as a base of operations, being scarcely accessible to the rest of the country by road, and so beyond all effective central authority. A backwater, it had also been spared much of the bitter civil wars raging elsewhere in Somalia, which meant that no pressing demands would be made on Hassan's fledgling organization to share its profits with any large feuding factions or clans. Instead, his proceeds—after bribes to a few local officials to ignore prizes being anchored offshore, plus payments to local suppliers—left ample funds to be re-invested into more sorties, as well as in procuring better equipment and recruits.

See Table 6.7 in Chapter 6, for a more detailed statistical breakdown on the upsurge in reported pirate attacks in Somali waters and the adjoining Gulf of Aden during this period.

Foreign observers soon noted how Afweyne's new southern marauders enjoyed better boats, armaments, even satellite phones and Global Positioning Systems to locate their targets. The ruthlessness of his criminal enterprise was exemplified by the hijacking of the UN-chartered aid ship *Semlow* on the evening of June 27, 2005 by 15 of his young gunmen aboard three fiberglass speedboats equipped with powerful outboard motors. This elderly, 920-ton Kenyan freighter had been plodding past northward about 30 miles offshore, bearing 850 tons of German- and Japanese-donated rice for the World Food Program or WFP to be distributed at Bosaso among survivors of a recent tsunami, when it was taken. Despite the public outcry, international condemnation, and suspension of all humanitarian shipments into starving Somalia as a result, Afweyne stubbornly held his prize at anchor for three months off Ceel Huur, 70 miles from Harardheere, until a reduced ransom of $135,000 was paid.

His organizational practices would spread north when such hired mercenaries as Garad Mohamed and Boyah returned to their lawless home port of Eyl, applying them to their own independent operations. Other imitators would also appear, especially as the ransoms increased in volume, producing tempting streams of cash into such poor and backward areas. The number of reported captures off Somalia jumped from two in 2004, to 35 by 2005, prompting worried foreign shipping-firms to shift their routes a couple of hundred miles out to sea, beyond the range of most pirate shore boats. This uptick was also noted by international observers, even attracting the attention of U.S. Navy officers patrolling much farther north in the Arabian Sea, as well as at the regional U.S. foothold in Djibouti. However, Washington's primary focus still remained its fight against terrorism and Islamic extremism, not an antipiracy campaign.

Textbook Case: Chance Rescue of a Dhow, January 2006

By January 16, 2006, the small Indian dhow *Safina Al Bisarat* had already run about 200 miles northeastward out of Kismaayo, bound toward Dubai in the United Arab Emirates to deliver a cargo of charcoal, when it was suddenly attacked by three small speedboats carrying 10 men brandishing AK-47s, RPG launchers, and pistols. They pulled alongside the dhow and used ladders to quickly swarm aboard, supposedly identifying themselves as the "Somali Marines." *Al Bisarat*'s Captain and 15 crewmembers were corralled on its forecastle under threats of physical violence while the pirate leader used the dhow's own radio to contact his headquarters ashore requesting further instructions (Report S/2006/229).

The three speedboats were then secured astern of the hijacked vessel and taken under tow, three pirates remaining aboard one of these boats, which contained their extra weapons, fuel, and provisions. The captive Indian captain was ordered to alter course farther out to sea, moving 200 miles out into the busy international shipping lanes where the pirates intended to use *Al Bisarat* as an inconspicuous "mother ship" to attack passing merchantmen. Over the next three days, they would make three such unsuccessful attempts, their final attack occurring on January 19, 2006, when they fired numerous rounds and rocket-propelled grenades at the Bahamian-registered bulk carrier *Delta Ranger*. This vessel reported its narrow escape by radio to the International Maritime Bureau in Kuala Lumpur, which in turn relayed this information to the U.S. naval authorities in Bahrain.

As the 380-man, 9,200-ton guided-missile destroyer USS *Winston S. Churchill* happened to be on patrol "against al-Qaeda elements" only about 100 miles away from the spot of this latest attack, its commander was diverted on the morning of January 20th to go in search of the pirate mother ship. *Churchill* located the suspect vessel that same afternoon, tracking its movements throughout that moonless night. The noise of its helicopter engine caused the pirates to panic at dawn, immediately ordering the dhow steered west toward the distant Somali coast, in hopes of reaching its territorial waters. Yet *Churchill* easily shadowed the small vessel, coming menacingly up over the horizon with the sunrise on January 21, 2006. By 8:00 a.m., the 16 captive Indian crewmen could be plainly seen huddled on its forecastle, holding up a piece of plywood with these spray-painted words: "SIR PLEASE HELP US" (Raffaelle).

The U.S. warship thereupon attempted to raise the dhow by both ship-to-ship radio and over loudspeaker, directing that its crew be released aboard the two small boats which could be seen trailing astern (the third pirate craft having parted company during the night). The gunmen ignored these instructions and pressed westward so that—with Somali territorial waters now only four hours ahead—*Churchill* closed in and at a range of 500 yards, fired a burst of 25mm shells across *Al Bisarat's* bow at 11:30 a.m. The dhow stopped, yet its captors still refused to cooperate. *Churchill* threatened to open fire once more at 1:00 p.m., then loosed off another burst at 2:20 p.m., which finally convinced the pirates to reply by radio and begin releasing their captives a half-hour later. Armed U.S. Navy personnel then went aboard *Al Bisarat* and secured its 10 pirate captors, who had tossed most of their weapons overboard during the pursuit, although an AK-47 was subsequently found hidden in its wheelhouse.

Late that same afternoon of January 21, 2006, the flagship for *Churchill's* strike group—the 40,000-ton amphibious assault ship USS *Nassau*—joined both vessels, securing the pirates in its brig. The two U.S. warships thereupon resumed their antiterrorist patrols, while U.S. Central Command in Bahrain was consulted as to the prisoners' fate. It was decided to hand them over to the authorities in Kenya to stand trial for piracy, which was eventually done a month later at Mombassa, on February 25, 2006. Eventually, all 10 were sentenced to seven years in prison.

Deliberate Targeting of Prizes

Yet while U.S. and allied naval forces would continue to concentrate on defending the contentious waters off distant Iraq, as well as containing any spread of Islamic extremism throughout the region, the business of profit-motivated seizures took root unchallenged along the barren stretches of central Somalia, accompanied by a palpable increase in the sophistication and organization of some of these piratical strikes, which—in the words of a UN intelligence report compiled in May 2006—left the commercial-shipping world "reeling with concern" (Report S/2006/229, p. 25). The opportunistic and scattered attacks once launched close inshore by roving boatloads of local clansmen were being superseded by directed ventures, backed by:

- land-based headquarters to plan, direct, and control any distant vessel seizures by radio
- informal yet effective information-relaying networks, often embedded throughout neighboring countries, to advise on any rich merchant-ship departures and their intended routes
- sufficient funds to ensure that these new pirate bands could put out to sea manned by competent sailors and reliable gunmen, all adequately armed and provisioned, many additionally equipped with satellite phones and GPS systems.

The UN monitoring group noted that such new expeditions usually consisted of about 10 pirates, some seamen and the remainder gunmen, distributed aboard two speedboats and a provisions-boat. They would often target a harmless-looking dhow, trawler, or coastal trader close inshore, to use as a mother ship for venturing farther out, into the international shipping lanes. There, they would employ their captive vessel's radar "to monitor ship movements up to 60 miles away," while lying in wait for a choice victim (ibid., p. 26).

The disciplined focus and deliberate targeting by such strike groups, also meant that coastal traders could often purchase an exemption from attack. The UN report described maritime traffic at other Somali seaports such as Berbera, Bosaso, El Ma'an, Kismaayo, and Marka as "thriving," noting that:

Cargo ships laden with all types of foodstuffs, clothing, hardware items, oils and lubricants, fuel, building materials, and electronic goods, arrive regularly at Somali seaports. Somali businessmen have links with traders in South America, China, India, the Far East, the Middle East, Mediterranean countries, and East and southern African countries. (ibid., p. 22)

Advance payments—euphemistically known as "safety fees," ranging from $50,000 per ship on upwards—plus other bribes once in port to local syndicates controlling the tugs, cranes, steve-dores, etc., ensured a welcome reception. El Ma'an, for example, was estimated to be receiving 30 merchantmen a month, and processing a total of two million metric tons of goods a year. Some unscrupulous local strongmen and officials even continued to sell fishing permits to foreign trawlers, at prices ranging from $80,000 a year and up. "Some permits are typed out on the previous gov-ernment's letterhead, while others bear the personal seals of war-lords" (ibid., p. 24).

Islamic Clampdown, Summer 2006

Surprisingly, the growing number of hijackings was abruptly curtailed by the sudden rise to power of a religious faction called the Islamic Courts Union (ICU), whose militiamen defeated vari-ous bickering warlords and fought their way into the capital Mogadishu by June 5, 2006. That same summer, ICU forces expanded beyond its district, pushing 300 miles northeastward to sweep uncontested into the remote pirate port-towns of Hobyo and Harardheere by mid-August 2006. Being long opposed to piracy on religious grounds, dismissing it as an unworthy path to unseemly wealth, the ICU ordered a halt to all such sorties, in addition to imposing other restrictions in accordance with strict Sharia law. The tiny local skiffs at these ports were mostly laid up at that time anyway, because the summer monsoon season is when high winds and seas typically rise along the East African coast, rendering any lengthy ventures out to sea dangerous from late April through early September (*Piracy Off the Somali Coast*, p. 15).

But few forays were attempted when that autumn came, while the ICU had also succeeded in reopening Mogadishu's air-port and seaport that same year to international traffic, for the first time more than a decade. It may well have been that the fun-damentalists genuinely intended to repress piracy throughout southern Somalia so as to help nurture the shattered region's maritime trade and economy back to life. Such religious leaders had long condemned the allure of piracy's ill-gotten wealth, advising their followers not to participate or support it, some even going so far as to assert that marriage to a pirate was null and void in the eyes of the law (ibid., p. 18).

The statistical downturn in reported pirate strikes out of Somalia is evident upon examining Table 6.7 in Chapter 6, under the year 2006.

When an intrepid British reporter visited the notorious seaport of Eyl three years afterward—with two captive merchantmen plainly visible offshore, prizes awaiting ransoms—a crowd nonetheless quickly gathered and one woman informed him:

> We are all against the pirates here. They have brought bad culture here. They come here with their shiny cars, collect their money, and leave. We worry that our children will be attracted to crime. We are very fearful of the pirates, and of the international community. We hear reports that the West will launch air-strikes against our town. (Harding)

U.S. Intervention

However, U.S. operatives at Djibouti and officials of the Bush administration in Washington were more concerned by reputed links between certain extremist elements within the ICU and the international pariah network of al-Qaeda, in particular the belief that three leaders involved in past terrorist attacks— including the bombings of the U.S. Embassies in Kenya and Tanzania in 1998—were being given shelter by certain ICU fundamentalists.

Covert U.S. support was therefore directed to help fund a counterinsurgency against Somalia's new Islamist rulers, led by a group of displaced and disaffected Mogadishu warlords, who banded into the so-called "Alliance for the Restoration of Peace and Counter-Terrorism." With the backing of Ethiopian troops, they defeated and drove the ICU from office by late December 2006, after which a U.S. airstrike with an AC-130 gunship was conducted that following month against al-Qaeda members embedded with ICU forces in southern Somalia, near Ras Kamboni. The aircraft carrier USS *Dwight D. Eisenhower* and other U.S. naval forces were even positioned off the coast to provide support, and prevent any al-Qaeda members from escaping by sea.

Yet regional and European governments noted how during its brief term in office, the ICU had effectively reduced Somali piracy—which once they were gone, revived and exploded into an unbridled wave of attacks. With only 10 pirate attacks reported in Somali waters during the ICU's six months in office, some analysts believed—and still insist—that the Islamists remain the best bet for restraining piracy off the Horn of Africa.

Unfettered Somali Piracy (2007–Present)

Following the expulsion of the ICU, the number of piratical depredations soon regained momentum, and strikes began to expand outward on a much more far-ranging scale than before. Attacks would no longer be confined to within 50 nautical miles of Somalia's coast, as many pirates began employing their small, fast skiffs to instead hijack innocuous coasters or trawlers as they plodded past near shore, and compelled their crews to tow them far out into the main shipping lanes. With these new tactics, attempts on merchantmen would escalate not only far out into the Indian Ocean, but also well into the Gulf of Aden, even as far as the mouth of the Red Sea.

America's Redefined Role (June 2007)

In response to allied and regional complaints, plus some criticism for its removal of the only Somali government apparently capable of restraining such piratical forays, the Bush administration issued a new policy statement in mid-June 2007, agreeing to address and treat security concerns off the Horn of Africa as a separate issue to its ongoing "War on Terror." After five-and-a-half years of coalition support for this U.S.-led offensive, Washington was willing to assist its partners against this spreading problem, which represented much more of a direct threat to their commercial and economic well-being.

Not that the redeployment of all allied warships in the "Combined Maritime Forces" division would have sufficed for such an immense task, as—even including U.S. assets—they were far too few in number to patrol any significant portion of such a vast arena. Although the coalition naval-contribution was drawn from sixteen different nations, the actual number of warships that they could muster in this distant theater at any given time varied from only between six to 10 vessels. Such slender strength could never possibly cover a sea expanse stretching over a couple of thousand miles from the Straits of Hormuz as far south as Kenya, nor would warships necessarily provide the best and sole solution.

Cautionary Case: *Golden Nori* Rescue

Some drawbacks to the U.S. Navy's participation in antipiracy patrols were soon to be revealed. Early on a Sunday morning,

October 28, 2007, the 280-man, 9,000-ton destroyer USS *Porter*—on routine patrol as part of the multinational Combined Task Force-150, although still officially part of the antiterrorist Operation "Enduring Freedom-Horn of Africa"—picked up a distress call from an unknown tanker in the Gulf of Aden, saying that it was being boarded from two pirate skiffs. The warship immediately steamed toward this signal's coordinates, which had originated some 80 nautical miles northwest of Caluula on the Somali coast. The captive vessel proved to be the 11,700-ton, Japanese-owned, Panamanian-flagged *Golden Nori*, which had been seized by pirates led by the notorious Farah Hirsi Kulan, better known as "Boyah," who was already sailing his prize toward Somalia's 12-mile limit, intending to round the Horn of Africa and anchor it several hundred miles farther south so as to extort a ransom from near his stronghold of Eyl.

But when *Porter* overtook this fleeing vessel in international waters that same Sunday afternoon, its gunners quickly destroyed the pair of skiffs being towed astern with a few bursts of 25mm rounds, isolating Boyah and his pirates on board. Washington then used its contacts with the tottering Transitional National Government in distant Mogadishu to secure authorization for the U.S. destroyer *Arleigh Burke* and other warships to join this pursuit into Somalia's territorial waters so that Boyah could not shake off the foreign squadron. Only the fact that *Golden Nori*'s 23-man crew was being held hostage and that the tanker was loaded with 40,000 tons of volatile chemicals—including extremely-flammable benzene—prevented an immediate assault.

However, a two-month standoff thereupon ensued, with two U.S. and a German warship maintaining watch over this cornered prize. Its Japanese owners finally started negotiations for their tanker's release in November 2007, after which Boyah managed to inch *Golden Nori* by December 4th into the harbor at Bosaso, Puntland's biggest port and most populous city. A ransom of $1.5 million was allegedly paid eight days later to free both ship and crew, at which point Boyah and his pirates escaped ashore. In order to maximize the benefits from this lengthy intervention, the U.S. and allied warships furthermore exerted pressure on the captors of four other anchored merchantmen in that area, securing their release and producing a brief downturn in local hijackings.

Yet although this rescue of *Golden Nori* and four other prizes was hailed as a victory over piracy, naval professionals realized that such lopsided encounters were hardly cost-effective. As an analyst from the Center for Strategic and Budgetary Assessments in Washington would comment during its aftermath: "Essentially, you don't want to use a billion-dollar DDG [guided-missile destroyer] to suppress pirates. That's a mission for a much smaller ship." He went on to note that although the U.S. Navy still had numerous vessels posted to the Horn of Africa region, "These are ships designed for high-end war fighting, not chasing pirates." Most U.S. warships remaining in that theater had originally been dispatched to fight a conventional war, equipped to do battle against modern aircraft, naval opponents, or missile strikes.

By way of contrast, Somali pirates ventured out to sea in bare, 30-foot, open skiffs with high freeboards, powered by outboard motors. Such craft were usually manufactured of fiberglass in Yemeni boatyards, and sold to coastal traders or fishermen for $2,500–$3,500 apiece. The most highly-regarded outboard motors for powering such craft were twin 150-horsepower Yamaha models, which allowed a skiff to attain speeds of 30 knots in relatively calm seas, with four people jostling onboard. Most of the pirates' handheld weaponry also originated out of Yemen, although a significant proportion came from Mogadishu. Typically, arms dealers or middlemen would receive a deposit on behalf of a group of pirates through a *hawala* broker, and a batch of weapons would then be driven into Puntland, where the balance would be paid upon delivery (*Piracy Off the Coast of Somalia*, p. 14).

NATO, EU, and UN Commitments

By the spring of 2008, the explosion of piratical sorties emanating out of such notorious lairs as Eyl, Hobyo, and Haradheere, would begin to reach alarming proportions and encompass ever-wider tracts of ocean, with ships seemingly being attacked anywhere pirates chose to strike. Already stretched too thin, U.S. Naval Forces Central Command had in early January 2008 detached a few coalition warships from its multinational Combined Task Force-150 to make random "Visit, Board, Search, and Seizure" inspections on dhows and oil tankers circulating near the Somali coast, a measure which had produced little benefit. As the toll of losses mounted, an international outcry arose—especially out of Europe—against this mushrooming rash of assaults, which not only threatened its commercial sea lines but were being launched with a purposefulness and brazenness that had caught many by surprise, and portended serious trouble for the foreseeable future.

When the French government was compelled to pay a $2 million ransom for the release of its luxury cruise ship *Le Ponant* in mid-April 2008, sharpshooters were sent aboard helicopters in pursuit of these Somali pirates as they escaped ashore, six being captured after a brief shootout and flown away to stand trial in Paris. The conservative British journal *The Economist* editorialized less than two weeks later in its April 23, 2008 issue, that "Sonalia's coastal waters are proving increasingly perilous for mariners," and joined the rising call from many quarters for vigorous counter-measures. A UN assessment later this same year would concur that "marine travel anywhere near the stretch of Somalia known as Puntland, has become the most dangerous waters in the world for merchantmen" (*Piracy Off the Coast of Somalia*, p. 14).

See Table 6.7 in Chapter 6, for a more detailed statistical breakdown on the surge in reported pirate attacks in Somali waters and adjoining Gulf of Aden during this period.

Because of the virtual eradication of piracy in the Strait of Malacca, the Horn of Africa had now become the major global hot spot, with reported attacks off its shores almost tripling in a single year between 2007 and 2008, rising from 44 to 111—this latter figure representing almost 40 percent of 2008's world total. After witnessing the onslaught of attacks during that spring, the regional Commander of U.S. Naval Central Command in Bahrain attempted to prepare for a second round of pirate strikes once the summer monsoon season ended by establishing a "Maritime Security Patrol Area" in the region as of August 22, 2008. This was to be a movable traffic-lane running through the Gulf of Aden, which could be regularly monitored and patrolled by U.S. and Combined Maritime Forces' warships and aircraft so as to afford some measure of protection for merchantmen who chose to transit along this route, until a more long-term solution could be instituted. Yet initial results did not seem promising, as "preliminary data indicates that the pirate success rate for hijacking is only slightly lower inside the MSPA, than outside" (*Countering Piracy*).

However, both Washington and U.S. Navy officials in the region were reluctant to divert any more of their strength 1,200 miles southwest from their advance-support roles near the Persian Gulf, especially to initiate a protracted new campaign against Somali pirates. In any event, the large U.S. warships would be wasted in pursuit of tiny skiffs, while the vast majority of victimized vessels were European, Asian, or African. With the Bush administration already into its last months in office, and a drawdown out of Iraq seeming ever more likely, U.S. interests would not be served by remaining for a thankless task of combating piracy. Instead, the U.S. government would assist the efforts of its allies, who were more directly affected by its consequences.

NATO "Operation Allied Provider"

As Somali pirates resumed their depredations with implacable vigor that same autumn of 2008, the international community at last began moving—with Washington's full approval and support—to assume a more direct responsibility and involvement in combating the problem off the Horn of Africa, coordinating all their efforts through the United Nations. First to commit a force would be the North Atlantic Treaty Organization (NATO), whose Council agreed in late October 2008 to a special request from the UN Secretary-General to dispatch more warships to temporarily supplement the few naval vessels already escorting chartered merchantmen through those pirate-infested waters, delivering World Food Program humanitarian shipments into starving pockets of Somalia. The UN was worried by the soaring number of pirate interceptions being made, publicly alluding to the "more than 80 such attacks so far this year, including 32 hijackings, compared with 31 attacks in 2007, according to the London-based International Maritime Bureau" (*UN News Centre* press release, November 11, 2008).

Consequently, "Standing NATO Maritime Group 2" was hastened out to assist the ongoing efforts of the lone Dutch frigate HNLMS *De Ruyter*. By October 28, 2008, Standing NATO Maritime Group 2's Greek frigate HS *Themistokles* was guiding its first chartered freighter into the anchorage at Merka, 60 miles southwest of Mogadishu, and would soon be joined by the rest of this force: the Royal Navy's HMS *Cumberland*; the Turkish frigate TGC *Gokova*; and the Italian Navy destroyer ITS *Luigi Durand de la Penne*, serving as Standing NATO Maritime Group 2's flagship under Rear Admiral Giovanni Gumiero. This first deployment to the Horn of Africa, codenamed Operation "Allied Provider," was to serve as a temporary protection force until December 2008, when NATO handed over responsibility for the WFP's extra protection to the European Union's Operation "Atalanta."

EU "Operation Atalanta"

In Brussels, the European Union's foreign ministers also agreed on November 10, 2008 to dispatch five to seven frigates, with the requisite number of support aircraft, into the Horn of Africa region within one month to protect merchant-shipping in addition to escorting WFP food-relief into Somalia (*UN News Centre* press release, November 11, 2008). Codenamed Operation "Atalanta," this expedition represented an unprecedented step, the first independent naval campaign ever launched by the EU—a financial, political, and cultural confederation—under the framework of its "European Security and Defense Policy."

The specific mandate for this squadron's operations was broader than NATO's initial deployment, specifying that it was to contribute toward:

- protection of vessels of the World Food Program, while delivering food-aid to displaced persons in Somalia;
- aiding vulnerable vessels sailing in the Gulf of Aden and off the Somali coast;
- employing all necessary measures—including the use of force—to "deter, prevent, and intervene in order to bring to an end acts of piracy and armed robbery which may be committed" in those waters.

As authorization, these actions were to be undertaken in compliance with Resolutions 1814, 1816, 1838, and 1846, all adopted that same year of 2008 by the United Nations Security Council.

This force, better known by its acronym of EUNavFor, would also establish the "Maritime Security Centre (Horn of Africa)" or MSC-HOA, an information hub for gathering and disseminating news on piratical activity in the Gulf of Aden, as well as tracking movements of merchantmen transiting through those troubled waters.

UN Intelligence Gathering

The United Nations was simultaneously hosting a gathering in mid-November 2008 in Nairobi, Kenya, of an "International Expert Group on Piracy off the Somali coast," to gather the most current and accurate information available to help "develop a coordinated response to the challenge of maritime piracy along the Somali coast." This assembly included veteran Somali hands, naval and police officers, relief organizations, legal scholars, security specialists, etc., who together offered considerable insight into the actual workings of Somalia's shadowy pirate groups, most of which information has subsequently proven to be quite accurate.

Creation of Combined Task Force-151

In support of the growing responsibility being shouldered by allied nations in their separate campaign against Somali piracy, Vice Admiral William E. Gortney, commander of U.S. Naval Forces Central Command and the U.S. Fifth Fleet, announced the formation on January 8, 2009 of a new coalition detachment—Combined Task Force-151—which had been split off from the already existing CTF-150, this new formation being crafted specifically to conduct counter-piracy operations. According to the original mandate which had sent coalition warships into the Indian Ocean theater as part of Operation "Enduring Freedom," the U.S.-led antiterrorist offensive, these vessels had been assigned to perform "Maritime Security" duties, which included the deterrence of destabilizing activities such as drug-smuggling or weapons-trafficking—yet did not encompass hunting pirates.

"Some navies in our coalition did not have the authority to conduct counter-piracy missions," Gortney explained. "The establishment of CTF-151 will allow those nations to operate under the auspices of CTF-150, while allowing other nations to join CTF-151 [and] support our [mutual] goal of deterring, disrupting, and eventually bringing to justice the maritime criminals involved in piracy events." The few U.S. Navy warships assigned to this newly created Combined Task Force-151, would be the first U.S. naval assets actually tasked with conducting antipiracy sweeps off the Horn of Africa region (Ploch, p. 4). Four days later, on January 12, 2009, CTF-151 was further cleared to operate under the UN Security Consul resolution mandate, although still under U.S. command.

UN "Contact Group on Piracy"

At the United Nations headquarters in New York City on January 14, 2009, in compliance with Security Council Resolution 1851, a "Contact Group on Piracy off the Coast of Somalia" was created "to facilitate discussion and coordination of actions among states and organizations, to suppress piracy off the coast of Somalia." Representatives from key nations such as Djibouti, Oman,

Saudi Arabia, Somalia's Transitional Federal Government, the United Arab Emirates, the United States, and Yemen were all included, as well as the African Union, European Union, and NATO. This mandate urged all to act jointly against piracy, which:

> disrupts critical humanitarian-aid deliveries to Somalia; increases shipping insurance-premiums along one of the world's most traveled routes to near-prohibitive levels; damages littoral economies by forcing the diversion of vessels around the Cape of Good Hope; and raises the prospect of an environmental disaster as ships fall prey to hostile intent. Piracy is a symptom of a wider lack of security and rule of law in Somalia, and continues to constitute a threat to regional stability. As important, piracy is symptomatic of the overall situation in Somalia, including the prevalence of illegal fishing and toxic-waste dumping off the coast of Somalia, which adversely affects the Somali economy and marine environment.

The Group was intended to serve as a clearinghouse for policy decisions, concentrating on six main areas:

- improving operational and information support to counterpiracy operations,
- establishing a counterpiracy coordination mechanism,
- strengthening judicial frameworks for arrest, prosecution, and detention of pirates,
- strengthening commercial shipping self-awareness and other capabilities,
- pursuing improved diplomatic and public information efforts,
- and tracking financial flows related to piracy.

Kenyan and Somali Prosecutions

Soon after beginning to make their first captures of Somali pirates and flying them home to stand trial, various European governments became aware of the expense and unforeseen legal complications in conducting such long-distance cases. As reluctance to host such trials spread, some naval patrols in that distant theater even resorted to letting a few intercepted pirates go, after simply confiscating their weapons—known as the "catch-and-release" method—rather than make insignificant yet potentially frustrating arrests.

In order to circumvent this problem, the European Union signed an agreement with the Kenyan government in Nairobi on March 6, 2009, whereby suspected pirates could be landed directly in that East African nation to face trial under the international statutes of the UN's "Convention on the Law of the Sea." Similar, less-formal deals were also struck with authorities in such semi-autonomous Somali states as Somaliland and Puntland, who—so long as the disembarked prisoners did not hail from that particular region—would condemn them without compunction, allowing both governments to claim an active role in the ongoing global campaign against piracy.

Western jurists worried about the legality of "dumping" such prisoners in a third country, yet it persists in practice.

NATO "Operation Allied Protector"

A second NATO effort was organized in March 2009, when its Standing NATO Maritime Group 1 was ordered to the theater as part of Operation "Allied Protector," with an openly declared mission to "deter, defend against, and disrupt pirate activities." This Group had originally been scheduled to perform such anti-piracy duties only temporarily, while in transit through the Horn of Africa region en route to a goodwill tour of Southeast Asia, as well as during its return passage back through those same waters toward Europe in June 2009.

However, NATO officials instead cancelled Standing NATO Maritime Group 1's planned visits to Singapore and Australia in April 2009 so as to perform one uninterrupted anti-piracy tour after starting its first patrols in late March 2009. This squadron consisted of the Portuguese flagship NRP *Corte Real*, Canada's HMCS *Winnipeg*, the Dutch HNLMS *Zeven Provinciën*, the Spanish warship SPS *Blas de Lezo*, and USS *Halyburton*, who would all remain on that station until June 20, 2009.

NATO "Operation Ocean Shield"

On August 17, 2009, NATO announced its third "contribution to international efforts to combat piracy off the Horn of Africa," once its Council had finalized approval for such a mission under the codename of Operation "Ocean Shield," to be conducted by the alliance's currently-constituted Standing NATO Maritime Group 2—this time around comprised of the Royal Navy frigate

HMS *Cornwall* as flagship; the Greek frigate HS *Navarinon*; the Italian frigate ITS *Libeccio*; the Turkish frigate TCG *Gediz*; and the American destroyer USS *Laboon*.

A specific new component of this particular effort was to be building up contacts and better relationships with regional governments so that they too might begin developing their own local counterpiracy contributions. For example, SNMG's flagship *Cornwall* would welcome aboard Somali maritime officials from the troubled State of Puntland, as well as visit the port of Bosaso in the country's northern province of Bari, for consultations with officials responsible for port security and maritime transportation.

Other International Contributions

Inspired by the multinational effort being gathered under UN auspices to address the problem of piracy off the heavily transited Horn of Africa, nations which seldom or never had participated in joint naval exercises in the past, yet whose merchantmen had been victimized—such as Russia, India, Japan, China, and South Korea—would dispatch individual warships to help bolster this campaign.

The end result would be an array of NATO, EU, regional, and other multinational naval forces conducting patrols near Somalia, in coordination with a U.S.-led task force.

Defensive Measures

U.S. naval officers had often deplored the lax security observed aboard many modern commercial ships traveling near the Horn of Africa, rendering even the largest and wealthiest vessel easy prey for a handful of pirates. As long ago as November 2008, Vice Admiral William E. Gortney—commander of the U.S. Fifth Fleet and coalition Combined Maritime Forces operating in the Indian Ocean—had complained of this shortsightedness, in a public statement which urged shipping firms to take basic measures to better protect their vessels, noting that 10 of the most recent 15 ships attacked in the Gulf of Aden, had not even been traveling within the patrolled corridor recommended by the UN's International Maritime Organization, and carried no kind of onboard security. "Companies don't think twice about using security guards to protect their valuable facilities ashore," Gortney added. "Protecting valuable ships and their crews at sea is no different" (Wadhams).

Patrolled Convoy Routes

The deployment of additional foreign warships into those waters, while wholly insufficient to sweep any significant portion of open ocean at least allowed for more effective monitoring of a narrow passage through the troubled Gulf of Aden. Dubbed the "International Recommended Transit Corridor," its use was promulgated in cooperation with the EU and UKMTO on February 1, 2009 and recommended to all transiting merchantmen by the U.S. Navy, allied forces, regional governments, and civilian shipping agencies. It parallels the Yemeni coastline, lying roughly between 12° North, 58° East, and 10° South, extending between the U.S. base in Djibouti and U.S. naval forces in the Arabian Sea. Westbound merchantmen are directed to tend toward the shipping channel on its northern side, eastbound ships toward its southern side.

In addition to the aerial and naval patrols, which regularly prowled this Corridor, convoys were also organized for slower moving vessels so that they might run through the Gulf of Aden with a naval warship nearby. Three types of such groupings were organized, depending on need:

- a Group Transit, usually merchantmen of similar speed, who would run through within sight of each other so as to summon help if one should be attacked;
- an Escorted Group Transit, a disparate group of freighters clustered near a warship;
- or a National Convoy, a group of vessels from a single country, often with their own accompanying warship.

Better-Defended Merchantmen

As the tempo of piratical attacks continued to soar off Somalia during early 2009, U.S. Admiral Bill Gortney would be moved to observe: "The most effective measures we've seen to defeat piracy, are non-kinetic and defensive in nature." Not surprisingly for the professional seamen involved, such as this veteran U.S. officer, boarding any large ship running on the high seas from a small skiff was no easy feat. With a few simple, extra steps that should meet with approval from even the most parsimonious shipping-firm, many modern vessels could be rendered a lot less vulnerable to assault. Even the notorious pirate chieftain Boyah himself guessed in April 2009, that only "20 to 30 per cent of attempted hijackings succeed" (Bahadur, "I'm Not").

Various concerned maritime associations had already compiled and circulated their own internal lists of suggestions, when the Commercial Crime Services division of the International Chamber of Commerce in London gathered up input from more than a dozen such groups, and published an industry-wide manual entitled "Best Management Practices to Deter Piracy." This information included materials previously published in the International Maritime Organization's *Circular MSC.1/Circ.1334*, as well as manuals from other organizations. All recommended certain common measures which merchant Captains might adopt before transiting through such perilous waters as the Gulf of Aden or Horn of Africa region, and which are summarized here below:

Prior to Departure

1. Register for access to restricted sections of the MSC-HOA Web site, so as to review the most current intelligence on pirate sightings and receive regular updates, plus special warnings or other advice.
2. Inform UKMTO Dubai, MARLO Bahrain, and MSC-HOA, either online or via e-mail or fax, of one's intended course, by filing a "Vessel Movement Registration" several days prior to actually entering into the endangered waterway.
3. Review ship contingency plans and procedures, conducting periodic drills to familiarize crewmembers with alarm bells, etc.
4. Prepare a reinforced "safe room" deep within the ship, without portholes and away from all external bulkheads so as to be able to retreat inside and await rescue, in case of being boarded.
5. Ensure that all doors, portholes, and vents that provide access into the interior of a ship from above, can be securely locked from the inside.
6. For a fairly low-speed vessel, consider delaying passage through more dangerous stretches of the Gulf of Aden so as to instead travel as part of a Group Transit, Escorted Group Transit, or National Convoy grouping.
7. However, if a vessel's sea-speed is more than eighteen knots, it is not recommended joining a slow and straggling convoy, but rather to run through the peril-zone alone.

8. Install whatever self-defense measures may be on board, such as razor-wire coils along low-freeboard railings, etc.
9. Consider traveling in rough weather, as wind-strengths over eighteen knots and waves higher than six feet will deter most pirate boats.
10. Plan on running through the most high-risk areas at night, if at all possible.

While Transiting through Dangerous Passages

11. Minimize all external communications via cell or satellite phones, radios, handsets, etc., as these might reveal a ship's position.
12. Rearrange watches so that extra lookouts are made available.
13. Restrict the amount of crew-work on deck, especially at night so as to avoid being surprised by pirates at an untimely moment.
14. Ensure that all access to and from the decks into the accommodations and internal work-areas, be reduced to a single point of entry, although without obstructing any necessary emergency exits.
15. Keep all overside ladders and lines securely fastened up on deck.
16. Transmit updates of ship progress every noon to UKMTO Dubai, and even more frequently while running past danger zones.
17. Keep essential emergency radio frequencies, phone numbers, and pre-arranged distress signals ready for instant use, such as permanently displayed beside the ship's communications panel.
18. Perhaps switch off the ship's Automatic Identification System.
19. Avoid straying into Yemeni territorial waters, where U.S. and allied warships cannot enter to effect a rescue.
20. Keep redundant auxiliary machinery, such as ship generators and steering motors, primed for instant use.
21. In danger zones, keep fire-hoses pressurized and ready for immediate discharge, particularly those near a ship's most vulnerable points.
22. Keep the ship dark at night, running along with only navigation-lights illuminated.
23. Provide lookouts with night-vision optics, if possible.

24. Immediately report any sightings of suspected pirate "mother ships" to UKMTO Dubai and the IMB PRC.
25. Maintain special vigilance astern, in particular at dawn and dusk, when most pirate attacks occur from that quarter.

If Attacked

26. Immediately upon detecting an approaching pirate craft, advise the UKMTO and MSC-HOA listening posts, which are manned round the clock.
27. Reactivate the ship's AIS, if this system has been switched off.
28. Make distress calls on Navy-monitored VHF channels 16 or 8, as well as via Digital Selective Calling system and Inmarsat-C, or by cell phone directly to UKMTO.
29. If possible, increase speed and perhaps begin small zig-zags (although this latter tactic can reduce distance covered over the water).
30. If an attack occurs at night, illuminate all deck-lighting so as to attract attention from any nearby vessels.
31. Immediately gather all off-duty hands within the safe-room.
32. If fired upon, maintain full sea-speed so that the pirates must risk boarding the rapidly moving vessel.
33. As boarders come aboard, stop the main engine, and all remaining personnel should retreat inside the safe-room. (*Best Management Practices*)

Applied together, such measures could prove surprisingly effective in averting many attacks, and some of these tactics were also employed to good effect by the crew of the U.S. container ship *Maersk Alabama*, in resisting the attempted seizure of their vessel.

Rarest of Encounters: The *Maersk Alabama* Incident

Given the historic changes which had transpired over the past several decades in the world's shipping industry, such as:

— a drastic contraction of the U.S. Merchant Marine,
— the manning of commercial vessels with minimal, low-cost crews,

— the expansion of Asian and Third-World fleets,

— and the widespread adoption of "flags of convenience,"

it was truly remarkable to find an find an American-flagged merchantman running out of the Gulf of Aden during the spring of 2009. This was the 17,500-ton, 500-foot container ship *Maersk Alabama*, which was making its regular run southward from Salalah in Oman, down the troubled East African coast toward Mombassa, Kenya.

Unusual Presence

Originally a Taiwanese-built ship launched in 1998 as the *Alva Maersk* for the Danish conglomerate A. P. Moller-Maersk Group— the largest shipping-firm in the world—this smallish container ship had been re-flagged as an American vessel in 2004 so as to take advantage of Department of Defense contracts being issued in support of the occupation of Iraq. As these contracts gave preference to U.S.-owned ships with American crews, operating under the Maritime Security Program, ownership had been transferred by the corporation on paper to its subsidiary Maersk Line, Limited, of Norfolk, Virginia, and twenty American officers and seamen had been flown out to replace the previous crew and operate this vessel in the Indian Ocean.

Although no longer under Pentagon contract during this particular run down toward Mombassa in early April 2009, *Maersk Alabama* nonetheless remained under U.S. government charter, having been hired to carry 8,150 metric tons of United States Agency for International Development or USAID humanitarian cargo, which—again according to the U.S. Congress's Cargo Preference Act of 1954, as well as the 1985 amendment to the Merchant Marine Act—required that 75 percent of all such shipments be transported aboard American-flagged carriers. More than 5,000 metric tons of UN World Food Program provisions had also been loaded onboard the *Alabama*, yet the ship was riding rather high in the water, being only partially full.

With the northeastern monsoon season now at an end, tiny pirate craft were once more reemerging, in ever greater numbers and farther out to sea, as the spring weather cleared along the Somali coast. Multiple warnings about attempted and actual attacks were already being issued by both the United Kingdom Maritime Trade Organization, a joint military command coordinating anti-piracy efforts around the Horn of Africa, as well as private security firms such as the Virginia-based SecureWest out of Norfolk, which were all recommending that transiting merchantmen try to keep at least 600 nautical miles offshore.

Maersk Alabama nevertheless continued on its original heading, roughly half that distance from Somalia, despite reports arriving daily of other vessels being seized along this same route. Capt. Richard Phillips would later say that he hoped the speed and high freeboard of his ship would spare it from outright capture, although he had already informed his crew to be prepared for just such an attempt, as it was only "a matter of when, not if" (Kahn).

Pursuit

At mid-afternoon on Tuesday, April 7, 2009, the container ship was spotted by a pirate mother ship, which launched three skiffs in pursuit. A couple soon gave up in the rough seas, although the third hung on grimly until within a mile, before finally turning back as well, and disappearing into the churning wake. Around 3:45 a.m. on Wednesday morning, April 8, 2009, another mother ship was spotted on *Alabama*'s 24-mile radar, which hailed them over VHF radio: "Stop ship. Stop ship. This is Somali pirate" (Murphy).

Phillips increased speed to 18 knots and slightly altered course so that this second contact soon faded from the scope as well. Yet at 6:48 a.m., a new contact was faintly detected, only three-and-a-half miles away. Amid the growing light and over a perfectly smooth sea, a tiny fibreglass skiff could be seen boring in at 26 knots, with four armed gunmen aboard. *Alabama*'s Chief Mate Shane Murphy fired two red flares in the direction of this approaching craft yet was otherwise powerless to slow its advance.

Boarding

By 7:13 a.m. on that Wednesday morning, April 8, 2009, the pirates had come along *Alabama*'s port side, tossing grappling hooks over its midship railings so that a pair of gunmen could start clambering up its sheer plates while the other two fired warning shots into the air. Most of the crew were immediately ordered below decks so as to be safe from any chance rounds. It took several minutes for the first two pirates to gain the main deck, and they then had to shoot their way past a locked mesh-cage door over the ladder-well, as well as other locks on the outer ladders, before eventually gaining the bridge and capturing Captain Phillips, Third Mate Colin Wright, the ship's Bangladeshi-American helmsman Abu Tasir Mohammed "Zahid" Reza, and Seaman Cliff Lacon.

However, control of the ship had been taken over by Chief Engineer Mike Perry from down below in the engine room so that *Alabama* could no longer be steered from the bridge. As one pirate gunman returned amidships with a pair of prisoners at 8:30 a.m., to have them rig the rope "pilot ladder" so that their two comrades might climb up and join them, First Engineer Matt Fisher down in the engine room swung *Alabama*'s rudder around violently from side to side so that the skiff was unexpectedly swamped and then capsized, leaving all four pirates stranded on board. Immediately thereafter, Perry shut down every system so that the entire vessel "went black" and was left adrift in hissing silence.

Resistance

Fourteen of the U.S. seamen below decks had been directed by Perry into a locked "strong room," which had been fortified earlier in the ship's stern, while he joined *Alabama*'s second-in-command, Chief Mate Murphy, in covertly observing the pirate quartet from atop one of the towering deck-cranes before both officers returned below. Despite having seized the bridge and a few prisoners, as well as looting the ship's safe and cabins, the boarders could not control their huge prize and were fearful of descending into its dark hold. The captive Third Mate was released to order the crew up on deck, yet he naturally disappeared. Then one of the pirates—later identified as Abduwali Abdukhadir Musé—was persuaded by the helmsman "Zahid" Reza, a fellow Muslim and a resident of West Hartford, Connecticut, to go below together.

Musé first handed his pistol to a colleague, apparently because the Somalis were concerned about losing a weapon to an ambush in the darkness. And indeed, the tiny pirate was suddenly jumped in a passageway by Chief Engineer Perry—a very fit man in his 60s—who stabbed and subdued him along with Reza's help. By 9:00 a.m., the wounded Musé had been tied up with wire restraints, gagged, and bundled into one of the safe-rooms (Casella).

The remaining three armed pirates up above became very agitated when their comrade failed to reappear, threatening to shoot Captain Phillips, yet such menaces could not force anyone to emerge, while the Somalis remained even more fearful than before of venturing below. Meanwhile, the elusive Chief Mate Murphy managed to slide some drinks and a medical kit down to the men sweltering inside the unventilated safe-room, before sneaking up four decks into the Captain's ransacked cabin to retrieve a VHF radio and a cell phone, then returning into his hidden vantage-point atop the crane to use these to begin making a series of distress calls by 1:00 p.m.—which the pirates on the bridge could plainly overhear yet not prevent.

Having lost their skiff and one gang member, as well as being unable to control the huge drifting ship, Captain Phillips talked this trio by 4:00 p.m. into retreating back out to sea aboard *Alabama*'s 18-foot rescue boat so as to at least regain their mother ship with what booty they had pilfered. After informing his hidden crewmen by radio, Phillips descended into this open boat with his three captors, allowing Murphy and Perry to reoccupy the bridge and main deck. The U.S. seamen also agreed to winch down some food, water, and diesel to supply the pirates bobbing on the waves below, an electrician named John White later declaring: "They couldn't get off the ship without our help" (Bone).

Hostage Taking

But the pirates then stalled the rescue boat's engine so that the bigger 28-foot, bright-orange, enclosed lifeboat had be lowered instead and motored across to them. These protracted operations did not conclude until 7:00 p.m. that same Wednesday, April 8, 2009, at which point it only remained for the pirates to free Captain Phillips in exchange for their captive comrade so that the Somalis might make away together into the night, leaving *Alabama*'s complement intact. However, Chief Mate Shane Murphy would later describe how this trade went awry, for as the injured Musé clambered down a rope ladder, Murphy called to Phillips to start climbing back up:

> He just stood there looking up at us, the pirates pointing guns at him. "Captain," I shouted, "get on the ladder!"
> "I'm just going to show them how to drive the boat," Captain Phillips said. The door closed, and then,

the Captain told me later, the pirates drew down on him.
(Murphy)

Since Musé had been reunited with his colleagues, the pirate band failed to honor the bargain, and instead puttered off slowly into the evening with their hostage.

Since *Alabama*'s engines and systems had been brought fully back on line, the container ship was easily able to follow this low-powered craft, illuminating it with a searchlight. Murphy, now in command of *Alabama*, even arranged for a fighter-jet from an approaching coalition warship to buzz the lumbering lifeboat at low altitude, as a warning that naval reinforcements were close at hand. Yet as darkness fell at 9:00 p.m., a good deal of Somali VHF chatter could also be heard on the radio as other pirates tried to steer their prizes to their comrades' assistance, who were using their own satellite-phone to request help. Around 1:00 a.m. on April 9, 2009, Phillips radioed back to Murphy, saying that his captors would shut down the lifeboat's engine for the night, if *Alabama* did the same, which was agreed upon.

Standoff

Shortly thereafter, the 270-man, 9,200-ton guided-missile destroyer USS *Bainbridge* of Cmdr. Francis X. Castellano appeared out of the night, having raced more than 300 miles in twelve hours from the Gulf of Aden to the rescue, closely followed by other American warships. Commander Castellano transferred a guard detail of 18 armed U.S. Navy sailors aboard *Alabama*, and the container ship was directed to proceed with its interrupted voyage toward Mombassa under Murphy, arriving there uneventfully by 8:30 p.m. that Saturday evening.

Meanwhile, the pirates' land-based commander, the notorious Abdi Garad, was glibly informing an Agence France-Presse reporter by telephone from the lawless port of Eyl on Thursday morning, April 9, 2009, that: "We are planning to reinforce our colleagues, who told us that a Navy ship was closing in on them" ("U.S. Navy"). Despite the vast disparity in firepower, as well as a P-3 Orion surveillance plane circling lazily overhead, the four pirates somehow still hoped to link up with other cohorts at sea who were holding a variety of Russian, German, and Filipino hostages aboard numerous other merchant prizes off Somalia. Yet it was clearly suicidal for them to brave the massing U.S. forces, so that pirate threats soon dwindled away to nothing. SEAL sharp-shooters were in the meantime parachuted into the sea unseen one night, to be taken aboard *Bainbridge* and concealed in position for a possible shootout.

On April 10, 2009, Phillips attempted to escape from the life-boat by suddenly leaping into the sea, only to be recaptured and tethered by his captors. The pirates also threw away a phone and two-way radio previously dropped to them by the U.S. Navy, apparently fearful that the Americans were somehow manipulating this equipment to relay instructions to their hostage. Other warships, including the 225-man, 4,100-ton guided-missile frigate USS *Halyburton* and 1,100-man, 41,500-ton amphibious assault ship USS *Boxer*, hastened onto the scene. Negotiations were resumed between the pirates and the Captain of the *Bainbridge*, who was being advised by FBI hostage negotiators, while the cornered Somalis continued communicating in vain with other pirate vessels by satellite phone.

Rescue

On Sunday morning, April 12, 2009, the wounded pirate Musé asked to come aboard *Bainbridge* for medical treatment, reportedly telling its U.S. officers that his three companions were prepared to kill their hostage, if they were not all granted safe passage out of this predicament. The rising seas were meanwhile carrying the lifeboat inexorably closer to Somalia's territorial waters, and as the weather began to deteriorate further, U.S. Navy negotiators offered to steady the rolling lifeboat by towing it along behind *Bainbridge*. A 200-foot line was therefore reeled out and attached to it, but—unnoticed amid the heavy wave-action—it was then very slowly inched back in, until the lifeboat was only trailing 75 feet astern of the warship.

As evening fell that Easter Sunday, SEAL snipers watching through night-vision rifle scopes from their positions of conceal-ment along *Bainbridge*'s fantail, saw a pair of pirates poke their heads out of the lifeboat hatch at 7:19 p.m., apparently getting some fresh air. The third, visible through a window, was pointing his AK-47 at Phillips's back, as the Captain moved to one side of the boat to relieve himself over its side. Commander Castellano of the *Bainbridge* gave the order, and each sharpshooter took a single shot, killing all three pirates simultaneously. When a rescue party hastened aboard the lifeboat, they found Phillips still tethered to its interior.

The Captain and crew of the *Alabama* were to return home to a euphoric heroes' welcome, while the lone surviving pirate was flown into New York City eight days later, to be paraded past news-cameras and charged in court with 10 counts related to piracy, carrying the death-penalty. In the interim, his Somali chieftain Garad had threatened to exact revenge, some of his minions apparently chasing and firing at another U.S. freighter, the *Liberty Sun*, on the evening of April 14, 2009. However, this merchantman easily outran its pursuers and next dawn, French Marines swooped in aboard a helicopter from the 3,000-ton frigate *Nivôse* of the EU's Operation "Atalanta," snapping up all eleven pirates and their "mother ship" to stand trial in Kenya.

Current Status and Future Outlook

Although no other American merchantman would be captured that year, this was chiefly due to a lack of U.S.-flagged ships throughout that region, as 2009 otherwise proved to be a record year for piracy. As early as September 14, 2009, the U.S. State Department was announcing that at least 156 attacks had already been recorded off the Horn of Africa since January, including 33 successful hijackings. Attacks remained concentrated in the Gulf of Aden between Yemen and the north coast of Somalia, as well as along its eastern coastline, while the UN Secretary-General had further warned in July 2009 that because of the enhanced foreign naval presence in the Gulf, pirates were opting for more daring strikes, prowling "further seawards, towards the Seychelles, and using more sophisticated weaponry."

Ransoms paid to such profit-driven pirates and their backers were estimated to have totaled at least $30 million in 2008, while some Kenyan officials suggested that the figure may have actually been as high as $150 million (Karon). This was a powerful inducement in such an impoverished nation, fueling the escalating number of forays in 2009. The International Maritime Bureau's "Piracy Reporting Centre" in Kuala Lumpur announced in January 2010, that it had recorded 406 incidents of piracy or armed sea robbery during that preceding year: 153 vessels having been boarded, 49 hijacked, 84 weathering attacks, and 120 vessels fired upon (compared to only 46 ships fired upon in all of 2008).

The total number of incidents specifically attributed to Somali pirates stood at 217, with 47 vessels hijacked and

867 crewmembers taken hostage—more than half the world's totals for 2009. The ominous shift in their area of operations was confirmed, for while most attacks had previously been clustered in the Gulf of Aden, more merchantmen were now being targeted far away from the eastern shores of Somalia. In fact, since October 2009 alone, the IMB declared, thirteen incidents—including four ship hijackings—had occurred well beyond the recommended commercial safety line of 60° East, roughly 1,000 nautical miles out into the Indian Ocean.

Six Basic Elements

The reason for this piratical shift was apparent, as the more robust NATO, EU, and CTF-151 presence guarding the Gulf of Aden sea lanes, was making piratical raids more difficult in that busy corridor so that more distant yet softer areas were being tried. The joint new allied deployments in and around the Gulf had also been accompanied by more concerted contacts ashore, achieving some of the six basic goals required for a successful antipiracy effort:

> *(1) Accurate intelligence*, which had allowed foreign services to acquire a clearer understanding of pirate operations, sometimes to the extent of being able to monitor certain notorious bases and tracking covert departures;

> *(2) International commitment*, including participation by every major maritime power, plus logistical and surveillance support from already existing U.S. assets;

> *(3) Regional cooperation*, which included willing partners in such fringe Somali states as Somaliland and Puntland, who were eager to prosecute captured pirates from outside their jurisdiction, in return for material assistance from the alliance;

> *(4) Local involvement*, the only weak link in the allied operation, as the most pirate-prone districts of central Somalia still remained closed to outside influences, serving as havens for hijacked merchantmen;

> *(5) Denial of prey*, which had been achieved through better security measures aboard many large transiting merchantmen, as well as better adherence by commercial shipping to patrolled passages;

(6) Legal recourses, as several deals had quietly been struck by European representatives to deposit any captured pirates to stand trial in Kenya, Somaliland, or Puntland, where they would receive discouragingly harsh sentences without the expense and trouble of a distant Western prosecution.

By April 2010, the International Maritime Bureau was able to announce a significant decline in reported pirate attacks during the first quarter of this year, a worldwide total of 67 incidents having been logged from January to March 2010, compared to 102 during the same period during the previous year. A "dramatic decline" was highlighted in attacks in the Gulf of Aden and its adjacent seas, only 17 incidents having been recorded, in contrast to the 41 during the first three months of 2009.

U.S. Viewpoint

Yet despite such positive signs, the struggle against Somali piracy is far from over. The expense of sustaining so many warships on patrol will soon prove vexing, while many legal issues still remain unresolved. For example, a lawsuit has been filed in Berlin on behalf of a Somali suspect delivered up to the Kenyan authorities by a German warship, suing for the inhumane treatment which he has received since being handed over. And moreover, the core issue of grinding poverty, devastated local resources, and absence of any responsible government in central Somalia, will continue to send desperate rovers out to sea. "Most experts believe that the reestablishment of government authority in Somalia, is the only guarantee that piracy will not persist or reemerge as a threat" (Ploch, p. i).

Little has changed since Bile Mohamoud Qabowsade, an adviser to the President of Puntland, explained that pirates had even built up considerable political influence, as being one of the few local sources of wealth:

> Many people like the pirates, for their pockets. They have money, and give to their relatives and friends. That money goes through many hands, which in return gives them support among the community. ("Somali Piracy")

In some parts, pirate ransoms still remain welcome. News that some cash bags have been brought ashore, often under cover of darkness, spreads quickly throughout neighboring towns and villages.

Next day, the pirates will take over a large restaurant or expensive hotel, where they invariably start their celebration by chewing the best *khat*. A procession of well-wishers then starts to arrive: Friends and relatives, as well as local traders and elders owed money for their assistance or supply of provisions during the operation. "You see many people coming into the hotel visiting them, they are busy paying money to the visitors for a whole day, and they spend half of their time talking on their expensive cell phones. They look like big company bosses," observed Ali Haji Yusuf, a local hotel owner in Garowe (ibid.).

As U.S. forces draw out of Iraq and reduce their footprint in this volatile region, no new involvement in a protracted and potentially costly campaign against pirates would be welcome.

Sources

Bahadur, Jay. " I'm Not a Pirate, I'm the Saviour of the Sea." *The Times Online* [UK], April 16, 2009.

Best Management Practices to Deter Piracy in the Gulf of Aden and Off the Coast of Somalia. London: Commercial Crime Services division of the International Chamber of Commerce, 2009.

Bone, James. "*Maersk Alabama* Crew Return to U.S. to Tell of Somali Pirate Ordeal." *The Times Online* [UK], April 18, 2009.

COMUSNAVCENT "Command" and "History," www.cusnc.navy.mil, official U.S. Navy Web site GILS#002176.

Curran, John. "Mutiny: Crew Blames Richard Phillips, *Maersk Alabama* Captain, for Ignoring Pirate Warnings." *Huffington Post Online*, December 2, 2009.

"Don't Give Up the Ship!: Quick Thinking and a Boatload of Know-how Saves the *Maersk Alabama*." *Marine Officer* (Summer 2009), 18 pp.

Harding, Andrew. "Postcard from Somali Pirate Capital." *BBC News*, June 16, 2009.

International Crisis Group. *Somalia: The Problem with Puntland.* Africa Briefing No. 64, August 12, 2009.

Kahn, Joseph P. "Uncharted Waters." *Boston Globe Online*, August 29, 2009.

Karon, Tony. "Battling the Somali Pirates: The Return of the Islamists." *Time Magazine*, November 25, 2008.

Murphy, Shane, as told to Sean Flynn. " I'm Your Worst F**king Nightmare." *GQ Online*, November 18, 2009.

Piracy Off the Somali Coast: Workshop Commissioned by the Special Representative of the Secretary-General of the United Nations to Somalia, Ambassador Ahmedou Ould-Abdallah. Nairobi, Kenya, November 2008.

Ploch, Lauren, et alia. *Piracy Off the Horn of Africa.* Washington, D.C.: "Congressional Research Service" Report for Congress, September 28, 2009.

Raffaelle, Paul. "The Pirate Hunters." *Smithsonian Magazine*, August 2007.

Report S/2006/229 of the U.N. Monitoring Group on Somalia, Submitted to the Security Council on May 4, 2006. New York: United Nations Security Council, 2006.

"Somali Piracy: 'We're Defending Our Waters.' " *Mail & Guardian Online* [UK], October 14, 2008.

"US Navy Closes Grip on Somali Pirates." *Agence France-Presse*, April 8, 2009.

4

Chronology

We are not pirates. We are gentlemen, defending our shores against foreign fishermen. It did become a business, but it was forced upon us, because we were attacked. We have bills to pay and families to care for.

—Jamal Akhmed, condemned to a life sentence at Bosaso,
June 2009

The following listing intersperses some major milestones associated with the evolution of modern piracy, with a selection of some of the more representative or unusual depredations committed in recent years upon the high seas. The sheer number of attacks which have been reported, amid such a broad variety of geographic settings and circumstances, make any coherent compilation impossible. Piracy remains as chaotic and opportunistic today, as in bygone eras.

December 10, 1982
After nine years of negotiations and drafting, the United Nations's "Convention on the Law of the Sea" is finally passed and signed in Jamaica's Montego Bay. However, it will not actually come into effect until November 16, 1994, a year after the 60th-member nation has signed on and agreed to its terms.

October 7, 1985
While steaming peacefully from Alexandria toward Port Said in Egypt, the Italian liner *Achille Lauro* is hijacked by four members of a faction known as the Palestinian Liberation Front. Diverting the vessel toward Tartus in Syria, they threaten to start killing

October 7, 1985 (*cont.*) captives unless Israel releases 50 prisoners. Rebuffed, the gunmen next afternoon shoot Leon Klinghoffer, an elderly American Jew confined to a wheelchair, then throw his body overboard before reversing course for Port Said.

Unaware of this murder, the Egyptian government ends the hostage standoff on October 9th by granting the hijackers safe passage toward Tunisia. Instead, U.S. naval fighters intercept the Egyptian airliner over the Mediterranean, forcing it to land at a NATO base in Sicily. The four Palestinians are separated from among the passengers and—over American objections—put on trial by the Italian authorities, while Cairo angrily protests to Washington about the mid-air interception.

This high-profile incident reveals unresolved differences, the U.S. government accusing the hijackers of piracy, although a great deal of public opinion does not concur, especially in the Arab and nonaligned world.

May– June 1988 Because of repeated reports that armed piratical attacks have occurred in the East China Sea, specifically off the coast of Zhejiang Province during which many fishing vessels have been plundered of their catches, fishermen assaulted and kidnapped, vessels blown up, and threats used to force sales at reduced prices, Chinese officials announce the arrest of six pirate ships based out of Fujian Province.

January 1, 1989 U.S. mariners are warned to be alert for the possibility of vessels being boarded and hijacked by armed pirates while transiting through or anchored in the waters of Southeast Asia.

February 7, 1990 On the global stage, the Cold War begins to end when an exhausted Soviet Union simply implodes from stagnation, its once all-powerful Central Committee agreeing to relinquish political power, after which East and West Germany move toward reunification and other Warsaw Pact satellites peacefully regain their independence. The United States is left as the lone superpower in the world.

August 8, 1990   The U.S. government warns its mariners to exercise caution while sailing near the coast of Liberia, as rebel ships might attempt to board merchantmen. Information received indicates that these rebels will be flying two flags: The national colors, plus the flag of the National Patriotic Front of Liberia, being red with a black scorpion displayed.

November 11, 1990   While under way at about 2:00 a.m. in Singapore's Phillip Channel, the American-flagged, 80,000-ton tanker *Ocean City* is boarded by four robbers armed with long knives. A crewman confronts them near the Master's stateroom and office, only to be bound and gagged. The pirates then steal the ship's safe and other personal items before escaping, this incident being reported by VHF radio to the harbor police.

January 26, 1991   Unnoticed amid the great realignment shaking world politics, President Mohamed Siad Barre is driven from power in Somalia's capital of Mogadishu by rebel factions. He nonetheless flees to his power base to fight on from among the Marehan clan in the southwestern Gedo region so that this impoverished nation quickly fragments into hostile enclaves continuously at odds with one another for the next two decades.

December 25, 1991   The Soviet Union dissolves, and the world begins moving into the post-Cold War Era.

November 3, 1993   Reports indicate that within the past week in the Bay of Bengal, pirates have attacked about 50 fishing vessels, looting their catches and throwing some 20 crewmembers into the sea.

November 16, 1994   The United Nations's "Convention on the Law of the Sea" legally comes into effect, its 320 articles defining

November
16, 1994
(*cont.*)

many boundaries and issues related to commercial exploitation of natural resources. However, its eight articles related to piracy will only be spottily enforced.

**August
10, 1995**

At 7:30 p.m., while under way about 40 nautical miles southeast of Hong Kong, a lookout aboard the American-flagged container ship *President Harrison* sights an approaching speedboat, so that the ship takes evasive action and outmaneuvers its pursuer.

**December
6, 1995**

An unknown vessel fires twice upon the U.S.-flagged yacht *Kelly Marie*, while it is lying at anchor overnight off the Hanish Islands in the southern Red Sea, which are being disputed between Yemen and Eritrea.

**April 10,
1996**

According to news reports from Jakarta, the Indonesian Navy has sent eight warships and a helicopter to the Natuna Islands after unidentified gunmen shot and killed the captain of a private boat in that area. They add that fishermen have refused to venture into those waters since assailants in a speedboat shot Captain Saryadi with automatic rifles on April 6th, fleeing without taking anything from his boat. Colonel L. Soetanto of the Indonesian Navy is quoted as saying the shooting will be difficult to investigate, because it occurred near the waters of Vietnam, the Philippines, and Malaysia, all of which are infested with pirates.

**November
4, 1997**

This morning in the Singapore straits area of the Straits of Malacca, the 43,398-ton Danish-flagged tanker *Northsea Bellows*—en route from the Arabian Gulf toward Japan—is stealthily boarded by three intruders who are discovered onboard and leap overboard after doing some minor damage to the ship's accommodation and two doors.

**November
8, 1997**

The Australian-flagged yacht *Poloflat* is fired upon by pirates while on the Red Sea off Eritrea, close to the Zubayr Islands, suffering damage to its sails but no injuries to any personnel. The yacht's skipper defends himself with homemade Molotov cocktails until the attackers desisted.

November
18, 1997

As the tanker *Atlanta 95* is steaming early this morning through the Indonesian strait named Selat Riau, en route to the Arafura Sea to serve as a bunkering station for fishing vessels, it is boarded by armed pirates. The crew is locked in their cabins, and the vessel steered into the Gulf of Thailand, some captives being ordered to assist in the engine room. Upon arriving, the tanker's entire cargo of marine oil is transferred to another vessel on December 1st, after which the prize gets under way again and steams in the vicinity of the Tow Islands for several days.

The tanker is finally abandoned by the pirates at 19:20 p.m. on December 7th, after which its crew force their way out of their locked cabins and regain control. Before departing, the pirates destroy all charts and damage the radio sets, so that the vessel limps into Singapore by December 10th with the aid of a spare VHF, and an old chart from the Master's cabin. During its captivity, *Atlanta 95*'s name has also been painted over by the pirates, and its funnel altered with black paint.

October
10–11,
1998

The local cruise boat *Ma Foroe* is boarded during the night by five men armed with knives from a small boat in Port Moresby Harbor, Papua New Guinea, its 150 passengers being threatened, punched, and struck with bottles while being robbed of money and valuables.

October
27, 1998

While steaming along at 3:20 a.m. in a rainstorm north of the Sunda Strait, the Danish-flagged cargo ship *Thor Marie* is boarded between Indonesia's Belitung and Bangka Islands by five persons armed with knives and a pistol. The chief mate having just completed a security inspection and searchlight sweep, the door of the starboard bridge wing is unlocked, where the intruders suddenly appear. They force the chief mate to call the captain to the bridge, on the pretext of a navigation problem. He has his hands tied and is forced back to his cabin, where he is compelled to open the safe, which contains only medicine and papers. The captain is therefore forced to turn over

October
27, 1998
(*cont.*)

his personal cash, a suitcase, the photocopy machine, a video recorder, two cartons of cigarettes, a camera, and his watch. He is left tied up on deck behind the funnel, while the thieves escape in a boat, the entire incident having lasted about 20 minutes.

**November
9, 1998**

While departing about three miles from the port entrance buoys of Soyo, Angola, the Cypriot-flagged cargo ship *Innes* is confronted by a barrier of fishing boats connected by a line, which is being towed into position in the channel ahead in an apparent attempt to stop the vessel and board it. The exiting ship maneuvers around this obstacle and escapes out to sea, while calls to port control go unanswered.

**November
26, 1998**

Ten days after the Panamanian-flagged bulk carrier *Cheung Son* has cleared Shanghai on a voyage with a cargo of furnace slag destined for Port Kelang, Malaysia, the International Maritime Bureau issues an alert for this overdue vessel. It is eventually learned that the ship has been hijacked by pirates, the Public Security Bureau of China announcing the arrest on January 13, 1999 of a gang implicated in the murder of all its 23 Chinese crewmembers.

Having earlier in the week identified three of six bodies—found bound, gagged, and weighted in fishermen's nets off Shantou, China—as being those of the *Cheung Son* crew, the authorities press capital charges. The arrested men reportedly admit to having seized the ship for $11,000 apiece and are found to have photos showing a celebratory party on board.

**December
28, 1998**

While underway at 20:15 p.m. off Belitung Island in the North Java Sea, en route toward Singapore, the Maltese-flagged bulk carrier *Patroclus* is approached by a speedboat with 10 people on board. Three pirates board using lines and grappling hooks, before the attack is repelled by the crew.

**January
15, 1999**

The Singapore-flagged container vessel *Vira Bhum* is boarded at 2:00 a.m. while underway in the South

Java Sea off the southeastern tip of Sumatra, by five pirates armed with knives and wearing masks. The vessel had departed Panjang, Indonesia earlier that day and was en route to Singapore. The pirates entered the bridge, tied up the duty officer, and a seaman, then went to the master's cabin to seize $2,348 and other valuables. The master was held hostage while the chief officer, second engineer, fourth engineer and cadet were robbed of cash and valuables worth $2,500. Two walkie-talkies and two binoculars were taken before the attackers left.

And also this same morning, while running through the Strait of Malacca en route to Pasir Gudang, Malaysia, the Panamanian-registered chemical tanker *Shoryu Emmy* is boarded by stealth at 4:50 a.m., while off Riau Island, its master being attacked in his cabin by an unknown number of assailants armed with long knives who tie him up and steal cash and other valuables.

March 2, 1999   The 131,654-ton, French-flagged tanker *Chaumont* is attacked in the Phillip Channel, in Indonesian waters near Singapore, by boarders who threaten its watch officer with a machete and bind his hands. The tanker reportedly wanders off course while under the pirates' control.

March 17, 1999   The Panamanian-flag cargo ship *Marine Master* is attacked and hijacked at 2:00 a.m. in the Indian Ocean-Andaman Sea. The Master and 20 crew were placed on nine small inflatable rafts March 21 and rescued on March 27 by a passing Thai fishing boat. The hijacked ship was carrying a cargo of bagged soda ash from Nantong, China to Calcutta, India. A July 21, 1999 report states that the *Nuevo Tierra* was detained in Fangcheng, China on July 20th by port officials. It is believed that the *Nuevo Tierra* is in fact the *Marine Master*. *Nuevo Tierra* was last reported discharging a cargo of soda ash in Shantou, China.

March 21, 1999   A cargo ship is reportedly boarded at 9:05 p.m., while steaming through Indonesia's Selat Karimata Strait,

March 21,
1999
(*cont.*)
bound from Jakarta toward Singapore. The boarding takes place in light rain, as the mate and seaman on watch are monitoring a small group of nearby fishing-boats.

Five masked men armed with knives appear suddenly on the bridge. They tied the crewmembers's hands with plastic cord when seven more masked men entered the bridge. The mate was taken to his cabin and the captain's cabin where various items were stolen, including $1,000. The mate was taken by the pirates to where two boats were tied when he escaped and was attempting to untie the AB. He was retaken and later found unconscious but otherwise unhurt on deck.

**April 9,
1999**
The Lithuanian-flag refrigerated cargo ship *Orionas* is attacked by armed intruders after sailing from Matadi, Congo Republic. Two speedboats opened fire and at 2:30 p.m. the vessel was stopped. Fifteen men boarded taking about $5,000 cash and other valuables and stores. Attackers left the vessel at 4:25 p.m. No injuries were reported.

**April 11,
1999**
The Antigua-flagged container ship *Karin S* is intercepted, fired upon with light weapons, and pursued off Somalia's east coast. The attack was made from one of two boats, which approached from shore-ward as the *Karin S* passed another ship. One of the attacking boats was described as wood with an outboard motor, while the second was steel hulled. The attack began at 1:35 p.m., when six or seven armed men waved their weapons as a signal to the ship to stop. The ship's master altered course to sea-ward and increased speed. After about three minutes' pursuit, during which shots were fired, the boats gave up chase. Damage was reported to bridge windows and deck crane but no crew were injured.

And this same day, three fishermen are killed in an attack on their anchored boat near the Basilan Straits in the Southern Philippines, these attackers stealing the engine and other equipment. The provincial Governor orders increased military and police patrols in the area, which is plagued by armed separatist groups.

April 26, 1999

The Norwegian-flag bitumen tanker *Rathrowan* is boarded by armed thieves while underway off Lepar Island, Indonesia. Six men with heavy knives entered the bridge through the only unlocked door and forced the bosun to take them to the master's cabin. The master barricaded himself in his cabin but slipped the key to the ship's safe under the door when the intruders threaten to kill the bosun. The robbers ransacked the ship's office, stealing valuables and $3,500. The bosun and the second mate suffered wrist abrasions and shock from being tied up. The bosun also suffered a small knife wound in the arm and was punched by the thieves.

April 28, 1999

The 22,009-ton Bahamas-flag bulk carrier *Sidrela* is boarded while underway at full speed (approx. 16 knots) in Selat Bangka off Sumatra, Indonesia. The attackers attempted to stop the ship and, when theattempt failed, left with $10,000 from the ship's safe. The next day another attempt at an illegal boarding was repelled by the crew using fire hoses. No serious injuries were reported from either attack.

May 1, 1999

Somali gunmen kidnap two Finnish tourists from a yacht off Bosaso on the Gulf of Aden coast. The Somali Salvation Democratic Front claims responsibility for this hostage taking.

May 27, 1999

Six pirates armed with long knives board a vessel in Selat Baur, off the west coast of Belitung Island, and held the master as hostage. They stole $18,700 from the ship's safe and $8,000 cash and valuables from the master before escaping on a small open craft.

June 5, 1999

The Malaysian-flagged tug *Galaxy I* and barge *Galaxy II* are reported missing from their anchorage at Kota

June 5, 1999 (*cont.*)	Kinabalu, Malaysia. Vessels are suspected to have changed name, color, and flag, and may be used for piracy attack and armed robbery.

June 24, 1999

Somali Salvation Democratic Front militiamen, operating from a speedboat, kidnap four German tourists from a yacht off the north coast of Somali, about 100 miles east of Bosaso. The kidnappers take the hostages to the coastal village of Bolimog, holding them for $50,000 ransom.

July 13, 1999

A small bitumen tanker navigating off the Guinea-Bissau coast is intercepted by a launch equipped with a large gun on its aft deck and forced to stop in international waters by threat of arms from government forces. The ship is then boarded and ordered to sail into Bissau, where it is accused of violating pollution regulations, so that it is held in port for a week while these charges are processed. In order to secure the tanker's release, a negotiated settlement is reached, local authorities agreeing to accept a payment of $150,000—reduced from the original fine of $1 million.

July 20, 1999

A group of about twenty armed men board the 4,497-ton Bahamanian-flagged tanker *Kilchem Oceania* off Lagos, Nigeria. After stealing numerous items from the vessel, the attackers force two Russian seafarers, the ship's third officer and an oilman, to join them as they leave the ship. The attackers demand that the vessel return to the same spot in two days' time, to exchange additional goods as ransom for the release of the two seafarers. A September 1st, 1999 report indicates that the two Russian hostages were released at Port Harcourt on August 26, 1999, following extensive negotiations.

July 28, 1999

In Indonesia's Selat Gelasa, the strait between the islands of Bangka and Belitung, four pirates armed with knives board a merchant vessel and threaten its captain, inflicting an injury on his hand.

July 31, The 11,748-ton, Panamanian-flagged cargo ship *Sabrina I*
1999 is reported missing by its owners. Having left Tanjong
Priok, Indonesia, on July 17th with a cargo of bagged
cement destined for Al Mukalla, Yemen, its Captain
reported a leak in a cargo hold July 31st, saying that
he was steering for Mogadischu's outer anchorage to
await a tug from Kenya. The ship did not make this
rendezvous, and its owners fear that their ship may
be in some Somali port under control of a warlord.

August 19, Pirates armed with guns board a vessel from a boat
1999 while it is underway off Jawa, along the north coast
of Indonesia. Its duty officer first notices them when
they appear on the bridge wing, firing three shots that
shatter the windows. The duty officer, armed with a
gun himself, crouches down and fires eight shots in
return so that the pirates flee. No injuries are reported.

August 27, Pirates in a 25-foot, rusted speedboat with a gun
1999 mounted on its foredeck approach a merchant vessel
in the South China Sea, intending to board. The ship
sounds its foghorn and alerts all nearby vessels by
radio so that after a few minutes, the pirate boat alters
course and gives up the chase.

August 31, Guyanese authorities report nearly a dozen cases of
1999 robbery from fishing boats along its coastline and rivers, as well as the killing of one robber aboard a ship
moored at Georgetown. On a single day in August
alone, six fishing boats working within a 30-square-
mile area have been robbed of engines, fish catches,
equipment, and left adrift, while the robbers flee back
toward Venezuela, reputedly working from border
towns in Suriname and Venezuela.

September While underway through the Selat Sunda off Eastern
16, 1999 Sumatra in Indonesia, the 16,927-ton, Malaysian-
flagged bulk carrier *Alam Aman* is boarded from a
wooden boat by four pirates armed with knives. They
handcuff the master and chief engineer then steal
cash, binoculars, and expensive equipment.

September 16, 1999 (*cont.*)	This same day in the nearby Selat Leplia, the 14,063-ton, Singapore-flagged container ship *Maersk Atlantic* is also boarded by pirates armed with knives who enter the bridge and tie up its master, chief engineer, and lookout. These pirates then take the master at knifepoint to his cabin, where they steal the vessel's cash and other valuables before taking the master as a hostage to the starboard quarter and escaping over the side. No injuries to the crew are reported.
September 25, 1999	About 50 miles off Mullaittivu, a known stronghold of the Liberation Tigers of Tamil Eelam, the 9,182-ton, Chinese-flagged freighter *Yu Jia*—on a voyage from Aqaba, Jordan, with a cargo of fertilizer for Madras, India—is attacked with rocket-propelled grenades fired from boats. It suffers several holes near its waterline and is briefly boarded by the Liberation Tigers of Tamil Eelam fighters before Sri Lankan Navy units intervene and destroy four rebel craft. One crewmember is reportedly injured aboard the Chinese ship.
	Also this same day, the 21,030-ton, Bahamian-flagged bulk carrier *Aspidoforos* is pursued near the Strait of Hormuz by two speedboats, each carrying four persons, which make several attempts to come alongside. The ship's general alarm is therefore sounded, crew put on high alert with fire hoses pressurized, and zig-zag maneuvers begin. After 10 minutes, the boats break off their pursuit, this incident being reported to the United Arab Emirates's Coast Guard and other nearby vessels.
October 13, 1999	Three days after the 137-ton, Hong Kong-owned, Nigerian-flagged fishing boat *Unicorn 1* has departed Port Harcourt and cleared the Bonny River for Conarky, Guinea (intending to sail via Monrovia and Freetown), it is reportedly hijacked by Nigerian pirates, its four-man crew being unharmed.
October 23, 1999	While steaming toward Miike, Japan, bearing a cargo of 7,000 tons of aluminum ingots, the 7,762-ton,

Panamanian-registered cargo ship *Alondra Rainbow* is intercepted by pirate speedboats in the vicinity of Kuala Tanjung, Indonesia. Ten pirates come aboard armed with pistols, knives, and swords, who set the ship's 15 crewmen adrift in life rafts on October 29th, to be rescued 10 days later by friendly fishermen off Phuket, Thailand.

Eventually, the hijacked *Alondra Rainbow* is recovered off Goa by the Indian Coast Guard and Navy on November 16th. Upon being sighted, the pirates attempt to scuttle their prize by setting it afire and flooding its holds. Fifteen suspects are nonetheless arrested, and 3,000 tons of its cargo is found to be missing, believed to have been bartered in Cambodia or Thailand for weapons destined to support the Tamil Tiger insurgency in Sri Lanka.

November 19, 1999 The 47-foot sailing vessel *Leopard Star* is boarded near Jabal Attair in the Southern Red Sea by eight men armed with AK-47s who demand money and passports. They are given fuel and drink only, and then leave the vessel, no casualties being reported.

December 6, 1999 The 19,925-ton, Liberian-flagged tanker *Louise*, while adrift about eighteen miles off the Guinea coast, is approached by a gray craft armed with fixed machine-guns. Fifteen persons can be seen on board, all wearing brown uniforms. They close upon the tanker as if to board so that *Louise*'s master gets underway, standing away from the coast at full speed. The attackers open fire with their machine guns, aiming at the ship's accommodation, bridge, and radio room. Extensive damage is inflicted, bullets piercing through the steel bulkheads and penetrating the accommodation. As the distance between the tanker and its pursuer increases to about two-fifths of a mile, the attackers switch to rocket fire, then abort their attack altogether after the distance widens to about three-fifths of a mile. Their assault has lasted for about 30 minutes of continuous gunfire, yet miraculously no crewmen are injured.

September 11, 2001	New York City and Washington, D.C. are struck by devastating terrorist attacks. The administration of President George W. Bush will retaliate with an invasion of Afghanistan by U.S. and allied forces in pursuit of the al-Qaeda mastermind Osama bin Laden, followed during the ensuing months by a sweeping counteroffensive throughout the Near and Far East codenamed "Operation Enduring Freedom."
February 2002	Warships from more than a dozen allied nations having arrived to bolster the U.S. Fifth Fleet in the Indian Ocean, they are formed up into a separate "Combined Maritime Forces" division under U.S. Naval Forces Central Command out of Bahrain.
October 2002	U.S. authorities sign an agreement with the government of Djibouti, to establish a fortified advance base outside their capital for use by the "Combined Joint Task Force-Horn of Africa," a Marine contingent intended to detect and disrupt Islamic extremists in the desert expanses of northeastern Africa.
March 20, 2003	The U.S. aerial bombardment of Iraq begins, and twin fast-moving armored columns quickly bring about the fall of Baghdad by April 9th, and an end to all conventional fighting six days afterward. The large number of U.S. Navy battle-groups and major warships deployed into the Arabian Sea for this invasion is quickly drawn down, while lighter American and coalition warships are moved up closer to Iraq to protect its vulnerable offshore oil-installations, patrol its porous borders, and escort supply-convoys.
May 6, 2003	The refurbished 88-acre compound in Djibouti is occupied by 2,000 U.S. Marines and Naval personnel, with offshore support from the allies' Combined Task Force-150.
June 20, 2005	The Joint War Committee of Lloyd's Market Association in London, list the Strait of Malacca as one of several global danger-zones, branding it a passage "highly prone to piracy, war strikes, terrorism, and

related perils for ocean shipping." This sudden declaration quickly shoots up insurance-premiums by as much as 30 percent, galvanizing the three nations that control the Strait—Singapore, Malaysia, and Indonesia—into a fast-paced series of reforms intended to combat piracy and restore the lower insurance rating.

June 27, 2005   This evening, the small and elderly Kenyan freighter *Semlow*, chartered by the UN to carry 850 tons of donated rice to Bosaso for distribution among survivors of a recent tsunami, is seized about 30 miles off the Somali coast by three speedboats manned by 15 young gunmen. They take *Semlow* to an anchorage off the coast, phoning a ransom demand to the ship's owners in Mombassa, despite global outrage over this hijacking of a humanitarian shipment. Eventually, a reduced ransom will be paid so that the freighter is towed into a safe port by October 2nd.

August 11, 2005   After a successful yearlong campaign by Singapore, Malaysia, and Indonesia to reduce incidents of piracy in their shared Strait of Malacca, the Joint War Committee of Lloyd's Market Association removes this waterway's name from the list of global danger-zones so that insurance premiums are restored to previous levels.

April 4, 2006   The South Korean fishing vessel *Dong Won* comes under rocket attack off the coast of Somalia and two patrolling ships of the Combined Task Force 150—the Dutch warship *Zeven Provinciën* (F802) and U.S. guided-missile destroyer *Roosevelt* (DDG-80)—immediately respond. However, the hijacked vessel has already been carried into Somali territorial waters by the time that they arrive, the pirates threatening its captive crewmembers.

June 5, 2006   After a month of bitter fighting against rival Somali warlords, a religious faction known as the Islamic Courts Union (ICU) gains control over the capital of Mogadishu and its surrounding district. Jowhar also

June 5, 2006 (*cont.*)	falls to ICU militiamen nine days later, securing much of the weaponry available in this impoverished country.
Mid-August 2006	ICU militiamen sweep into the Somali port-towns of Hobyo and Harardhere, 300 miles northeast of Mogadishu, without opposition.
November 17, 2006	As part of its imposition of strict Sharia law, the fundamentalist ICU bans the addictive, leafy *khat* for the entire month of Ramadan, sparking riots at Kismaayo and other ports.
December 8, 2006	Fighting erupts between ICU militiamen and Somali counterforces loyal to its Transitional Federal Government, backed by Ethiopian troops and covert American support. The hard-pressed ICU soon calls for jihad against Ethiopia so that international Mujahideen volunteers begin arriving in Somalia, but the Islamists are quickly defeated and driven from the capital Mogadishu by December 28th.
January 2007	An American airstrike is conducted with an AC-130 gunship against al-Qaeda members embedded with the defeated ICU forces near Ras Kamboni in southern Somalia, while the aircraft carrier USS *Dwight D. Eisenhower* and other naval forces remain poised off the coast to provide support and prevent any escape out to sea.
February 25, 2007	Around 9:30 a.m. on this Sunday morning, the freighter *Rozen* is boarded by Somali pirates near Bargal, north of Hafun in the State of Puntland. Manned by a crew of six Sri Lankans and six Kenyans, this ship has been chartered by the World Food Program to deliver 1,800 tons of humanitarian aid into the ports of Berbera and Bosaso, and is running back empty toward its home port of Mombasa. Deliveries of World Food Program aid are temporarily suspended until after 40 days and the payment of a ransom, the captive vessel is released two miles off the fishing village of Dhighdhiley.

October 15, 2007	Armed clashes escalate in Somalia, when a Somaliland-aligned faction of the Dulbahante clan attacks their Puntland-aligned clansmen in Las Anod, capital of a disputed region encompassing Sool, Sanaag, and Cayn. This latter faction has ruled over the town since 2003 after driving out their opponents. Regular Somaliland forces mobilize from their base in the town of Adhica-deeye, west of Las Anod, tipping the balance in this latest clan conflict. Puntland proves slow to respond due to its weak economy and feeble, overstretched military.
October 28, 2007	While on routine patrol as part of the multinational Combined Task Force 150, the guided missile destroyer USS *Porter* picks up a distress call from the Japanese tanker *Golden Nori*, reporting that it is being boarded in the Gulf of Aden from two pirate skiffs. *Porter* overtakes this same afternoon, destroying the pirate skiffs being towed astern, isolating the notorious Farah Hirsi Kulan, better known as "Boyah," and his minions on board.
	The Transitional National Government in distant Mogadishu grants permission for the American destroyer and other foreign warships to continue this pursuit into Somalia's territorial waters, but they are unable to storm the vessel because of its cargo of highly-volatile chemicals and 23 hostage crewmen. A two-month standoff ensued until Boyah finally manages to inch his prize into the harbor at Bosaso, where a ransom of $1.5 million is finally paid to secure the release of both ship and crew.
January 4, 2008	Ships of the multinational Combined Task Force 150 routine "Visit, Board, Search, and Seizure" operations on passing dhows and oil tankers near the Somali coast.
April 11, 2008	Having been paid a ransom of some $2 million, the Somali pirates holding the French cruise ship *Le Ponant* release their hostages in good condition, then escape ashore. Some disperse upon reaching land, but six get into a 4×4 truck. French helicopters pursue this vehicle until a sniper is able to halt it by firing

April 11, 2008 (*cont.*) into its engine. Two helicopters then land nearby and take the six Somalis into custody, recovering part of the ransom as well. One week later, formal criminal proceedings will begin against these six captured pirates in France.

August 22, 2008 The U.S. and coalition Combined Task Force 150 establishes a "Maritime Security Patrol Area," a narrow corridor within the Gulf of Aden routinely patrolled by its warships and aircraft so as to deter attacks and hijackings of merchant ships passing through these troubled waters.

September 17, 2008 The Danish warship *Absalon*, acting as temporary flagship for Combined Task Force 150, captures 10 pirates in two small ships who are found to be in possession of ladders and other implements for boarding ships, as well as rocket launchers, machine guns, and grenades. After consulting with the Danish Ministry of Justice and other task-force members, it was determined by the Danish Ministry of Foreign Affairs that the pirates could only be prosecuted in Copenhagen, partly because the pirates would have faced the death penalty in nearby states, and Danish law prohibits extraditing criminals when they might be so condemned. Eventually, the pirates were freed, since the Danish authorities were concerned that it would prove difficult to deport them back to Somalia once their sentences were served. The pirates were allowed to keep their ships, although not their weapons.

October 23, 2008 India, concerned by the increasing threat posed by piracy in the Gulf of Aden, since most of its shipping trade-routes pass through those waters, deploys a warship into the region, after calling for a UN peacekeeping force under unified command to tackle this problem off Somalia.

Late October 2008 The North Atlantic Treaty Organization (NATO) agree to a special request from the Secretary-General of the United Nations to send some warships to help escort World Food Program humanitarian shipments through pirate-infested waters into starving Somalia, an effort which will be designated "Operation Allied Provider." The Greek frigate *Themistokles* guides the first such chartered merchantman into the anchorage at Merka by October 28th.

November 10, 2008	An UN-sponsored gathering of an "International Expert Group on Piracy off the Somali Coast" meets at Nairobi, Kenya, producing a report 11 days later which gives a fairly comprehensive picture as to how pirate operations are being conducted.
November 11, 2008	The European Union announces that the previous day, its foreign ministers have agreed to dispatch five to seven frigates and support aircraft to the Horn of Africa region within a month to protect merchant shipping and humanitarian food-relief into Somalia from pirates, an expedition codenamed "Operation Atalanta."
November 21, 2008	The Indian Navy receives UN approval to enter Somali waters to combat piracy.
December 2008	*Absalon* is involved in the rescue of suspected Somali pirates, found adrift for several days some 90 miles off Yemen, with rocket-propelled grenades and AK-47 assault rifles aboard. These weapons are seized, their craft sunk, and the prisoners turned over to the Yemeni Coast Guard.
January 2009	The United Nations establishes a multilateral "Contact Group on Piracy off the Coast of Somalia" to coordinate the antipiracy efforts by various American, NATO, European Union, regional, and other naval forces patrolling the waters off the Horn of Africa. It will be criticized for only meeting sporadically and not including the two main groups that are central to this problem: Owners and operators of the small coastal craft that make up the bulk of victims in the Gulf of Aden, as well as the Somalis themselves.
February 1, 2009	MSCHOA establishes the "Internationally Recommended Transit Corridor" through the pirate-plagued

February 1, 2009 (*cont.*)	waters of the Gulf of Aden, which is to be regularly patrolled by naval warships and aircraft to protect transiting merchantmen.
Late March 2009	NATO authorizes a second antipiracy campaign in the Horn of Africa region, designated Operation "Allied Protector," by diverting its Standing NATO Maritime Group 1 on an extended tour.
April 6, 2009	Near the Seychelles, Somali pirates capture the Taiwanese fishing vessel *Win Far 161*, using it as a "mother ship" to launch other strikes, including the attack on the American container ship *Maersk Alabama*.
April 23, 2009	UN donor nations pledge over $250 million to help stabilize Somalia, including $134 million to increase the African Union peacekeeping force from 4,350 to 8,000 troops, and $34 million to upgrade security forces of the Somali Transitional Federal Government. Secretary-General Ban Ki-moon tells delegates that "Piracy is a symptom of anarchy and insecurity on the ground," and that "more security on the ground will make less piracy on the seas."
April 24, 2009	In an effort to project an air of reform against pirates, the newly-elected President Abdirahman Farole of Puntland—concerned about rumored international plans to bomb their bases within his district—announces the start of a police campaign, who raid two suspected pirate safe-houses in the capital of Garowe and confiscate four AK-47s, 327 bottles of alcohol, and roughly $10,500 in cash.
May 8, 2009	Islamist forces from the breakaway al-Shabaab and Hizbul Islam factions attack Somalia's capital of Mogadishu, driving out its more moderate Islamic Courts Union government after eight days of intense fighting, during which hundreds of casualties are inflicted.
	However, the ICU government gains support from the powerful warlord Yusuf "Indho Ade" Mohamed

Siad and successfully counterattacks by May 22nd, setting off a summerlong round of fighting in which the luckless capital changes hands several more times. These clashes finally subside after al-Shabaab and Hizbul Islam turn on each other in early October during their own power struggle around Kisimayo.

August 17, 2009　NATO announced its third "contribution to international efforts to combat piracy off the Horn of Africa," by authorizing the dispatch of its Standing NATO Maritime Group 2 into that region on a campaign designated as Operation "Ocean Shield."

February 5, 2010　The Danish warship *Absalon*, operating in the Gulf of Aden as part of NATO's "Operation Ocean Shield," responds to a distress call from the merchantman *Ariella*, which has been boarded by armed pirates. *Ariella*'s crew having all withdrawn inside a locked safe room, Danish Marines board the vessel and regain control, as well as detaining the pirates.

February 11, 2010　Somali pirates finally release the Taiwanese fishing vessel *Win Far 161*, three of its 30 crewmen having died during their 10-month detention.

March 14, 2010　After five months in captivity, the small Iranian cargo dhow *Saad 1* stands away from the Somali coast, its pirate captors compelling its crew to steer out into busy sea lanes, so that they might launch a strike from this "mother ship." However, the Italian warship *Scirocco* of Commander Massimiliano Giachino—which has been monitoring pirate camps ashore—follows and closes in two days later, chasing the dhow back toward the Somali coast.

As the pirates hastily flee ashore on the evening of March 17th, the dhow escapes out to sea, being met by *Scirocco*. The Italians repair its radio, provide 1,000 liters of fuel, plus provisions and water for *Saad 1* to return home.

March 23, 2010   A European Union Naval Force spokesman announces that after the Spanish frigate *Navarra* has responded to a distress signal from a United Arab Emirate-owned cargo ship pursuing the three pirate boats which tried to attack it, they capture six perpetrators and find a seventh pirate dead on board—believed shot by hired private guards aboard the United Arab Emirate vessel.

5

Biographical Sketches

Piracy cannot be beaten offshore. It has to be eradicated on the ground.

— Abdirahman Mohamed Farole, President
of the Somali region of Puntland, June 2009

Afweyne

See Hassan Hayir, Mohamed Abdi

Bi'ir, Owkeh (fl. 2009), Minor Somali Pirate Commander

When the newly-elected President of the Somali region of Puntland, Abdirahman Mohamed Farole, inaugurated his administration in January 2009 with a loudly-trumpeted drive to "stamp out" piracy, it was alleged that his electoral campaign had in fact been partially financed with proceeds from extorted piratical ransoms, and that his own nephew Bi'ir was a well-known pirate commander.

Boya or Boyah

See Kulan, Farah Hirsi

Dhegey, Mohamed Hidig (fl. 2009), a Somali Pirate Gunman

Although not a major figure, this veteran raider was nonetheless contacted by telephone in April 2009 at Garowe—a town lying almost 100 miles inland from the main Somali pirate hotbed of Eyl—to be interviewed by Mustafa Haji Abdinur, a reporter for Agence France-Presse stationed in Mogadishu.

During their conversation, Dhegey offered the following idealized account of the rules of conduct observed among the various pirate groups prowling offshore:

> If any one of us shoots and kills another, he will auto-matically be executed and his body thrown to the sharks. If a pirate injures another, he is immediately discharged, and the network is instructed to isolate him. If one aims a gun at another, he loses five percent of his share of the ransom. (Abdinur)

Little else is known about Dhegey's participation in any piratical ventures beyond this single chance interview.

Garad, Abdi (fl. 2008–Present), Somali Pirate Chieftain Involved in the *Maersk Alabama* Incident

The first mention of this leader occurred in October 2008, when he gave a telephone interview "from an undisclosed location in the semi-autonomous breakaway region of Puntland," to an Agence France-Presse reporter stationed in Mogadishu ("Somali Piracy").

Garad began by declaring: "I have been on the ocean for a long time, not to fish but to hunt down ships in our territorial waters, which nobody will guard if I don't do it" (ibid.). He went on to justify such depredations by claiming that:

> We're defending our waters from foreigners dumping toxic waste, and plundering our sea resources. I hope the world can understand this is the responsibility of

Somalis, and we shall one day be rewarded for our efforts. (ibid.)

Apparently, Garad had already begun profiting handsomely from his chosen career, for he added: "We enjoy life with the money we get as a ransom." His own personal shares had allowed him to marry two additional wives, buy a fine apartment, several vehicles, plus many other luxuries. He regarded his occupation as a business, declaring: "We care about it, just like anyone would care about their job" (ibid.).

Nothing more would be heard from Garad until seven months later, when he became embroiled in the tense standoff following a failed pirate attempt to seize the American container ship *Maersk Alabama* on April 8, 2009. Having lost their skiff and retreated back out onto the ocean aboard a lifeboat that same night, with Captain Richard Phillips as their hostage, the four assailants then used a satellite phone to contact fellow gunmen operating in the vicinity, as well as their leaders on shore, seeking help from both in extricating themselves from this predicament. Garad was apparently the nominal leader of this group, and informed the AFP reporter during another telephone interview from the port of Eyl:

> We are planning to reinforce our colleagues, who told us that a Navy ship was closing in on them, and I hope the matter will soon be solved. They are closely monitored by a Navy ship, and I think it will be difficult for us to reach the area promptly. But we are making final preparations, and will try our best to save our friends. ("US Navy Closes Grip")

Garad was soon in contact with U.S. authorities as well, insisting upon payment of a reputed $2 million for ending this standoff. "We are demanding to get ransom and to return home safely, before releasing the Captain," Garad explained during yet another telephone interview next day, adding that his men were adamant that they should not "be arrested if they release the Captain, and the American officials will hopefully fulfill that condition, otherwise the Captain will not be released" ("Pirates Demand Ransom").

On April 11, 2009, Garad announced that there were still no new developments in the impasse, beyond the fact that his followers were "planning to transfer the hostage onto one of the ships our friends are holding around Garacad area, so that we can wait" there for the eventual American acquiescence. However, in light of a recent French assault which had freed the captive yacht *Tanit*—resulting in the deaths of a hostage and two pirates—Garad noted: "I'm afraid this [*Maersk Alabama*] matter is likely to create disaster, because it's taking too long, and we are getting information that the Americans are planning rescue tricks like the French commandos did" ("Pirates Issue New Threat").

Indeed, three of his pirates were killed next day by U.S. Navy SEAL sharpshooters, while the fourth was arrested and detained to stand trial, and Captain Phillips was freed. "The American liars have killed our friends, after they agreed to free the hostage without ransom," Garad ranted impotently over the phone, "but I tell you that this matter will lead to retaliation, and we will hunt down particularly American citizens travelling our waters" (Watts). Two days later, some of his minions apparently attempted to act upon this threat, when a boatload of pirates chased and fired at the American freighter *Liberty Sun* on the evening of Tuesday, April 14, 2009, yet failed to get aboard. Garad nonetheless declared:

> The aim of this attack was totally different. We were not after a ransom. We also assigned a team with special equipment to chase and destroy any ship flying the American flag, in retaliation for the brutal killing of our friends. ("French Warship")

Yet this second pirate assault would also end in failure, for the 3,000-ton French frigate *Nivôse* of the EU Operation Atalanta had already detected the pirates' "mother ship" that same evening. After *Liberty Sun* escaped, French Marines swooped in aboard a helicopter on Wednesday morning to snap up all 11 pirates and their craft, who were then handed over to Kenyan authorities by April 22, 2009 to stand trial.

One week later, Garad attempted to give a more responsible veneer to his men's activities at sea. In one final interview with the AFP reporter Mustafa Haji Abdinur, he alleged that all of Puntland's rovers maintained a secret mountain retreat at Bedey, a few miles from Eyl, where their leaders could confer and resolve internal differences. "We have an impregnable stronghold, and when there is a disagreement among us, all the pirate bosses gather there," Garad declared. "We have a kind of mobile court that is based in Bedey. Any pirate who commits a crime is charged and punished quickly, because we have no jails to detain them" (Abdinur).

Nothing more is known about Garad's role in such activities.

Gortney, William Evans (1955–Present), Vice Admiral and Commander of U.S. Naval Forces Central Command in Bahrain

Born on September 25, 1955, at La Jolla, California, Bill Gortney graduated from Elon College in North Carolina with a Bachelor of Arts in History and Political Science in the spring of 1977. He thereupon entered the U.S. Navy as an aviation officer candidate, receiving his commission as an ensign in the United States Naval Reserve by September 2, 1977, and his wings of gold after successfully completing training at the Naval Aviation Schools Command in Pensacola, Florida, by December 1978.

He was then assigned to the Naval Air Station at Beeville in Texas until June 1980, and had his first fleet assignment with Attack Squadron 82 (VA-82) onboard the carrier USS *Nimitz* from April 1981 to March 1984. After a three-and-a-half-year stint at Naval Air Station Lemoore in California, he was promoted to lieutenant-commander and served a second fleet assignment from November 1987 to July 1989 with Strike Fighter Squadron 87 (VFA-87) on board the carrier USS *Theodore Roosevelt*. As an aviator, he would eventually log over 5,360 mishap-free flight hours and make 1,265 carrier-landings, primarily in the A-7E Corsair II and FA-18 Hornet.

After serving as aide and flag lieutenant from July 1989 to March 1991 to the Assistant Chief of Naval Operations for Air Warfare in Washington DC, Gortney became executive officer of Strike Fighter Squadron 132 (VFA-132) on board the USS *Forrestal* until June 1992, then held the same posting for VFA-15 on board USS *Theodore Roosevelt* through October 1993. Now a full Commander, his first command tour ensued on this latter carrier until January 1995, after which he graduated in March 1996 from the Naval War College at Newport, Rhode Island with a Master of Arts in International Security Affairs. A second command our followed until July 1997 with VFA-106—the East Coast FA-18 Fleet Replacement Squadron at Naval Air Station Cecil Field in Florida—after which Gortney served as Operations Officer of J-33 Joint Operations

Department CENTCOM or Central Command Division, from July 1997 until July 1999.

Promoted to Captain, his first overseas tour ensued from October 1999 until February 2000 as Deputy Commander for Current Operations of Joint Task Force Southwest Asia in Riyadh, Saudi Arabia, after which Gortney deployed in May 2000 as deputy commander of Carrier Air Wing 7 on board the carrier USS *Dwight D. Eisenhower*, assuming command over this Wing and shifting his flag aboard the USS *John F. Kennedy* for the opening phase of "Operation Enduring Freedom." He also served as chief of Naval and Amphibious Liaison Element to the Combined Forces Air Component Commander of U.S. Central Command during the opening months of the Iraqi invasion, then after its conclusion, as chief of staff for the Commander of Naval Forces Central Command and the U.S. Fifth Fleet as of February 2003. His first flag tour as Rear Admiral then ensued at Norfolk, Virginia, as deputy chief of staff for Global Force Management and Joint Operations, Fleet Forces Command, from 2004 to 2006.

Rear Admiral Gortney returned to the Mideast theater as commander of Carrier Strike Group 10 on board the USS *Harry S. Truman*, patrolling in support of Maritime Security Operations from 2007 before being promoted to Vice Admiral and succeeding Kevin J. Cosgriff as Commander of Naval Forces Central Command in early July 2008. Within a month, Somali pirate attacks began expanding northward into the Gulf of Aden, prompting Gortney to authorize the establishment of a "Maritime Security Patrol Area" through its waterways, a concentrated yet movable traffic-lane where his limited number of warships and aircraft could maintain more regular surveillance, thus affording merchantmen a greater measure of protection. A veteran naval officer, Gortney recognized and has often repeated that piracy cannot be entirely defeated at sea, but must be addressed on land.

Hassan Hayir, Mohamed Abdi (fl. 2003–Present), Ground-Breaking Pirate Organizer at Harardheere

More commonly known by the nickname of *Afweyne* or "Big Mouth," Hassan was a penniless ex-civil servant who in 2003 sought to transform the forays being randomly launched by diverse gangs against passing targets offshore into a united and profitable business venture.

Ironically, Hassan came from a town and region with relatively little inclination toward piracy—Harardheere, an impoverished town located some 12 miles inland from the ocean, in the Somali province of South Mudug or Galmudug—as well as from a clan that until then had not been involved in any such activities, the Suleiman branch of the extensive Hawiye clan group. Previously, piracy had been a phenomenon mainly occurring in neighboring Puntland and dominated by the Majerteen clan, although a few outsiders (some with matrilineal as opposed to patrilineal ties to the Majerteen) had also been allowed to participate.

Afweyne nonetheless scraped together what money he could from a few financial supporters, and used this small cache to travel into Puntland in 2003 and recruit veteran pirates, choosing rovers with the greatest local notoriety. Famous leaders such as Garad Mohamed, Farah Hirsi "Boya" Kulan, and Farah Abdullahi were lured south by Hassan's inducements, to serve him—both as active pirates offshore, as well as instructors for new local recruits. Afweyne himself had no experience, a colleague later recalling:

> He had no clue about the sea. On technical matters related to boats, I had to teach him from scratch, and the first times we went out to sea, he was sick all the time. (Mojon)

Afweyne nonetheless managed to cobble together a tightly-knit corps of hand-picked pirates, the entire purpose of his enterprise being to waylay foreign vessels and patiently hold them while extorting large ransoms, with proper logistical support ashore so as to ensure eventual success, and thus secure a significant inflow of cash for future operations. His organization was given a self-serving veneer of legality by proclaiming itself to be a "National Volunteer Coast Guard," supposedly created to prevent illicit fishing and dumping in Somalia's territorial waters, although this was merely a cover. What actually ensued was a notable upswing in offshore seizures starting in 2004, as dozens of prizes were soon being intercepted and brought to anchor along the lonely, unpoliced stretch of coastline between Harardheere and Hobyo, to patiently await the payment of ransoms from their distant owners.

Harardheere's very remoteness proved advantageous to Afweyne as a base of operations, being barely accessible to the rest of the country even by road, being connected by only a few dirt tracks. This bleak, sun-baked town therefore lay beyond all effective central authority, and furthermore was spared much of the bitter civil wars raging elsewhere in Somalia—which meant that no pressing demands could be made on Hassan's fledgling organization, either, to share its profits with any of the large feuding factions. Instead, proceeds were spent on bribes to a few officials, as well as payments to local suppliers, so that ample funds were left over to be re-invested in more sorties, as well as procuring better equipment and recruits.

Foreign observers soon noted how Afweyne's new southern marauders enjoyed better boats, armaments, even satellite phones and Global Positioning Systems. The small number of pirates actually engaged in his raids also minimized frictions and ensured an informal alliance between the Suleiman clan of Mudug and the Majerteen of Puntland, both groups cooperating as they profited from this compact yet lucrative joint venture. "Later, members of other clans with a local presence—especially the Saad clan—were to join, but Suleiman and Majerteen still dominate Somali piracy today" (Hansen, p. 25).

The ruthlessness and scope of Afweyne's criminal enterprise soon made itself felt, exemplified by his hijacking of the UN-chartered aid ship *Semlow*. On the evening of June 27, 2005, this elderly 920-ton freighter was plodding north about 30 miles offshore, bearing 850 tons of German- and Japanese-donated rice for the World Food Program or WFP, to be distributed at Bosaso among survivors of a recent tsunami. Suddenly, *Semlow* was fired on from three fiberglass speedboats equipped with powerful outboard-motors, then boarded by fifteen barefoot young men wearing shorts and T-shirts—although armed with an abundance of AK-47s and rocket-propelled grenade launchers. The freighter's Sri Lankan Captain Sellathurai Mahalingam noted that all were very calm, and some even told him that "this was the 20th ship they had hijacked this year" (Robinson).

After stealing $8,500 from the captain's safe and ransacking the cabins of the Tanzanian engineer and eight Kenyan deckhands, the pirates ordered their prize steered for the town of Ceel Huur, 70 miles from Harardheere, where it dropped anchor within sight of land. Three days after its hijacking, a man came aboard with a note instructing Mahalingam to radio *Semlow*'s Kenyan owners in Mombassa, relaying two telephone numbers: one for a mobile phone, the other a Thuraya satellite phone. The director of the Motaku Shipping Agency received this call and was eventually told that he would have to pay $500,000 for the return of his ship and crew. Unable to raise such a sum, he left negotiations to diplomats from Kenya, Sri Lanka, Tanzania, and the United Nations—yet who could only deal through officials of Somalia's ineffectual Transitional Federal Government at Mogadishu, not directly with Afweyne or any of his representatives.

More captures ensued offshore, while outrage mounted over the hijacking of a humanitarian shipment. After the WFP suspended all traffic into starving Somalia on July 4, 2005, Hassan granted a telephone interview three days afterward to a reporter, during which he blandly lied: "We are not pirates and we are not after any financial gain, as people are claiming." Yet he refused to release the prize, and his men aboard the distant *Semlow* remained relaxed throughout this interlude—passing the time by cleaning their weapons, occasionally marching in haphazard parades on deck, chewing the mildly narcotic leaf known as *khat* or *miraa*, and sniping at any boats that drifted too close. The merchant crew was kept confined to the rear of the ship, resorting to fishing when their food-supplies began to run low, and rationing their water. But Afweyne's organization ensured that his pirates were kept regularly supplied with goats, potatoes, tomatoes, and onions bought from local farmers and sent aboard, as well as by cooking some of the WFP's rice cargo. Every four or five days, a fresh group of guards would arrive to relieve their colleagues.

After two months of fruitless negotiations, Afweyne wished to exert more pressure, so had a regional commissioner from Harardheere named Mohamed Sheikh Ali grant another telephone interview to a French reporter from Agence France-Presse, during which this official threatened to put the captive crew on trial for illegal fishing and dumping of chemical wastes in Somali territorial waters. Hassan then got on, and added his own comment that: "The owners of the ship and WFP seem to be less concerned about the crew, than the cargo" ("Somali Warlord").

A tentative deal finally seemed within reach by mid-September 2005, so that the captive *Semlow* was steamed to the port of El Ma'an near Mogadishu for offloading and exchange.

Unsatisfied with the final terms, though, Afweyne ordered it back toward Harardheere by September 22nd. While en route, its frustrated pirate prize crew spotted the Egyptian cement ship *Ibn Batuta* passing by farther out at sea, so jumped into their speedboats to capture it as well. Both prizes were then sailed directly to Harardheere, where Captain Mahalingam and his Tanzanian engineer were taken ashore and driven 30 miles inland, to meet with Hassan and other pirate bosses. "At that stage, I realized that all the coastal villages were involved," Mahalingam would later declare (Robinson).

Finally, the Kenyan owners agreed to pay $135,000 for *Semlow*'s release, and Afweyne relented. Since the freighter was now completely out of fuel, it had to be towed toward El Ma'an behind *Ibn Batuta*. Along the way, the pirate guards abandoned both prizes on Sunday, October 2, 2005, speeding away on their skiffs, leaving the pair to limp into safety three days afterward.

Afweyne's successful yet heartless business was dealt a setback next summer, when the fundamentalist Islamic Courts Union or ICU fought its way into power at Mogadishu, then pushed its militia northeastward to sweep uncontested into Hobyo and Harardheere by mid-August 2006. Being opposed to piracy on religious grounds, the ICU ordered a halt to such sorties, so that almost no pirate skiffs were able to put out to sea when the summer monsoon season ended that September. But an American-backed invasion drove the ICU from power by the end of 2006, so that Afweyne's interrupted operations were free to resume next spring with a vengeance.

Dozens of vessels would be taken by his pirates and ransomed for millions during the ensuing couple of years, so that Afweyne became a very rich man—without ever having to personally venture out to sea. When the Libyan dictator Muammar al-Gaddafi hosted lavish celebrations in Tripoli in August 2009 to mark his 40 years in power, one of the invited dignitaries would be the newly wealthy and influential Afweyne, described by one Western reporter present as "a confessed leader of one of the largest pirate gangs that has been terrorising shipping off the Horn of Africa" (Howden). An exiled Somali press-group in Stockholm further identified Hassan as "a big tycoon" with commercial interests in India, Dubai, and Kenya, in addition to Somalia, and even noted that: "In Dubai, his business is managed by his cousin called Yolah, and in India it is managed by a man called Abdirhaman" (Waagacusub).

Hayeysi, Dahir Mohamed (fl. 2009), Rank-and-File Pirate Gunman from Harardheere

This otherwise unremarkable 25-year-old Somali rover gave a telephone interview to Mohamed Olad Hassan of the BBC News in April 2009, describing his participation in various piratical forays over that previous couple of years, and summarizing his career in the following simple language:

> I used to be a fisherman, with a poor family that depended only on fishing. The first day [that] joining the pirates came into my mind, was in 2006. A group of our villagers, mainly fishermen I knew, were arming themselves. One of them told me that they wanted to hijack ships, which he said were looting our sea-resources. He told me it was a national service, with a lot of money in the end. Then I took my gun, and joined them. (Olad Hassan)

Hayeysi felt that such depredations were justified because of the years of illegal fishing and dumping of toxic wastes by foreign vessels, which had eroded Somali fish stocks to the point that it had ruined their meager livelihoods.

He claimed to have first ventured out as a pirate early that following year, helping intercept the freighter *Rozen* near Bargal, north of Hafun off the State of Puntland, at 9:30 a.m. on a Sunday morning, February 25, 2007. This ship, manned by a crew of six Sri Lankans and six Kenyans, had been chartered by the World Food Program to deliver 1,800 tons of humanitarian aid into the ports of Berbera and Bosaso, and was running empty back toward its home port of Mombassa when it was boarded and seized. After 40 days of extortionate negotiations by his bosses and the payment of a ransom, it was released two miles from the fishing village of Dhighdhiley.

Unconcerned by the fact that *Rozen*'s detention had caused a temporary suspension of World Food Program aid into starving Somalia, Hayeysi participated in three more piratical expeditions over the next couple of years, declaring his ambition was simply "to get a lot of money so that I can lead a better life" (ibid.). He proudly informed the reporter that he now owned two trucks, a luxury car, and had started his own small business, and only wanted "one more chance in piracy to increase my cash assets, then I will get married and give up" (ibid.). Rather defensively, he went on to add:

> We have local support; most of the people here depend on pirates, directly or indirectly—because if there is a lot of money in the town, they can get some through friendship, relatives, or business. Also, our work is seen by many in the coastal villages as legal, and we are viewed as heroes. (ibid.)

The only way piracy could ever be stopped, he concluded, would be through restoration of a truly effective national government for Somalia, which could protect its fishing trade. "Then we will disarm, give our boats to that government, and will be ready to work" (ibid.).

Hussein, Moktar Mohamed (fl. 2006), Teenage Somali Pirate Convicted in Kenya

When the U.S. guided-missile destroyer USS *Winston S. Churchill* ran down a suspected pirate mother ship in January 2006, it proved to be a hijacked Indian dhow named *Safina Al Bisarat*, with sixteen captive crewmen and ten pirates on board. The latter were deposited on February 25th at Mombassa, to be tried that same October at a maximum-security prison an hour's drive north of the Kenyan capital.

An American reporter briefly interviewed 17-year-old Moktar Mohamed Hussein and an 18-year-old codefendant, the day before their trial started. They stated that they were merely fishermen, whose boat had broken down, so that they had sought help from the dhow. When asked why they were carrying AK-47s and RPG launchers, Hussein replied: "Every man in Somalia carries such weapons for his protection" (Raffaelle). They had steered the dhow away when the American warship first appeared over the horizon, they added, as they feared being suspected of being members of Al-Qaeda. "We just want to go home," Hussein concluded softly.

Next afternoon, proceedings commenced before Judge Beatrice Jaden, all 10 Somali prisoners being charged with committing "acts of piracy on the high seas." The defense counsel objected to this trial on grounds that nobody involved—victims, defendants, or their American captors—was a Kenyan, to which the prosecutor Margaret Mwangi "countered that the UN's Convention on the Law of the Sea allows Kenya to prosecute pirates of any nationality, under the corresponding section of the Kenyan penal code," and requested the death penalty for these charges. A fortnight later, all ten were found guilty, and sentenced to seven years in prison apiece (Raffaele).

Ilkacase, Ahmed (fl. 2009), Member of a Somali Pirate Gang

Virtually nothing is known about this individual, beyond the fact that he was one of several pirates who granted an interview to a French reporter out of Mogadishu in April 2009, during the immediate aftermath of the *Maersk Alabama* incident—when worldwide interest in piratical activity off the Horn of Africa was running at an all-time high.

Ilkacase painted a glowing picture of piracy's rewards, relating how:

> The first pirate to board a hijacked ship is entitled to a luxurious car, or a house, or a wife. He can also decide to take his bonus share in cash. (Abdinur)

Moreover, he went on to defend the conduct observed by Somalia's rovers, apparently seeking to refute a universal stereotype of lawless gunmen violently plying the sea. Discipline was strictly enforced, Ilkacase insisted, alleging that:

> Anybody who is caught engaging in robbery on the ship, will be punished and banished for weeks. Anyone shooting a hostage, will immediately be shot. I was once caught taking a wallet from a hostage: I had to give it back, and then 25,000 dollars were removed from my share of the ransom. (ibid.)

Accounts from countless survivors victimized by Somali boarding parties would fly in the face of such glowing tribute, as intercepted ships are routinely pillaged of money immediately after their capture, before being sailed off to await the major payoff from a ransom demand. However, it is true that the syndicates who organize such forays do insist upon a measure of responsible conduct from their gunmen, so that foreign hostages are seldom ill-treated, as this would prove bad for business.

Kulan, Farah Hirsi (fl. 1994–Present), Somali Lobster Diver Turned Pirate Chieftain

More commonly known as "Boyah" or "Boya," Kulan is an imposingly tall, powerful, and menacing man of the sea. In the years immediately after the collapse of Somalia's central government early in 1991, he toiled as a humble lobster diver, working the reefs outside his home port of Eyl. However, foreign vessels—mostly Chinese, Taiwanese, and South Korean trawlers—took advantage of Somalia's subsequent power vacuum to begin overfishing its waters, even using steel-pronged dragnets and other illegal equipmentm which soon seriously depleted local lobster stocks.

His meager livelihood threatened, Boyah had turned to armed resistance by 1994, when he and several colleagues banded together and succeeded in capturing three foreign fishing vessels between 1995 and 1997, keeping their catches and ransoming the crews, and even receiving an $800,000 bounty for one particular ship. Undaunted, foreign fishing fleets countered by arranging for "protection" from local warlords ashore, so that armed guards and anti-aircraft guns soon became regular fixtures aboard foreign trawlers. Boyah's ill-armed makeshift group of followers were no match for such formidable targets, therefore increasingly began turning upon any passing commercial vessel, which proved easier prey.

Efforts as of 1999 by the regional government of Puntland to create a proper Somali Coast Guard, only worsened the fishermen's plight. The few craft deployed on patrol were often diverted to serve as private guard boats for foreign trawlers, who had purchased "fishing licences" and curried other favors from corrupt government officials. Boyah would later allege that such arrangements often caused serious confrontations, such as when he and his men seized several fishing vessels in 2001 "licensed" by Pres. Abdullahi Yusuf, which were being escorted by regional coast-guard craft. And all such halfhearted official efforts at restoring a proper control over Somalia's waters ended in dismal failure, anyway, with the inevitable dissolution of the contracting company and dismissal of its employees; who not only retained much of their equipment, but then ironically—having been left unpaid and unemployed—proved easy recruits for pirate bands.

When the novice organizer Mohamed Abdi "Afweyne" Hassan Hayir ventured north from Harardheere in 2003, seeking to hire veteran pirates to act as practical instructors in his own home waters, the formidable Kulan entered into his service. Somali piracy surged as a result of these professionalized criminal efforts, the trade becoming alluringly profitable as foreign commercial vessels were targeted farther and farther out at sea, and held for sizeable ransoms. Boyah quickly joined in on this trend, after returning home to Eyl to resume his own local operations. Any pretence of defending his home port's fishing banks against foreign interlopers was now long gone, as he brazenly prowled the commercial sea lanes of the distant Gulf of Aden seeking prizes.

In October 2007, Boyah captured the Japanese chemical tanker *Golden Nori* as it was transiting through the Gulf, immediately steering this captive vessel south toward Somalia's 12-mile limit, intending to round the Horn of Africa close inshore and eventually anchor it several hundred miles farther to the south, so as to await the payment of ransom near his own stronghold at Eyl. Instead, his lumbering prize was overtaken while still in the Gulf of Aden by the 9,000-ton destroyer USS *Porter*, which blasted his trailing pair of pirate skiffs to bits, isolating Boyah and his handful of pirates aboard the captive tanker. The tottering Transitional National Government in distant Mogadishu granted authorization for the American destroyer *Arleigh Burke* and other warships to continue this pursuit into Somalia's territorial waters, so that Boyah could not shake off the foreign squadron.

Only the fact that *Golden Nori*'s 23-man crew was being held hostage, and that the tanker was loaded with 40,000 tons of volatile chemicals—including extremely flammable benzene—prevented an outright assault. A two-month standoff nonetheless ensued, before Boyah finally managed to inch his prize into the harbor at Bosaso, Puntland's biggest port and most populous city. Eventually, a ransom of $1.5 million was paid to secure the release of both ship and crew, after which Boyah and his pirates escaped ashore.

Undeterred by this close call, Boyah's gang seized the French luxury yacht *Le Ponant* next April 2008, while it was en route back from the Seychelles toward the Mediterranean. Despite receiving a ransom payment and freeing its hostages, French helicopters then tracked Boyah's disembarked pirates as far as the village of Jariban, where Special Forces sharpshooters disabled their get-away vehicle and French commandos captured six pirates, who were later flown off to Paris to face trial.

Public support for piracy in Somalia was furthermore shaken during that same summer of 2008, when a delegation of clan and religious leaders visited Eyl, announcing that all dealings with pirates were *haram* or "religiously forbidden" according to Islamic law. Even the grizzled Boyah began to sense some disapproval, so issued a public statement calling for an end to all hijackings, while continuing about his business more discreetly. He also pointedly mentioned during an interview that several local officials were complicit in receiving large percentages from his piratical ransoms, sometimes totalling as much as 30 percent (*Garowe Online*, August 28, 2008).

Still, Boyah assured a Western reporter in April 2009 that he hadn't been on a piratical foray in more than two months, because: "I got sick [with tuberculosis] and became rich" (Bahadur, "I'm Not"). That same May 27, 2009, the pirate chieftain told the *Puntland Post* in another interview that he had "reformed," because piracy was "unlawful in religion." He nonetheless remained a formidable figure among the criminal-syndicates organizing such ventures, despite delegating active sea-duties to his subordinates.

Ludwig, Daniel Keith (1897–1992), American Shipping Billionaire and Developer of the First Supertankers

Born far from the sea on June 24, 1897 in South Haven, Michigan, the only child of a real-estate agent, young Daniel left school after the eighth grade and by age 19 had gone into a chartering business, with $5,000 raised mostly on his father's credit. Ludwig bought an old steamer and converted it into a barge for hauling molasses on the Great Lakes, struggling financially throughout the Great Depression of the late 1920s and early 1930s (Shields).

Moving to New York City, he finally began to prosper during the late 1930s in the expanding world oil trade, specifically by lining up long-term charters with major oil companies, then turning these agreements over to a bank or insurance company as collateral for a loan, which would cover his costs for building a new tanker— without requiring him to actually put up any of his own money toward its construction. When World War II erupted, Ludwig also built a tiny shipyard near Norfolk, Virginia, where he developed a process for welding rather than riveting tankers, which allowed him to rapidly and cheaply build a fleet of vessels for the U.S. government.

Once that conflict ended, Ludwig was given back these tankers and moved to expand his fortune globally, by seeking out inexpensive foreign labor. He rented the huge Kure naval yards from the defeated Japanese government in 1950 at bargain-basement prices and was among the first to recognize the profitability of transporting bulk cargoes of oil on ever-bigger ships with minimal crews. Early on, he had begun escalating into larger tankers, and after the temporary closure of the Suez Canal in 1956, became known as the "father of the supertanker." Over the next couple of decades, Ludwig would compete in a building race with Greek rivals such as Aristotle Onassis, launching six mammoth 335,000-ton crude carriers to transport oil from the Persian Gulf to Ireland. By the mid-1970s, Ludwig owned 5–6 million in deadweight tonnage, spread among some 60-plus tankers and bulk carriers operated by his Universe Tankships subsidiary. As a further cost-saving measure, most were registered under Liberian or Panamanian flags of convenience (ibid.).

The success of his shipping business, built entirely on credit, not only provided Ludwig with huge amounts of collateral and cash for other giant enterprises, it made him one of the richest men in the United States, and spawned a host of commercial imitators. By 1980, Ludwig ranked only third in his control over global tonnage, having been surpassed by the Chinese ship owners Y. K. Pao and C. Y. Tung. An eccentric loner, Ludwig spent much of his later life developing a huge project on the Jari River, far up the Amazon, to meet what he anticipated would be world shortages of food, lumber, and wood pulp for papermaking. This proved to be an economic and ecological failure, yet by the time Ludwig died of heart failure on August 27, 1992, he could still leave behind a huge fortune, most of it dedicated to cancer research.

Ludwig's single-minded drive toward developing the most cost-effective way of transporting vast amounts of crude oil over the high seas, had resulted in an unexpected by-product: huge, rich, yet thinly manned tankers roaming the world's oceans, easy prey for even tiniest bands of armed pirates.

McLean, Malcolm or Malcolm Purcell (1913–2001), American Shipping Magnate and Developer of the Container Ship

Born on November 14, 1913 in Maxton, North Carolina, young Malcolm received only a high-school education and pumped gas at a service station during the Great Depression, managing to save enough money to buy a secondhand pickup truck by 1934 for $120. He, his sister Clara, and brother Jim then founded the McLean Trucking Company, hauling empty tobacco barrels out of Winston-Salem.

Within 15 years, it had become the second-largest trucking firm in the United States, yet by the early 1950s McLean wished to further expand his operations into an all-encompassing land- and sea-service. Legend had it that he had originally conceived such an idea while still a young driver, sitting in his truck at a port waiting for a ship to be unloaded, yet his project was also very similar to already existing methods: For example, Seatrain Lines of New Jersey had been shunting railway cars on and off multi-decked ships for transportation to and from Cuba since the 1930s, while the Dover-Calais ferries had carried trucks for years, just as many Army trucks had also been transported at sea during World War II. However, McLean intended to apply this technique to a global commercial venture.

Since U.S. regulations at that time prohibited any trucking company from owning a steamship line, McLean sold his trucking firm in 1955 for $25 million and purchased the Pan-Atlantic Steamship Corporation and Gulf Florida Terminal Company from Waterman Steamship Corporation, with the aim of creating his own unique line of "trailer-ships"—vessels which could receive trailers detached from semitrucks, so as to be driven out of their holds by different truck cabs once they reached their destination. Securing a bank loan for $22 million, he bought two or three

World War II-vintage T-2 tankers in January 1956, beginning to transform them by the erection of wooden spar-decks several feet above their weather decks, a technique known as "Mechano" decking (a common wartime practice for carrying oversized cargos, such as aircraft). When his intended idea of driving truck trailers directly on board was deemed too wasteful of valuable cargo space, McLean refined his concept further, to instead hoisting specially reinforced, stackable containers off a trailer onto the deck, so that only these "boxes" or containers need be conveyed at sea—such vessels consequently becoming known as *container ships* or "box" ships.

McLean's first extemporized container ship—the 10,500-ton SS *Ideal X*—set sail from Port Newark in New Jersey on April 26, 1956, bearing 58 trailer-boxes on its six-day run to Houston, Texas. Other shipping firms soon began experimenting with this concept, but loading and unloading nonetheless remained difficult and slow throughout the industry, because of a lack of standardized containers. It would not be until 1961 that 20- and 40-foot metal shipping units could be widely agreed upon, designated as TEUs or "Trailer Equivalent Units." But McLean's system only truly came to excel during the Vietnam War of the late 1960s and early 1970s, delivering such prodigious amounts of supplies in a streamlined operation to U.S. forces in Asia, that many imitators now began adopting his method. In May 1969, he furthermore sold his company—since renamed Sea-Land Service, Inc.—to the R. J. Reynolds Tobacco Company for $530 million in cash and stocks, personally reaping $160 million from this sale, and a seat on Reynolds's board. Unhappy with this corporation's subsequent management of Sea-Land, though, he resigned and severed all ties with Reynolds by 1977.

Instead, McLean next year purchased the United States Lines, and set out to build a globe circling fleet of huge 4,400-TEU container ships, the largest afloat. However, these diesel-driven behemoths—laid down in South Korean yards in the aftermath of the 1970s oil shortages —proved fuel-efficient but slow, unable to compete against faster and more reliable competitors. United States Lines therefore went bankrupt by 1987, and McLean took very personally the criticisms heaped upon him for its collapse, along with having to file for Chapter 11 protection against a debt of some $1.3 billion. He nonetheless rebounded to found a small new company at the age of 78, in 1991, to operate between Puerto Rico, the Dominican Republic, and Jacksonville, Florida. He died at his home on the East Side of Manhattan on May 25, 2001, honored throughout the world's shipping industries.

By then, McLean's innovative container ship design and intermodal practices had become universally adopted, producing an enormous boom in the volumes of seaborne commerce. Wholly unexpectedly, though, his creation of such large, sparsely manned merchantmen had also resulted in rich, vulnerable targets at sea for a new generation of modern pirates.

Mohamed, Garad or Garaad Mohamud (fl. 2002–Present), Somali Fisherman Turned Pirate Chieftain

Details about his birth and early career have been deliberately kept obscure by the secretive Mohamed, even his real name being unknown: *Garaad* being an honorific nickname taken from the Somali term for a "clan elder," a sign of status among his piratical colleagues. He apparently began as a lowly fisherman from the port of Eyl, watching as its meager offshore stocks were stripped bare by foreign trawlers during the 1990s, and so became a teenage gunman.

Mohamed insisted to a Canadian reporter that his own independent forays had only begun as of 2002, and "with the sole objective of defending his livelihood and that of his fellow fishermen" (Bahadur, "Pirate King"). He had nonetheless soon gained such local notoriety as a successful rover, that when Mohamed Abdi "Afweyne" Hassan Hayir traveled north next year to hire veterans to act as piratical instructors in his home waters off Harardheere, Garaad Mohamed was among those chosen for this service. The profits from targeting foreign commercial vessels farther out at sea and holding them for hefty ransoms soon proved so alluring, that Somali piracy surged as a result.

Garaad Mohamed certainly participated in this upswing, after returning to Eyl and resuming his own local operations. Any pretence of defending its fishing banks against foreign trawlers was long since gone, yet he still tried to maintain a low profile as a pirate chieftain. One of the few exceptions occurred in late January 2006, after the U.S. guided-missile destroyer USS *Winston S. Churchill* had intercepted the captive Indian dhow

Safina Al Bisarat, arresting ten pirates and sending them to face trial in Mombassa, Kenya. In a telephone interview with the Mogadishu radio station *Shabelle*, Mohamed claimed to be commander of the "National Volunteer Coast Guard group" and threatened henceforth to kill anyone found aboard captured ships unless the U.S. Navy released his colleagues unconditionally. "No one has been killed in these hijackings so far, but we are now starting to kill anyone we catch in Somali waters, unless our men are freed," he blustered, going on to add that America had no business in Somalia or the Indian Ocean.

Such an outburst was unusual, though, and Mohamed soon resumed his shadowy existence of facilitating sorties by other pirates. He has acknowledged being involved in the capture of the Japanese-owned bulk carrier *Stella Maris*, which was intercepted in the Gulf of Aden in July 2008, and held for 11 weeks before being released for a ransom of $2 million. A reporter who interviewed him early in 2009 at a hotel on the outskirts of the northern Somali port city of Bosaso, described Mohamed as a well-dressed man in his mid-30s, although with a ragged face and "eyes scratched raw by constant rubbing—a textbook case of *khat* withdrawal" (ibid.).

Murphy, Shane Michael (1975–Present), Chief Mate of the *Maersk Alabama*

Born at South Weymouth, Massachusetts, on June 12, 1975—the son of a local merchant skipper—Murphy would later say that he got his first taste of the sea as a toddler on his father's lobster boat, operating out of Plympton. As a teenager, young Shane attended Silver Lake Regional High School in nearby Kingston from 1989, graduating four years later. While majoring in English at the University at Massachusetts-Dartmouth, he continued to remain close to the sea, working as a mess cook on Martha's Vineyard, as well as serving aboard a ferry, before enrolling at the age of 22 in the Massachusetts Maritime Academy at Bourne, graduating by 2001.

His father, Capt. Joseph S. Murphy II, had become a professor at this same institution as of 1984, and was already the well-known author of a series of U.S. Coast Guard deck-officer study guides known as *The Murphy Books*. Yet despite such a seafaring pedigree, young Shane would later mention: "Nobody in my family wanted me to get involved—it's tough being away from family and friends for so long" (Casella).

However, immediately after graduating he went to work on East Coast ships, soon earning his Chief Mate's license, and by the spring of 2008 had accumulated enough experience to be hired permanently to serve aboard the *Maersk Alabama* on its distant East African runs. After returning home that winter on leave, Murphy was to play a leading role in the successful resistance mounted against four Somali pirates who boarded that container ship at sea on April 8, 2009. Left in command when they departed in a lifeboat with Capt. Richard Phillips as their hostage, Murphy was directed next dawn from the USS *Bainbridge* to proceed toward Mombassa, bringing *Maersk Alabama* safely into that port by April 11th.

Returning home along with all other crewmembers to a heroes's welcome, Murphy spoke publicly in favor of permitting at least some defensive arms aboard merchantmen, for use in emergencies. He now serves as a spokesman for the private security firm Nexus.

Musé, Abduwali Abdukhadir (1992?–Present), Captured Somali Pirate Brought to New York City for Trial

He was born far from the sea, in the large and divided inland city of Gaalkacyo, whose northern portion falls within the jurisdiction of Puntland—one of two troubled semi-autonomous states that comprise central Somalia. The exact date of Musé's birth remains in some dispute, his father telling his American defense-attorneys that his son was born on November 20, 1993, while Musé's mother says that Abduwali was born in 1992—both dates which would make him a juvenile at the time of his arrest, thus exempt from trial as an adult in American courts. However, U.S. authorities refute such claims, offering numerous statements made by Musé himself which indicate that he was born in 1990, if not earlier. His diminutive size, being only five-foot, two-inches tall, adds to his general impression of youthfulness.

Details about Musé's early life and career remain sketchy. Given the arid country where he had been born and raised, it seems obvious that he had never been a seafarer, so presumably was recuited through clan connections to serve as a gunman by one of the syndicates organizing forays off the distant coastline— most likely for the group directed out of Eyl by the notorious Abdi Garad. When Musé was later brought to New York City and underwent further investigation, two additional sets of charges would be filed against him on January 12, 2010: one alleging that he and several comrades had participated in boarding and seizing an unnamed vessel in the Indian Ocean in March 2009, threatening its crew. The second that Musé and his colleagues had thereupon hijacked yet another ship, a fishing vessel, on April 6, 2009—believed to be the Taiwanese *Win Far 161*—and used it as their "mother ship" to launch their ill-fated strike against the passing *Maersk Alabama*.

It was apparently this captive fishing vessel which had been detected around 3:45 a.m. on Wednesday morning, April 8, 2009, by *Alabama*'s 24-mile-range radar, and which hailed the American ship over VHF radio with the words: "Stop ship. Stop ship. This is Somali pirate" (Murphy). *Alabama*'s Captain Richard Phillips instead increased speed and altered course slightly, yet Musé and three colleagues nonetheless managed to creep under its radar sweeps in their tiny skiff, emerging within three-and-a-half miles of their target and charging in at a speed of 30 miles an hour at 6:48 a.m.

Within 25 minutes, they had come along *Alabama*'s port side, tossing grappling hooks over its railings so that two gunmen could clamber aboard, while the other pair fired rounds menacingly into the air. It took several more minutes for these first two boarders to gain the main deck, shoot their way past some locked doors, and capture Captain Phillips along with three other seamen on the bridge. But when one gunman then returned amidships with a pair of prisoners at 8:30 a.m., to order them to secure a rope ladder over the side so that the other two pirates might climb up, *Alabama*'s rudder was swung around so violently from down in its engine room, that the waiting skiff capsized and left all four pirates stranded on board. Every system on the huge ship was then shut down so that *Alabama* drifted to a stop in eerie silence.

Despite looting the Captain's safe and crew cabins, the boarders could not control their prize and were fearful of descending into its dark hold, where most of the crew still remained hidden. The captive American third mate was released with instructions to order everyone up on deck, yet simply disappeared. It was therefore shortly before 9:00 a.m., after the Third Mate had failed to return, that Musé was persuaded by *Alabama*'s Bangladeshi- American helmsman—a resident of West Hartford, Connecticut, named Abu Tasir Mohammed "Zahid" Reza—to accompany him below decks unarmed, in a second attempt to contact the hidden crew.

> I convinced him, I told him: "Trust me. I am Muslim, you are Muslim. Trust me, Abdul. I am from Bangladesh, you are from Somalia. So we are brothers." (Bone)

Musé agreed to go, first handing his pistol to a colleague, apparently because the Somalis were concerned about losing any weapon to an American ambush in the darkness. And indeed, the tiny pirate was jumped in a dark passageway by Chief Engineer Mike Perry, who along with Reza stabbed Musé several times in subduing him. The helmsman would later relate how:

> I saw the pirate lying on the floor, and the Chief Engineer on his back with the knife. He was having [a] hard time to control him. I jumped over the pirate and stabbed him, and the Chief Engineer also stabbed him in the back. I was attempting to kill him, [but the] Chief Engineer said: "No, no, no, don't. We need him alive." (Bone)

Musé was trussed up and thrust into a safe room under guard, spending the remainder of that day sweltering in the boiling heat of close confinement, along with the American crew.

Finally at 4:00 p.m., the captive Phillips up on the bridge had talked the remaining trio of pirates into retreating back to sea aboard one of *Alabama*'s boats, to regain their mother ship with whatever booty they had looted. The American crew was informed of this arrangement by radio, so that as the three pirates went down into a boat, *Alabama*'s crew emerged to reclaim the bridge and main deck. After three hours of preparations, Musé was brought up to be exchanged for the American captain, prior to the pirates' actual departure. However, Chief Mate Shane Murphy would later describe how this trade went awry, for as the injured Musé clambered down a rope ladder, Murphy called to Phillips to start climbing back up:

He just stood there looking up at us, the pirates pointing guns at him. "Captain," I shouted, "get on the ladder!"

"I'm just going to show them how to drive the boat," Captain Phillips said. The door closed, and then, the Captain told me later, the pirates drew down on him. We didn't realize right away that they'd screwed us, and snatched the Captain. The lifeboat puttered away, and I was holding out hope that Captain Phillips was just going to do a quick loop, and come back to the ladder. But the distance between us and them kept opening up. (Murphy)

Musé had been reunited with his colleagues, and they had come away from *Alabama* with a valuable hostage, for whom their land-based leader Garad would soon begin demanding a hefty ransom. Yet despite using a satellite phone to contact other pirates roaming at sea and request their help, the appearance at dawn of April 9, 2009 of the 9,200-ton destroyer USS *Bainbridge* effectively dashed any hopes they had of escaping. The low-powered, bright-orange lifeboat simply could not get away from such a formidable warship, and as even more American vessels gathered, the four pirates began bartering by radio for simple safe-passage home, in exchange for Phillips.

On Easter Sunday, April 12, 2009, the weather got up, so that the reeling lifeboat was steadied by being taken under tow by *Bainbridge*. The pirates also requested that Musé be brought aboard to receive medical attention for his wounds, and while still on board that evening, Navy SEAL sharpshooters killed his three companions in the lifeboat with simultaneous shots, freeing Phillips. The unarmed Musé was consequently taken prisoner, and eight days later landed in a cold driving rain in New York City, to be paraded past an array of flashing news cameras and driven to FBI headquarters at 26 Federal Plaza in lower Manhattan.

Next morning, he was brought into the U.S. Southern District Court of New York to answer 10 charges, eight of which carried a maximum sentence of life in prison: piracy; possession of a machine gun while seizing a ship by force; hostage taking; conspiracy to commit hostage taking; possession of a machine gun during hostage taking; kidnapping; conspiracy to commit kidnapping; and possession of a machine gun during kidnapping. The remaining two charges carried a maximum of 20 years each, these being seizing a ship by force, and conspiracy to seize a ship by force. As noted previously, two additional sets of charges would also be filed against Musé on January 12, 2010, for his involvement in the two other piratical seizures off the coast of Somalia, prior to his encounter with the *Alabama*.

Still incarcerated, Musé's trial is believed to be "the first prosecution on piracy charges in the United States, since the 1861 trial of the crew of the Confederate privateer *Shenandoah*" ("A Pirate").

Phillips, Richard, American Merchant Captain Rescued from Somali Pirates

Originally from the town of Winchester, only eight miles north of Boston, Phillips grew up in a large family along with seven brothers and sisters, attending Winchester High School from 1969–1973, where he excelled in various sports.

Entering the University of Massachusetts with vague notions of studying international law, he dropped out after only a year, finding temporary employment driving a Boston taxi. Picking up a fare from the airport one day in 1974, his passenger—a merchant seaman home on leave—gave such a glowing account of a sailor's life, that Phillips enrolled next year in the Massachusetts Maritime Academy at Bourne, graduating by 1979 with a degree in Marine Transportation. Over the next three decades, he would sail the world's oceans in a variety of merchant vessels: tankers, container ships, freighters, and military transport charters. He met his future wife—a nursing-student named Andrea Coggio— in a bar outside Fenway Park, and they were married in 1987, soon buying an old farmhouse in the small rural town of Underhill in Vermont, from where she worked in the emergency room at nearby Burlington. Eventually, they would have two children, Mariah and Daniel.

Phillips won promotion to his first Captaincy in 1991, proving to be a strict and exacting commander at sea, while in the employ of a professional placement firm called LMS Ship Management. After a routine home-leave during the winter of 2008–2009, Phillips was flown out to the United Arab Emirates, and two weeks later relieved Captain Larry Aasheim at Djibouti in command of the *Maersk Alabama* on March 30, 2009. This vessel was a 17,500-ton, 500-foot-long container ship capable of transporting 1,100 cargo units known as TEUs. Originally a Danish ship, it had been reflagged five years previously to serve as an American vessel, and was registered with Norfolk, Virginia, as its home port. Although operated by Waterman Steamship Corporation, it ownership on paper was by the U.S. company Maersk Line, Limited, itself a subsidiary of the global Danish conglomerate A. P. Moller-Maersk Group—the largest shipping firm in the world.

Maersk Line is one of the Department of Defense's primary contractors, and also operates U.S.-flagged ships with American crews for the Maritime Security Program, run by the Department of Transportation's Maritime Administration. Although not under Pentagon contract at the time of its ill-fated run down toward Kenya, *Maersk Alabama* had been chartered to transport U.S. Agency for International Development humanitarian cargoes into that region, which by law must be mostly carried on American vessels. Its regular route, known as "Maersk's East Africa 4," was to run between Salalah in Oman and Mombassa, Kenya, through waters which had become perilously prone to Somali pirate attacks.

With the northeastern monsoon season at an end, tiny pirate craft were reemerging in ever greater numbers along this route, and multiple sightings were already being reported. Phillips would later say he hoped the speed and high freeboard of his ship would spare it from capture, although he had already informed his crew to be prepared for an attempt, as it was only "a matter of when, not if" (Kahn). *Maersk Alabama* was briefly pursued by three skiffs from a pirate mother ship on the afternoon of April 7, 2009, so that Phillips's written orders for that overnight watch read:

> After today's incident, there's no need to say where we are, and what's required: early observation and notification. We're in Apache territory, with no cavalry in sight. Keep a wary eye. Call me if in doubt, or if needed.

Indeed, he was summoned back to the bridge around 3:45 a.m. on Wednesday morning, April 8, 2009, when another pirate mother ship was spotted on *Alabama*'s 24-mile radar, radioing them to stop.

Phillips increased speed to 18 knots and altered course slightly, so that this second contact soon faded. Yet at 6:48 a.m., a new contact was detected only three-and-a-half miles away, a tiny

fibreglass skiff racing at 26 knots across a smooth sea in the growing light, with four armed gunmen aboard. They drew along
Alabama's port side by 7:13 a.m., two gunmen firing rounds at
the racing ship, while the other pair tossed grappling hooks over
its midship railings and started to clamber up. Phillips warned
his crew over their portable radios, so that most took cover below
decks. By the time the boarders shot their way past several locked
gates and stormed the bridge, only the Captain, Third Mate Colin
Wright, the helmsman, and a seaman remained to be captured.

However, ship-controls had been taken over from down in the
engine room, and when a rope ladder was lowered at 8:30 a.m.
for the pair of pirate gunmen waiting in the boat to climb up, *Alabama*'s rudder was swung around so violently that their skiff capsized, leaving all four pirates stranded on board. Immediately
thereafter, every system was shut down, so that the entire vessel
"went black" and drifted to a halt in eerie silence. Fearful of
descending into its dark hold, the pirates released the captive
Third Mate to order the hidden crewmen up on deck, yet he quite
naturally failed to reappear. Then at 9:00 a.m., the helmsman persuaded one of the pirates to accompany him below decks
unarmed, who was seized in a dark passageway and captured.

Phillips bravely bore the brunt of the pirates's wrath up on
the bridge, relaying their threats by radio to his crew below, yet
without suggesting that they surrender. Chief Mate Shane Murphy succeeded in securing a VHF radio and a cell-phone, and
from a vantage point began making a series of distress calls by
1:00 p.m., advising the world of *Maersk Alabama*'s plight. When
initial reports of this attack reached the United States, stating that
Phillips was being held captive by the pirates and not his crew,
family members mistakenly assumed that he had volunteered to
bear this burden for all. "What I understand is that he offered
himself as the hostage," the half-sister of Phillips's wife would tell
the press that same afternoon. "That is what he would do. It's just
who he is, and his responsibility as a Captain" (Houreld).

Eventually, as the torrid heat of the day built, Phillips talked
the remaining trio into retreating back out to sea aboard *Alabama*'s
lifeboat, so as to at least regain their mother ship. Preparations
were concluded by 7:00 p.m., at which point it only remained
for the captive pirate to clamber down a rope ladder, and Phillips
to be freed in exchange. But the switch went wrong, the wounded
Musé entering the lifeboat, after which the reunited pirates
refused to release Phillips, instead shutting the hatch and

puttering off slowly into the evening. Since *Alabama*'s engines and systems had been brought fully back on line, the container ship easily followed the low-powered craft, illuminating it with a searchlight.

Phillips would spend a difficult four days being held hostage aboard the bobbing lifeboat. He jumped into the sea once, in an unsuccessful attempt to escape toward the trailing American warships, only to be hauled back in and secured. Eventually on Sunday morning, April 12, 2009, the wounded pirate was transferred aboard USS *Bainbridge* for medical treatment, and his three companions were killed that evening by Navy SEAL sharpshooters.

Phillips was freed, and returned home to a tumultuous national welcome, for the undoubted bravery which he had displayed throughout this ordeal. However, he also felt uncomfortable at the well-intended misconception of having volunteered for captivity on behalf of his crew, repeatedly correcting this fact. His newfound fame was also spoiled when some former crewmen filed a lawsuit, for having steered *Alabama* into harm's way.

Shukri, Hasan (fl. 2009), Low-Level Member of a Pirate Gang Operating Out of Harardheere, Somalia

During a telephone interview conducted in April 2009 by Mustafa Haji Abdinur, a reporter for Agence France-Presse stationed in Mogadishu, this rover gave a brief description of the loose-knit organizational practices observed by the various coastal-groups involved in offshore raids:

> There are hundreds of small cells, linked to each other. We talk every morning, exchange information on what is happening at sea and if there has been a hijacking, we make onshore preparations to send out reinforcement, and escort the captured ship closer to the coast. (Abdinur)

Virtually nothing else is known about this particular individual.

Siad, Yusuf Mohamed (fl. 2002), Somali Warlord Suspected of Past Associations with Piracy

This mercurial chieftain, widely known by his nickname of "White-Eyed Joseph" or *Yusuf Indho Ade* (variously spelled Inda'ade, Inda'adde, Indha'adde, Indhaccade, etc.), had acquired a power base in 2002 in the Lower Shabelle region, which stretches southwestward from the beleaguered national capital of Mogadishu.

Born into the Ayr subclan, itself part of the Habar Gidir, a branch of the larger Hawiye clan, Yusuf was suspected by U.S. authorities of condoning piratical forays out of Shabelle's principal seaport of Marka, during the general upsurge in depredations all along Somalia's coastline from 2000 to 2005. However, Yusuf was to become more deeply embroiled in his nation's land-based civil wars over the next several years, rather than maritime matters, and often switching sides from his strategically placed province. He joined the rising fundamentalist Islamic Courts Union movement late, in September 2006, emerging as its Defense Chief.

After the ICU's defeat by the end of that same December 2006, Yusuf would fight on with fellow warlords against the Ethiopian occupation of central Somalia. In January 2008, he joined the hard-line resistance movement named Hizbul Islam, yet soon fell out with his leadership, and subsequently defected to the Transitional National Government, eventually becoming Somalia's current "State Minister for Defense Affairs."

Sources

Abdinur, Mustafa Haji. "Life in Somalia's Pirate Army." *National Post* [Canada], April 30, 2009.

"A Pirate Comes to New York." *The World Newser: ABC World News' Daily Blog*, April 21, 2009.

Bahadur, Jay. "I'm Not a Pirate, I'm the Saviour of the Sea." *The Times Online* [UK], April 16, 2009.

Bahadur, Jay. "The Pirate King of Somalia." *Globe & Mail [Canada]*, April 26, 2009.

Bone, James. "*Maersk Alabama* Crew Return to US to Tell of Somali Pirate Ordeal." *The Times Online* [UK], April 18, 2009.

Casella, Robin. "Seekonk Sailor Recalls Experience at the Helm of *Maersk Alabama*." *Taunton Daily Gazette*, June 25, 2009.

Davis, Paul. "Chief Mate on Pirated Ship Sought Adventure and Found It Off Somalia." *The Providence Journal Online*, April 14, 2009.

"French Warship Captures Pirates." *BBC News*, April 15, 2009.

Hansen, Stig Jarle. *Piracy in the Greater Gulf of Aden: Myths, Misconceptions, and Remedies*. Oslo: "Report 2009:29" of the Norwegian Institute for Urban and Regional Research, 2009.

Houreld, Katharine. "*Maersk Alabama* Seized: Somali Pirates Overrun Danish Ship." *Huffington Post Online*, April 8, 2009.

Howden, Daniel. "Gaddafi's Forty Years in Power Celebrated with a 'Gallery of Grotesques.'" *Belfast Telegraph* [Northern Ireland], September 2, 2009.

Kahn, Joseph P. "Uncharted Waters." *Boston Globe Online*, August 29, 2009.

Mojon, Jean-Marc. "Harardhere: The Cradle of Somali Piracy." *Middle East Online* [UK], October 29, 2009.

Murphy, Shane, as told to Sean Flynn. "'I'm Your Worst F**king Nightmare.'" *GQ Online*, November 18, 2009.

"Pirates Demand Ransom as US Captain's Escape Bid Fails." *France 24 International News*, April 10, 2009.

"Pirates Issue New Threat Over US Hostage." *Sky News Online* [UK], April 11, 2009.

Raffaele, Paul. "The Pirate Hunters." *Smithsonian Magazine* 38, Number 5 (August 2007), pp. 38–44.

Robinson, Simon, with Xan Rice. "In Peril on the Sea." *Time Magazine*, November 7, 2005.

Shields, Jerry. *The Invisible Billionaire: Daniel Ludwig*. Boston: Houghton Mifflin, 1986.

"Somali Piracy: 'We're Defending Our Waters.'" *Mail & Guardian Online* [UK], October 14, 2008.

"Somali Warlord Threatens to Try Crew of UN Ship." *Associated Press*, August 24, 2005.

"US Navy Closes Grip on Somali Pirates." *Agence France-Presse*, April 8, 2009.

Waagacusub Independent Somali Journalists. "The Boss of Somali Pirates Sighted in Libya." *Waagacusub Media* [Sweden], August 29, 2009.

Watts, Alex. "Backlash Fear After US Navy Shoots Pirates." *Sky News Online* [UK], April 13, 2009.

6

Data and Documents

Whenever ten guys get paid ransom-money, twenty more pirates are created.

—Osman Hassan Uke, police chief of Bosaso, Somalia, June 2009

The Data reproduced here below includes tables illustrating the wholesale shifts in world commerce which facilitated a resurgence of modern piracy, as well as the best statistics available on the number of attacks inflicted in recent years. However, it should be noted that reliable information on modern depredations is almost impossible to affix precisely, given the reluctance by many shipping firms—as well as certain countries—to report every single negative encounter. Consequently, these figures should be regarded as representative samples, useful for identifying trends—such as rising or falling activity in certain zones—rather than complete statistical records of every global attack.

As for the Documents, many sensationalized accounts on piracy can be found in all sorts of media, so that the materials included here below have been selected for the more sober judgment which they shed on this problem: official materials revealing some of the very real considerations—such as expense and legal complexities—entailed in fighting piracy in the world today.

Data

Table 6.1: Global Shipping Totals, September 1939 and June 1946

The information here below dramatically illustrated the commanding position in which U.S. merchant shipping had emerged from World War II, thanks to enormous wartime production and the country's safe remove from the catastrophic losses endured by other major combatants. During the ensuing decade, though, U.S. percentages would begin to plummet precipitously, as thousands of surplus merchantmen were sold off to the highest bidder, while American owners furthermore turned to "reflagging" their vessels with less-demanding foreign registers.

Country	1939 Tonnage	Percent	1946 Tonnage	Percent
United States	11,682,000	14.5	55,071,000	55.5
British Empire	24,054,000	29.9	21,167,000	21.3
Japan	7,145,000	8.9	1,427,000	1.4
Norway	6,931,000	8.6	4,197,000	4.2
Germany	5,177,000	6.4	1,160,000	1.2
Italy	3,911,000	4.9	692,000	0.7
France	2,999,000	3.7	1,473,000	1.5
Greece	2,791,000	3.5	856,000	0.9

Source: New York Times, October 27, 1946 edition, p. 85.

Table 6.2: Disappearance of the U.S. Merchant Fleet, 1955–2005

The downward spiral in the number and global percentage of American-flagged merchantmen is vividly summarized by the following table. In fact, these figures here below even include Great-Lake carriers—vessels which are intended solely to operate in inland waterways—so that the U.S. absence from international ocean trade is even more profound. Virtually every major Western merchant fleet has contracted in a similar fashion, their services being replaced by vast fleets of assorted, less-expensive, multinational transports, more vulnerable to piracy.

Year	Number of Ships	Avg. Deadweight Tonnage	Percent of U.S. Ocean Trade	Percent of Total World Tonnage
1955	1,072	12,688	33.8	23.6
1960	957	13,945	26.4	11.1

1965	912	15,293	21.4	7.5
1970	764	18,080	20.7	5.6
1975	534	25,556	17.5	5.4
1980	543	34,893	14.4	3.8
1985	401	42,394	14.9	4.4
1990	449	42,041	15.5	3.9
1995	331	45,773	13.6	3.9
2000	262	44,966	7.6	2.6
2005	249	Not available	Not available	2.0

Source: U.S. Maritime Administration.

Table 6.3: Leading "Flag of Convenience" Nations, 2008

The preponderance of merchantmen plying today's commercial lanes are not only foreign-built, a significant majority are furthermore registered on the books of "flag of convenience" nations—a practice originally devised to reduce shippers' taxes and operating costs, yet which has since resulted in fleets of under-regulated vessels, more vulnerable to pirate attacks. The following are the principal "open-register" nations, which between them are responsible for administering most modern-day international shipping, however ill-prepared or motivated to do so.

Country	Registered Ships	Foreign-owned	Percent Foreign
Panama	5,764	4,949	86
Liberia	1,948	1,904	98
Malta	1,281	1,197	93
Bahamas	1,213	1,134	93
Antigua & Barbuda	1,059	1,021	96
Marshall Islands	990	857	95
Cyprus	868	724	83
Cambodia	586	463	79
St. Vincent & Grenadines	582	536	92
Belize	261	217	83
Gibraltar	216	201	93
Georgia	209	180	86
Netherlands Antilles	138	125	91
Bermuda	133	126	95
Cayman Islands	124	122	98
Mongolia	73	62	85
Barbados	71	67	94
Vanuatu	51	51	100

Source: CIA World Factbook, "Transportation," 2008.

Table 6.4: Distribution of the World's Piratical Attacks, 2003–2009

The following table offers the most recent "Total" figures for all pirate attacks reported throughout the world during a span of seven years, followed underneath each by a breakdown of actual numbers recorded in five main trouble-spots. It should be noted that only assaults reported officially to the International Maritime Bureau's piracy-monitoring center in Kuala Lumpur are included, many other incidents doubtless passing unnoticed. The lowest Total number in recent years occurred in 2006, when a crackdown by the Islamic Courts Union temporarily curtailed piracy out of Somalia, although it soon resurged dramatically.

	2003	2004	2005	2006	2007	2008	2009
Total	**445**	**329**	**276**	**239**	**263**	**293**	**406**
Indonesia	121	94	79	59	43	28	15
Strait of Malacca	28	38	12	11	7	2	2
Nigeria	39	28	16	12	42	40	28
Gulf of Aden	18	8	10	10	13	92	116
Somalia	3	2	35	10	31	19	80

Source: International Maritime Bureau.

Table 6.5: Reduction in Piracy, Indonesia and Strait of Malacca—Analysis

The IMB statistics extracted here below, illustrate a significant decline in reported piratical attacks in these once-troubled waters of Southeast Asia. As recently as 2005, the Strait of Malacca had been deemed so risky and "highly prone to piracy" by Lloyd's Market Association in London, that insurance premiums were raised by as much as 30 percent. This sudden jump in costs had thereupon galvanized a concerted policing-effort by all three nations adjoining the Strait, resulting in such improved security that Malacca's name was removed from the danger list by that very next year, and incidents of piracy continued to dwindle even afterward.

	2003	2004	2005	2006	2007	2008	2009
Indonesia	121	94	79	59	43	28	15
Strait of Malacca	28	38	12	11	7	2	2

Table 6.6: Persistent Piracy Problem in Nigeria—Analysis

Statistically, assaults somewhat misleadingly categorized as "piracy" have remained constant in Nigeria over the past decade. However, these are actually felonious sea robberies and extortions perpetrated in the river approaches to its petroleum installations deep inside the Niger Delta, as well as the looting of merchantmen at anchor off its capital of Lagos. Neither crime can be addressed by outside governments or foreign naval patrols, though, as they occur well within Nigeria's territorial waters, and so must be alleviated by local police or national military forces.

	2003	2004	2005	2006	2007	2008	2009
Nigeria	39	28	16	12	42	40	28

Table 6.7: Piracy Boom, Somalia and the Gulf of Aden—Analysis

The statistics below reveal a remarkable spike in piratical attacks off the Horn of Africa in recent years. This upsurge first became apparent as of 2005, largely due to the organized efforts to extort ransoms inaugurated out of Harardheere by the mastermind Mohamed Abdi "Afweyne" Hassan Hayir. An equally noticeable dip would ensue next year, when the fundamentalist Islamic Courts Union fought their way into power, and for ideological reasons clamped down on all Somali sorties. But with the ICU's defeat and dispersal that same December 2006, piracy has ballooned out of Somalia, even spreading over to infest the nearby commercial sea lanes of the Gulf of Aden. The statistics for 2008 actually represent a combined total of 111 strikes made in both bodies of water by Somali raiders, while the figures for 2009 do not include another 21 attacks which happened near the mouth of the Red Sea, bringing the total number to 217.

	2003	2004	2005	2006	2007	2008	2009
Gulf of Aden	18	8	10	10	13	92	116
Somalia	3	2	35	10	31	19	80

Documents

Excerpts from the UN Convention on the Law of the Sea

Amid a rising tide of territorial claims and competing demands from nations all around the globe in November 1967, Arvid Pardo—Malta's Ambassador to the United Nations—gave a speech before that body, asking that a third international conference be convened so as to create a firmer legal framework for regulating and protecting the oceans. Six years were to elapse before its first session was even held in New York City, and—with more than 160 nations participating—it would take another nine years of delegations shuttling through Geneva, Switzerland, before the United Nations Convention on the Law of the Sea was finally passed and signed in Jamaica's Montego Bay on December 10, 1982. It did not actually come into effect until November 16, 1994, more than a quarter-century after Pardo's appeal.

Most of the representatives who had originally helped draft this document were consumed with questions of expanding their own territorial waters so as to claim offshore resources and control fishing rights upon which their nations' future prosperity seemingly depended. Of the Convention's 320 articles, only eight dealt with the minor issue of piracy, plus another couple touching on it tangentially, all 10 being reproduced here below. As can be seen, the definition of piracy was kept succinct, as were the use of authorized countermeasures or remedies. Signatory nations agreed, in principle, to adapt these articles in keeping with their criminal codes.

For example, when 10 Somali prisoners were deposited at Mombassa in February 2006 by the guided-missile destroyer USS Winston S. Churchill, *then appeared before a judge that same October to be tried for committing "acts of piracy on the high seas," their defense counsel would object on grounds that nobody involved—victims, defendants, or their U.S. captors—was a Kenyan, to which prosecutor Margaret Mwangi had swiftly "countered that the UN's Convention on the Law of the Sea allows Kenya to prosecute pirates of any nationality, under the corresponding section of the Kenyan penal code" (Raffaele).*

Yet the application of such charges remained at the discretion of local justice officials, and would be subject to many interpretations over the intervening decades, often influenced by outside political events or agendas. Even today, piracy charges are still laid somewhat haphazardly and sporadically around the globe.

Article 100: Duty to cooperate in the repression of piracy

All States shall cooperate to the fullest possible extent in the repression of piracy on the high seas, or in any other place outside the jurisdiction of any State.

Article 101: Definition of piracy

Piracy consists of any of the following acts:

(a) any illegal acts of violence or detention, or any act of depredation, committed for private ends by the crew or the passengers of a private ship or a private aircraft, and directed:
   (i) on the high seas, against another ship or aircraft, or against persons or property on board such ship or aircraft;
   (ii) against a ship, aircraft, persons, or property in a place outside the jurisdiction of any State;

(b) any act of voluntary participation in the operation of a ship or of an aircraft, with knowledge of facts making it a pirate ship or aircraft;

(c) any act of inciting or of intentionally facilitating an act described in subparagraph (a) or (b).

Article 102: Piracy by a warship, government ship, or government aircraft whose crew has mutinied

The acts of piracy, as defined in article 101, committed by a warship, government ship, or government aircraft whose crew has mutinied and taken control of the ship or aircraft, are assimilated to acts committed by a private ship or aircraft.

Article 103: Definition of a pirate ship or aircraft

A ship or aircraft is considered a pirate ship or aircraft, if it is intended by the persons in dominant control to be used for the purpose of committing one of the acts referred to in article 101. The same applies if the ship or aircraft has been used to commit any such act, so long as it remains under the control of the persons guilty of that act.

Article 104: Retention or loss of the nationality of a pirate ship or aircraft

A ship or aircraft may retain its nationality, although it has become a pirate ship or aircraft. The retention or loss of nationality is determined by the law of the State from which such nationality was derived.

Article 105: Seizure of a pirate ship or aircraft

On the high seas, or in any other place outside the jurisdiction of any State, every State may seize a pirate ship or aircraft, or a ship or aircraft taken by piracy and under the control of pirates, and arrest the persons and seize the property on board. The courts of the State which carried out the seizure may decide upon the penalties to be imposed, and may also determine the action to be taken with regard to the ships, aircraft, or property, subject to the rights of third parties acting in good faith.

Article 106: Liability for seizure without adequate grounds

Where the seizure of a ship or aircraft on suspicion of piracy has been effected without adequate grounds, the State making the seizure shall be liable to the State the nationality of which is possessed by the ship or aircraft, for any loss or damage caused by the seizure.

Article 107: Ships and aircraft which are entitled to seize on account of piracy

A seizure on account of piracy may be carried out only by warships or military aircraft, or other ships or aircraft clearly marked and identifiable as being on government service, and authorized to that effect.

. . .

Article 110: Right of visit

1. Except where acts of interference derive from powers conferred by treaty, a warship which encounters on the high seas a foreign ship, other than a ship entitled to complete immunity in accordance with articles 95 and 96, is not justified in boarding it unless there is reasonable ground for suspecting that:
   (a)   the ship is engaged in piracy;
   (b)   the ship is engaged in the slave trade;
   (c)   the ship is engaged in unauthorized broadcasting and the flag State of the warship has jurisdiction under article 109;
   (d)   the ship is without nationality; or
   (e)   though flying a foreign flag or refusing to show its flag, the ship is, in reality, of the same nationality as the warship.

2. In the cases provided for in paragraph 1, the warship may proceed to verify the ship's right to fly its flag. To this end, it may send a boat under the command of an officer to the suspected ship. If suspicion remains after the documents have been checked, it may proceed to a further examination on board the ship, which must be carried out with all possible consideration.

3. If the suspicions prove to be unfounded, and provided that the ship boarded has not committed any act justifying them, it shall be compensated for any loss or damage that may have been sustained.

4. These provisions apply *mutatis mutandis* to military aircraft.
5. These provisions also apply to any other duly authorized ships or aircraft, clearly marked and identifiable as being on government service.

Article 111: Right of hot pursuit

1. The hot pursuit of a foreign ship may be undertaken, when the competent authorities of the coastal State have good reason to believe that the ship has violated the laws and regulations of that State. Such pursuit must be commenced when the foreign ship or one of its boats is within the internal waters, the archipelagic waters, the territorial sea or the contiguous zone of the pursuing State, and may only be continued outside the territorial sea or the contiguous zone if the pursuit has not been interrupted. It is not necessary that, at the time when the foreign ship within the territorial sea or the contiguous zone receives the order to stop, the ship giving the order should likewise be within the territorial sea or the contiguous zone. If the foreign ship is within a contiguous zone, as defined in article 33, the pursuit may only be undertaken if there has been a violation of the rights for the protection of which the zone was established.
2. The right of hot pursuit shall apply *mutatis mutandis* to violations in the exclusive economic zone or on the continental shelf, including safety zones around continental shelf installations, of the laws and regulations of the coastal State applicable in accordance with this Convention to the exclusive economic zone or the continental shelf, including such safety zones.
3. The right of hot pursuit ceases as soon as the ship pursued enters the territorial sea of its own State or of a third State.
4. Hot pursuit is not deemed to have begun unless the pursuing ship has satisfied itself by such practicable means as may be available, that the ship pursued or one of its boats or other craft working as a team and using the ship pursued as a mother ship, is within the limits of the territorial sea, or, as the case may be, within the contiguous zone or the exclusive economic zone or above the continental shelf. The pursuit may only be commenced after a visual or auditory signal to stop has been given, at a distance which enables it to be seen or heard by the foreign ship.
5. The right of hot pursuit may be exercised only by warships or military aircraft, or other ships or aircraft clearly marked and identifiable as being on government service, and authorized to that effect.

6. Where hot pursuit is effected by an aircraft:
   (a) the provisions of paragraphs 1–4 shall apply *mutatis mutandis;*
   (b) the aircraft giving the order to stop must itself actively pursue the ship until a ship or another aircraft of the coastal State, summoned by the aircraft, arrives to take over the pursuit, unless the aircraft is itself able to arrest the ship. It does not suffice to justify an arrest outside the territorial sea, that the ship was merely sighted by the aircraft as an offender or suspected offender, if it was not both ordered to stop and pursued by the aircraft itself, or other aircraft or ships which continue the pursuit without interruption.
7. The release of a ship arrested within the jurisdiction of a State and escorted to a port of that State for the purposes of an inquiry before the competent authorities, may not be claimed solely on the ground that the ship, in the course of its voyage, was escorted across a portion of the exclusive economic zone or the high seas, if the circumstances rendered this necessary.
8. Where a ship has been stopped or arrested outside the territorial sea, in circumstances which do not justify the exercise of the right of hot pursuit, it shall be compensated for any loss or damage that may have been thereby sustained.

Source: United Nations Convention of the Law of the Sea, December 10, 1982. Retrieved from http://www.un.org/Depts/los/convention _agreements/texts/unclos/closindx.htm. Retrieved on August 4, 2009. Reprinted with permission of the United Nations Publications Board.

Renewed U.S. Policy Against Piracy, June 2007

After more than five-and-a-half years of its global "War on Terrorism," the administration of President George W. Bush officially issued the following policy statement on June 14, 2007, outlining its new stance on the separate issue of piracy, which it had previously viewed conjointly. Henceforth, the U.S. government would unite with its allies in a specific series of coordinated measures, intended to reduce the growing problem of piratical attacks, especially off the Horn of Africa. This declaration was to be given "immediate implementation by all domestic and overseas branches of the U.S. government."

Policy for the Repression of Piracy and Other Criminal Acts of
Violence at Sea

I. Purpose

This document establishes U.S. Government policy and implementation actions to cooperate with other states and international and regional organizations, in the repression of piracy and other criminal acts of violence against maritime navigation.

II. Background

Piracy is any illegal act of violence, detention, or depredation committed for private ends by the crew, or the passengers, of a private ship and directed against a ship, aircraft, persons, or property on the high seas or in any other place outside the jurisdiction of any state. Piracy also includes inciting or facilitating an act of piracy, and any act of voluntary participation in the operation of a ship with knowledge of facts making it a pirate ship. Piracy is a universal crime, and all states are obligated to cooperate to the fullest possible extent in the repression of piracy.

Piracy threatens U.S. national security interests, and the freedom and safety of maritime navigation throughout the world; undermines economic security; and contributes to the destabilization of weak or failed state governance. The combination of illicit activity and violence at sea might also be associated with other maritime challenges, including illegal, unlawful, and unregulated fishing, international smuggling, and terrorism.

Criminal and terrorist activities not defined as piracy also occur at sea, and similarly threaten U.S. economic and national security interests. These acts of violence endanger the safety of maritime navigation and may involve weapons of mass destruction. The prevention, interdiction, and punishment of those acts occurring in territorial seas are generally the responsibility of the coastal state. Prevention and punishment of acts occurring in international waters likely will require international cooperation and adequate domestic legal systems, most recently reflected in the 2005 Protocols to the 1988 Convention for the Suppression of Unlawful Acts against the Safety of Maritime Navigation and the Protocol for the Suppression of Unlawful Acts against the Safety of Fixed Platforms located on the Continental Shelf.

The policy set forth in this annex fosters both increased interagency coordination and international cooperation, and is consistent with, supports, and builds upon existing maritime security efforts for piracy repression.

III. Policy

The United States strongly supports efforts to repress piracy and other criminal acts of violence against maritime navigation. The physical and economic security of the United States—a major global-trading nation with interests across the maritime spectrum—relies heavily on the secure navigation of the world's oceans for unhindered legitimate commerce by its citizens and its partners. Piracy and other acts of violence against maritime navigation endanger sea lines of communication, interfere with freedom of navigation and the free flow of commerce, and undermine regional stability.

Piracy endangers maritime interests on a global scale, and the responsibility for countering this threat does not belong exclusively to the United States. Consequently, the United States will engage states and international and regional organizations to develop greater resources, capacity, and authorities to repress piracy and maximize inclusion of coalition assets in piracy repression operations.

Piracy repression should include diplomatic, military, intelligence, economic, law enforcement, and judicial actions. Effectively responding to piracy and criminal activity sends an important deterrent message and requires coordination by all departments and agencies of the U.S. Government in order to ensure that those responsible are brought to justice in a timely manner.

It is the policy of the United States to repress piracy, consistent with U.S. law and international obligations, and to cooperate with other nations in repressing piracy through the following actions:

- Prevent pirate attacks and other criminal acts of violence against U.S. vessels, persons, and interests;
- Interrupt and terminate acts of piracy, consistent with international law and the rights and responsibilities of coastal and flag states;
- Reduce the vulnerability of the maritime domain to such acts and exploitation when U.S. interests are directly affected;
- Ensure that those who commit acts of piracy are held accountable for their actions by facilitating the prosecution of suspected pirates, and ensure that persons suspected of committing acts of violence against maritime navigation are similarly held accountable by flag and littoral states and, in appropriate cases, the United States;
- Preserve the freedom of the seas, including high seas freedoms;
- Protect sea lines of communication; and
- Continue to lead and support international efforts to repress piracy and other acts of violence against maritime navigation, and urge other states to take decisive action both individually and through international efforts.

Responses to these threats will vary according to geographic, political, and legal environments. The scope of the mission and the defined nature of the threat also will affect the choice of response.

IV. Implementation

The Assistant to the President for National Security Affairs, and the Assistant to the President for Homeland Security and Counterterrorism, shall lead an interagency process to accomplish the following tasks:

- Incorporate this policy into the Maritime Operational Threat Response Plan (Protocols), as appropriate;
- Oversee the development of specific guidance and protocols for the prevention of and response by the United States Government to piracy and other acts of violence against the safety of maritime navigation;
- Review existing U.S. laws against or relating to piracy, and prepare for consideration such amendments as may be necessary to enhance our ability to prosecute pirates in U.S. courts; and
- Seek international cooperation, consistent with the International Outreach and Coordination Strategy of the National Strategy for Maritime Security, to enhance the ability of other states to repress piracy and other criminal acts of violence against maritime navigation and to support U.S. anti-piracy actions.

Source: "Policy for the Repression of Piracy and Other Criminal Acts of Violence at Sea" press release. Retrieved from http://georgewbush -whitehouse.archives.gov/news/releases/2007/06/20070614-3.html. Retrieved on February 17, 2009.

UN Security Council Resolution 1816, Regarding Somali Piracy

As the pace of attacks off the Horn of Africa accelerated during the first half of 2008, with pirates indiscriminately preying upon any and all passing vessels, several governments began to express concerns about its long-term economic detriment, enough to consider underwriting a naval countereffort. Yet before embarking upon any such armed intervention, a series of United Nations Security Council resolutions would have to be passed first, clearly ensuring acquiescence from recognized Somali authorities. The following is one of these early resolutions, adopted on June 2, 2008, and which reads in its totality:

The Security Council,

Recalling its previous resolutions and the statements of its President concerning the situation in Somalia,

Gravely concerned by the threat that acts of piracy and armed robbery against vessels pose to the prompt, safe, and effective delivery of humanitarian aid to Somalia, the safety of commercial maritime routes and to international navigation,

Expressing its concerns at the quarterly reports from the International Maritime Organization (IMO) since 2005, which provide evidence of continuing piracy and armed robbery, in particular in the waters off the coast of Somalia,

Affirming that international law, as reflected in the United Nations Convention on the Law of the Sea of December 10, 1982 ("the Convention"), sets out the legal framework applicable to combating piracy and armed robbery, as well as other ocean activities,

Reaffirming the relevant provisions of international law with respect to the repression of piracy, including the Convention, and *recalling* that they provide guiding principles for cooperation to the fullest possible extent in the repression of piracy on the high seas or in any other place outside the jurisdiction of any state, including but not limited to boarding, searching, and seizing vessels engaged in or suspected of engaging in acts of piracy, and to apprehending persons engaged in such acts with a view to such persons being prosecuted,

Reaffirming its respect for the sovereignty, territorial integrity, political independence, and unity of Somalia,

Taking into account the crisis situation in Somalia, and the lack of capacity of the Transitional Federal Government (TFG) to interdict pirates or patrol and secure either the international sea lanes off the coast of Somalia or Somalia's territorial waters,

Deploring the recent incidents of attacks upon and hijacking of vessels in the territorial waters and on the high seas off the coast of Somalia, including attacks upon and hijackings of vessels operated by the World Food Program and numerous commercial vessels, and the serious adverse impact of these attacks on the prompt, safe, and effective delivery of food aid and other humanitarian assistance to the people of Somalia, and the grave dangers they pose to vessels, crews, passengers, and cargo,

Noting the letters to the Secretary-General from the Secretary-General of the IMO dated July 5, 2007 and September 18, 2007 regarding the piracy problems off the coast of Somalia, and the IMO Assembly resolution A.1002 (25), which strongly urged Governments to increase their efforts to prevent and repress, within the provisions of international law, acts of piracy and armed robbery against vessels, irrespective of where such acts occur, and *recalling* the joint communiqué of the IMO and the World Food Program of July 10, 2007,

Taking note of the Secretary-General's letter of November 9, 2007 to the President of the Security Council, reporting that the Transitional Federal Government of Somalia (TFG) needs and would welcome international assistance to address the problem,

Taking further note of the letter from the Permanent Representative of the Somali Republic to the United Nations, to the President of the Security Council dated February 27, 2008, conveying the consent of the TFG to the Security Council for urgent assistance in securing the territorial and international waters off the coast of Somalia for the safe conduct of shipping and navigation,

Determining that the incidents of piracy and armed robbery against vessels in the territorial waters of Somalia and the high seas off the coast of Somalia exacerbate the situation in Somalia, which continues to constitute a threat to international peace and security in the region,

Acting under Chapter VII of the Charter of the United Nations,

1. *Condemns and deplores* all acts of piracy and armed robbery against vessels in territorial waters and the high seas off the coast of Somalia;

2. *Urges* States whose naval vessels and military aircraft operate on the high seas and airspace off the coast of Somalia, to be vigilant to acts of piracy and armed robbery and, in this context, *encourages*, in particular, States interested in the use of commercial maritime routes off the coast of Somalia, to increase and coordinate their efforts to deter acts of piracy and armed robbery at sea, in cooperation with the TFG;

3. *Urges* all States to cooperate with each other, with the IMO and, as appropriate, with the relevant regional organizations in connection with, and share information about, acts of piracy and armed robbery in the territorial waters and on the high seas off the coast of Somalia, and to render assistance to vessels threatened by or under attack by pirates or armed robbers, in accordance with relevant international law;

4. *Further urges* States to work in cooperation with interested organizations, including the IMO, to ensure that vessels entitled to fly their flag receive appropriate guidance and training on avoidance, evasion, and defensive techniques, and to avoid the area whenever possible;

5. *Calls upon* States and interested organizations, including the IMO, to provide technical assistance to Somalia and nearby coastal States upon their request to enhance the capacity of these

States to ensure coastal and maritime security, including combating piracy and armed robbery off the Somali and nearby coastlines;

6. *Affirms* that the measures imposed by paragraph 5 of Resolution 733 (1992) and further elaborated upon by paragraphs 1 and 2 of Resolution 1425 (2002) do not apply to supplies of technical assistance to Somalia solely for the purposes set out in paragraph 5 above, which have been exempted from those measures in accordance with the procedure set out in paragraphs 11 (b) and 12 of Resolution 1772 (2007);

7. *Decides* that for a period of six months from the date of this resolution, States cooperating with the TFG in the fight against piracy and armed robbery at sea off the coast of Somalia, for which advance notification has been provided by the TFG to the Secretary-General, may:

   (a) Enter the territorial waters of Somalia for the purpose of repressing acts of piracy and armed robbery at sea, in a manner consistent with such action permitted on the high seas with respect to piracy under relevant international law; and

   (b) Use, within the territorial waters of Somalia, in a manner consistent with action permitted on the high seas with respect to piracy under relevant international law, all necessary means to repress acts of piracy and armed robbery;

8. *Requests* that cooperating states take appropriate steps to ensure that the activities they undertake pursuant to the authorization in paragraph 7, do not have the practical effect of denying or impairing the right of innocent passage to the ships of any third State;

9. *Affirms* that the authorization provided in this resolution applies only with respect to the situation in Somalia, and shall not affect the rights or obligations or responsibilities of member states under international law, including any rights or obligations under the Convention, with respect to any other situation, and underscores in particular that it shall not be considered as establishing customary international law, and affirms further that this authorization has been provided only following receipt of the letter from the Permanent Representative of the Somalia Republic to the United Nations, to the President of the Security Council dated February 27, 2008, conveying the consent of the TFG;

10. *Calls upon* States to coordinate their actions with other participating States, taken pursuant to paragraphs 5 and 7 above;

11. *Calls upon* all States, and in particular flag, port, and coastal States, States of the nationality of victims and perpetrators of piracy and armed robbery, and other States with relevant jurisdiction under

international law and national legislation, to cooperate in determining jurisdiction, and in the investigation and prosecution of persons responsible for acts of piracy and armed robbery off the coast of Somalia, consistent with applicable international law including international human rights law, and to render assistance by, among other actions, providing disposition and logistics assistance with respect to persons under their jurisdiction and control, such victims and witnesses and persons detained as a result of operations conducted under this resolution;

12. *Requests* States cooperating with the TFG to inform the Security Council within 3 months of the progress of actions undertaken in the exercise of the authority provided in paragraph 7 above;

13. *Requests* the Secretary-General to report to the Security Council within 5 months of adoption of this resolution, on the implementation of this resolution and on the situation with respect to piracy and armed robbery in territorial waters and the high seas off the coast of Somalia;

14. *Requests* the Secretary-General of the IMO to brief the Council on the basis of cases brought to his attention by the agreement of all affected coastal states, and duly taking into account the existing bilateral and regional cooperative arrangements, on the situation with respect to piracy and armed robbery;

15. *Expresses* its intention to review the situation and consider, as appropriate, renewing the authority provided in paragraph 7 above for additional periods upon the request of the TFG;

16. *Decides* to remain seized of the matter.

Source: United Nations Security Council Resolution 1816 (2008). Retrieved from http://ods-dds-ny.un.org/doc/UNDOC/GEN/N08/361/77/PDF/N0836177.pdf?OpenElement. Retrieved on February 15, 2009.

EU Approval for Launching "Operation Atalanta"

As concern mounted in international capitals about the economic threat posed to marine traffic off the Horn of Africa, by emboldened Somali pirates venturing ever farther offshore to capture large merchantmen and hold them for ransom, a movement began toward more direct engagement in that affected region. With the dwindling number of U.S. naval forces still being required around the Persian Gulf and Arabian Sea, it remained for various allied nations to respond to UN appeals, and furnish additional warships so as to bolster antipiracy patrols farther south, in the troubled sea lanes around the Gulf of Aden.

Given that Europe's economic well-being depended directly on safe-passage through those waters, the Council of the European Union adopted an act at Brussels on November 10, 2008, officially designated as Joint Action 2008/851/CFSP, which authorized a "military operation to contribute to the deterrence, prevention, and repression of acts of piracy and armed robbery off the Somali coast." This would mark the first occasion on which the European Union (EU)—a political, financial, and cultural association—would raise a joint naval task force, and dispatch it overseas. The complexities of organizing, managing, and sustaining a multinational squadron are reflected in the Act itself. Actual authorization to launch "Operation Atalanta" was given subsequently by the EU Council as "Decision 2008/918/CFSP" on December 8, 2008, which is also appended here below:

Having regard to the Treaty on European Union, and in particular Article 14, the third subparagraph of Article 25, and Article 28(3) thereof,

Whereas:

1. In its Resolution 1814 (2008) on the situation in Somalia, adopted on May 15, 2008, the United Nations Security Council (UNSC) has called on States and regional organizations, in close co-ordination with one another, to take action to protect shipping involved in the transport and delivery of humanitarian aid to Somalia and in activities authorized by the United Nations.

2. In its Resolution 1816 (2008) on the situation in Somalia, adopted on June 2 2008, the United Nations Security Counsel (UNSC) expressed its concern at the threat that acts of piracy and armed robbery against vessels pose to the delivery of humanitarian aid to Somalia, the safety of commercial maritime routes, and international navigation. The UNSC encouraged, in particular, States interested in the use of commercial maritime routes off the coast of Somalia to increase and coordinate their efforts, in co-operation with the Transitional Federal Government of Somalia (TFG), to deter acts of piracy and armed robbery at sea. It authorized, for a period of six months from the date of the resolution, States cooperating with the TFG, of which advance notification had been given by the TFG to the UN Secretary-General, to enter the territorial waters of Somalia and to use, in a manner consistent with relevant international law, all necessary means to repress acts of piracy and armed robbery at sea.

3. In its Resolution 1838 (2008) on the situation in Somalia, adopted on October 7, 2008, the UNSC commended the ongoing planning

process towards a possible European Union (EU) naval operation, as well as other international or national initiatives taken with a view to implementing Resolutions 1814 (2008) and 1816 (2008), and urged States that have the capacity to do so, to cooperate with the TFG in the fight against piracy and armed robbery at sea in conformity with the provisions of Resolution 1816 (2008). The UNSC also urged States and regional organizations, in conformity with the provisions of Resolution 1814 (2008), to continue to take action to protect the World Food Program (WFP) maritime convoys, which is vital to bring humanitarian assistance to the affected populations in Somalia.

4. In its conclusions of May 26, 2008, the Council expressed its concern at the upsurge of piracy attacks off the Somali coast, which affect humanitarian efforts and international maritime traffic in the region, and contribute to continued violations of the UN arms embargo. The Council also commended the sequenced initiatives of some Member States to provide protection to WFP vessels. It stressed the need for wider participation by the international community in these escorts in order to secure the delivery of humanitarian aid to the Somali population.

5. On 5 August 2008, the Council approved a crisis management concept for action by the EU, to help implement UNSC Resolution 1816 (2008), and for peace and international security in the region.

6. On 15 September 2008, the Council reaffirmed its serious concern at the acts of piracy and armed robbery off the Somali coast, deploring, in particular, their recent resurgence. As regards the EU's contribution to the implementation of UNSC Resolution 1816 (2008) on combating piracy off the Somali coast and to the protection, under Resolutions 1814 (2008) and 1816 (2008), of vessels chartered by the WFP and bound for Somalia, the Council decided to establish a coordination cell in Brussels with the task of supporting the surveillance and protection activities carried out by some Member States off the Somali coast. On the same day, it approved, on the one hand, a plan for the implementation of this military coordination action European Union Navy Office of Community Outreach (EU NAVCO) and, on the other, a strategic military option for a possible EU naval operation for which those Member States wishing to cooperate with the TFG under Resolution 1816 (2008) would make available military resources for the deterrence and repression of acts of piracy and armed robbery off the Somali coast.

7. On September 19, 2008, the Council adopted Joint Action 2008/749/CFSP on the European Union military coordination action, in support of UN Security Council Resolution 1816 (2008) (EU NAVCO) (1).

8. On the launch of the Atalanta military operation, the tasks of the military coordination cell will be exercised under this Joint Action. The coordination cell should then be closed.

9. The Political and Security Committee (PSC) should exercise political control over the EU military operation in order to help deter acts of piracy off the Somali coast, provide it with strategic direction, and take the relevant decisions in accordance with third subparagraph of Article 25 of the Treaty.

10. Under Article 28(3) of the Treaty, the operational expenditure arising from this Joint Action, which has military or defense implications, should be borne by the Member States in accordance with Council Decision 2007/384/CFSP of May 14, 2007 establishing a mechanism to administer the financing of the common costs of European Union operations having military or defense implications (Athena) (2) (hereinafter referred to as 'Athena').

11. Article 14(1) of the Treaty calls for Joint Actions to lay down the means to be made available to the European Union. The financial reference amount, for a 12-month period, for the common costs of the EU military operation constitutes the best current estimate, and is without prejudice to the final figures to be included in a budget to be approved in accordance with the rules laid down in the decision regarding Athena.

12. By letter dated October 30, 2008, the EU made an offer to the TFG, pursuant to point 7 of Resolution 1816 (2008), which contains proposals for States other than Somalia to exercise jurisdiction over persons captured in Somali territorial waters who have committed, or are suspected of having committed, acts of piracy or armed robbery.

13. In accordance with Article 6 of the Protocol on the position of Denmark annexed to the Treaty on European Union and to the Treaty establishing the European Community, Denmark does not participate in the elaboration and implementation of decisions and actions of the European Union, which have defense implications. Denmark does not participate in the implementation of this Joint Action, and therefore does not participate in the financing of the operation,

HAS ADOPTED THIS JOINT ACTION:

Article 1
Mission

1. The European Union (EU) shall conduct a military operation in support of Resolutions 1814 (2008), 1816 (2008), and 1838 (2008)

of the United Nations Security Council (UNSC), in a manner consistent with action permitted with respect to piracy under Article 100 *et seq.* of the United Nations Convention on the Law of the Sea signed in Montego Bay on December 10, 1982 (hereinafter referred to as "the United Nations Convention on the Law of the Sea") and by means, in particular, of commitments made with third States, hereinafter called "Atalanta" in órder to contribute to:
— the protection of vessels of the WFP delivering food aid to displaced persons in Somalia, in accordance with the mandate laid down in UNSC Resolution 1814 (2008),
— the protection of vulnerable vessels cruising off the Somali coast, and the deterrence, prevention, and repression of acts of piracy and armed robbery off the Somali coast, in accordance with the mandate laid down in UNSC Resolution 1816 (2008),
2. The forces deployed to that end shall operate, up to 500 nautical miles off the Somali coast and neighboring countries, in accordance with the political objective of an EU maritime operation, as defined in the crisis management concept approved by the Council on August 5, 2008.

Article 2
Mandate

Under the conditions set by the relevant international law and by UNSC Resolutions 1814 (2008), 1816 (2008), and 1838 (2008), Atalanta shall, as far as available capabilities allow:

(a) provide protection to vessels chartered by the WFP, including by means of the presence on board those vessels of armed units of Atalanta, in particular when cruising in Somali territorial waters;
(b) provide protection, based on a case-by-case evaluation of needs, to merchant vessels cruising in the areas where it is deployed;
(c) keep watch over areas off the Somali coast, including Somalia's territorial waters, in which there are dangers to maritime activities, in particular to maritime traffic;
(d) take the necessary measures, including the use of force, to deter, prevent, and intervene in order to bring to an end acts of piracy and armed robbery which may be committed in the areas where it is present;

(e) in view of prosecutions potentially being brought by the relevant States under the conditions in Article 12, arrest, detain, and transfer persons who have committed, or are suspected of having committed, acts of piracy or armed robbery in the areas where it is present, and seize the vessels of the pirates or armed robbers, or the vessels caught following an act of piracy or an armed robbery and which are in the hands of the pirates, as well as the goods on board;

(f) liaise with organizations and entities, as well as States, working in the region to combat acts of piracy and armed robbery off the Somali coast, in particular the "Combined Task Force 150" maritime force which operates within the framework of "Operation Enduring Freedom".

Article 3
Appointment of the EU Operation Commander

Rear Admiral Phillip Jones is hereby appointed EU Operation Commander.

Article 4
Designation of the EU Operational Headquarters

The EU Operational Headquarters shall be located at Northwood, United Kingdom.

Article 5
Planning and launch of the operation

The Decision to launch the EU military operation shall be adopted by the Council following approval of the Operation Plan and the Rules of Engagement, and in the light of the notification by the TFG to the Secretary-General of the United Nations of the offer of cooperation made by the EU pursuant to point 7 of UNSC Resolution 1816 (2008).

Article 6
Political control and strategic direction

1. Under the responsibility of the Council, the Political and Security Committee (PSC) shall exercise the political control and strategic direction of the EU military operation. The Council hereby authorizes the PSC to take the relevant decisions in accordance with Article 25 of the EU Treaty. This authorization shall include the powers to amend the planning documents, including the Operation Plan, the Chain of Command and the

Rules of Engagement. It shall also include the powers to take decisions on the appointment of the EU Operation Commander and/or EU Force Commander. The powers of decision with respect to the objectives and termination of the EU military operation shall remain vested in the Council, assisted by the Secretary-General/High Representative (hereinafter referred to as the 'SG/HR').

2. The PSC shall report to the Council at regular intervals.
3. The PSC shall receive reports from the chairman of the EU Military Committee (EUMC) regarding the conduct of the EU military operation, at regular intervals. The PSC may invite the EU Operation Commander and/or EU Force Commander to its meetings, as appropriate.

Article 7
Military direction

1. The EUMC shall monitor the proper execution of the EU military operation conducted under the responsibility of the EU Operation Commander.
2. The EUMC shall receive reports from the EU Operation Commander at regular intervals. It may invite the EU Operation Commander and/or EU Force Commander to its meetings as appropriate.
3. The chairman of the EUMC shall act as the primary point of contact with the EU Operation Commander.

Article 8
Coherence of EU response

The Presidency, the SG/HR, the EU Operation Commander, and the EU Force Commander shall closely coordinate their respective activities regarding the implementation of this Joint Action.

Article 9
Relations with the United Nations, neighboring countries, and other actors

1. The SG/HR, in close coordination with the Presidency, shall act as the primary point of contact with the United Nations, the Somali authorities, the authorities of neighboring countries, and other relevant actors. Within the context of his contact with the African Union, the SG/HR shall be assisted by the EU Special

Representative (EUSR) to the African Union, in close co-ordination with the presidency.

2. At operational level, the EU Operation Commander shall act as the contact point with, in particular, ship-owners' organizations, as well as with the relevant departments of the UN General Secretariat and the WFP.

Article 10
Participation by third States

1. Without prejudice to the decision-making autonomy of the EU or to the single institutional framework, and in accordance with the relevant guidelines of the European Council, third States may be invited to participate in the operation.
2. The Council hereby authorizes the PSC to invite third States to offer contributions and to take the relevant decisions on acceptance of the proposed contributions, upon the recommendation of the EU Operation Commander and the EUMC.
3. Detailed modalities for the participation by third States shall be the subject of agreements concluded in accordance with the procedure laid down in Article 24 of the Treaty. The SG/HR, who shall assist the Presidency, may negotiate such agreements on behalf of the Presidency. Where the EU and a third State have concluded an agreement establishing a framework for the latter's participation in EU crisis management operations, the provisions of such an agreement shall apply in the context of this operation.
4. Third States making significant military contributions to the EU military operation shall have the same rights and obligations in terms of day-to-day management of the operation as Member States taking part in the operation.
5. The Council hereby authorizes the PSC to take relevant decisions on the setting-up of a Committee of Contributors, should third States provide significant military contributions.
6. The conditions for the transfer to a State participating in the operation of persons arrested and detained, with a view to the exercise of jurisdiction of that State, shall be established when the participation agreements referred to in paragraph 3 are concluded or implemented.

Article 11
Status of EU-led forces

The status of the EU-led forces and their personnel, including the privileges, immunities, and further guarantees necessary

for the fulfillment and smooth functioning of their
mission, who:

— are stationed on the land territory of third States,
— operate in the territorial or internal waters of third States,

shall be agreed in accordance with the procedure laid down in Article
24 of the Treaty. The SG/HR, who shall assist the Presidency, may
negotiate such arrangements on behalf of the Presidency.

Article 12
Transfer of persons arrested and detained with a view to their prosecution

1. On the basis of Somalia's acceptance of the exercise of jurisdiction by Member States or by third States, on the one hand, and Article 105 of the United Nations Convention on the Law of the Sea, on the other hand, persons having committed, or suspected of having committed, acts of piracy or armed robbery in Somali territorial waters or on the high seas, who are arrested and detained, with a view to their prosecution, and property used to carry out such acts, shall be transferred:
   — to the competent authorities of the flag Member State or of the third State participating in the operation, of the vessel which took them captive, or
   — if this State cannot, or does not wish to, exercise its jurisdiction, to a Member States or any third State which wishes to exercise its jurisdiction over the aforementioned persons and property.
2. No persons referred to in paragraphs 1 and 2 may be transferred to a third State unless the conditions for the transfer have been agreed with that third State in a manner consistent with relevant international law, notably international law on human rights, in order to guarantee in particular that no one shall be subjected to the death penalty, to torture or to any cruel, inhuman, or degrading treatment.

Article 13
Relations with the flag States of protected vessels

The conditions governing the presence on board merchant ships, particularly those chartered by the WFP, of units belonging to Atalanta, including privileges, immunities, and other guarantees relating to the proper conduct of the operation, shall be agreed with the flag States of those vessels.

Article 14
Financial arrangements

1. The common costs of the EU military operation shall be administered by Athena.
2. The financial reference amount for the common costs of the EU military operation shall be EUR 8,300,000. The percentage of the reference amount referred to in Article 33(3) of Athena shall be 30 %.

Article 15
Release of information to the United Nations and other third parties

1. The SG/HR is hereby authorized to release to the United Nations and to other third parties associated with this Joint Action, classified EU information and documents generated for the purposes of the EU military operation up to the level of classification appropriate for each of them, and in accordance with the Council's security regulations (1).
2. The SG/HR is hereby authorized to release to the United Nations and to other third parties associated with this Joint Action, unclassified EU documents relating to Council deliberations on the operation which are covered by the obligation of professional secrecy pursuant to Article 6(1) of the Council's Rules of Procedure (2).

Article 16
Entry into force and termination

1. This Joint Action shall enter into force on the date of its adoption.
2. Joint Action 2008/749/CFSP shall be repealed as from the date of closure of the coordination cell put in place by that Joint Action. It shall be closed on the launch date of the operation referred to in Article 6 of this Joint Action.
3. The EU military operation shall terminate 12 months after the initial operating capability is declared, subject to the prolongation of UNSC Resolutions 1814 (2008) and 1816 (2008).
4. This Joint Action shall be repealed following the withdrawal of the EU force, in accordance with the plans approved for the termination of the EU military operation, and without prejudice to the relevant provisions of Athena.

Article 17
Publication

1. This Joint Action shall be published in the *Official Journal of the European Union.*
2. The PSC's decisions on the appointment of an EU Operation Commander and/or EU Force Commander, as well as the PSC's decisions on the acceptance of contributions from third States and the setting-up of a Committee of Contributors, shall likewise be published in the *Official Journal of the European Union.*

Source: Council Joint Action 2008/851/CFSP of November 10, 2008 on a European Union military operation to contribute to the deterrence, prevention and repression of acts of piracy and armed robbery off the Somali coast, published in the *Official Journal of the European Union*, L301, Vol 51, November 12, 2008, p 33. Retrieved from http://eur-lex.europa.eu/ LexUriServ/LexUriServ.do?uri=OJ:L:2008:301:0033:0037:EN:PDF. Retrieved on March 8, 2009. © European Union, http://eur-lex .europa.eu/. Only European Union legislation printed in the paper edition of the Official Journal of the European Union is deemed authentic.

Actual authorization to launch this operation was given subsequently by the EU Council, as "Decision 2008/918/CFSP" on December 8, 2008, and which reads in its entirety:

Having regard to the Treaty on European Union, and in particular Article 17(2) thereof,

Having regard to Council Joint Action 2008/851/CFSP of November 10, 2008 on a European Union military operation to contribute to the deterrence, prevention, and repression of acts of piracy and armed robbery off the Somali coast (ATALANTA), and in particular Article 5 thereof,

Whereas:

1. In its Resolution 1814 (2008) on the situation in Somalia, adopted on May 15, 2008, the UN Security Council called on States and regional organizations, in close coordination with one another, to take action to protect shipping involved in the transport and delivery of humanitarian aid to Somalia and UN-authorized activities.
2. In its Resolution 1816 (2008) on the situation in Somalia, adopted on June 2, 2008, the UN Security Council expressed its concern at the threat that acts of piracy and armed robbery against vessels pose to the delivery of humanitarian aid to Somalia, the safety of commercial maritime routes and international navigation. The UN Security Council encouraged, in particular, States interested in the use of commercial maritime routes off the coast of Somalia

to increase and coordinate their efforts to deter acts of piracy and armed robbery at sea in cooperation with the Transitional Federal Government of Somalia (TFG).

3. In its Resolution 1838 (2008) concerning the situation in Somalia, adopted on October 7, 2008, the UN Security Council commended the ongoing planning process towards a possible European Union naval operation, as well as other international or national initiatives taken with a view to implementing Resolutions 1814 (2008) and 1816 (2008), and urged all States that have the capacity to do so to cooperate with the TFG in the fight against piracy and armed robbery at sea, in conformity with the provisions of Resolution 1816 (2008). It also urged all States and regional organizations, in conformity with the provisions of Resolution 1814 (2008), to continue to take action to protect the World Food Program maritime convoys, which is vital to bring humanitarian assistance to the Somali population.

4. The Somali Transitional Federal Government informed the United Nations Secretary-General by letter dated November 14, 2008 of the offer made to it, in conformity with paragraph 7 of Resolution 1816 (2008).

5. The European Union may be brought to rely on subsequent UNSC resolutions regarding the situation in Somalia.

6. In accordance with Article 6 of the Protocol on the position of Denmark annexed to the Treaty on European Union and to the Treaty establishing the European Community, Denmark does not participate in the elaboration and implementation of decisions and actions of the European Union which have defense implications, and therefore does not participate in the financing of the operation,

HAS DECIDED AS FOLLOWS:

Article 1

The Operation Plan and the Rules of Engagement concerning the EU military operation to contribute to the deterrence, prevention, and repression of acts of piracy and armed robbery off the Somali coast, hereinafter referred to as "Operation Atalanta," are approved.

Article 2

Operation Atalanta shall be launched on December 8, 2008.

Article 3

The Commander of Operation Atalanta is hereby authorized with immediate effect to release the Activation Order in order to execute the deployment of the forces and start execution of the mission.

Article 4

This Decision shall take effect on the day of its adoption.

Article 5

This Decision shall be published in the *Official Journal of the European Union*.

Source: "Council Decision 2008/918/CFSP of December 8, 2008 on the launch of a European Union military operation to contribute to the deterrence, prevention and repression of acts of piracy and armed robbery off the Somali coast (Atalanta)," published in the *Official Journal of the European Union*, L330, Vol 51, December 9, 2008, p 19. Retrieved from http://eur-lex.europa.eu/LexUriServ/LexUriServ.do?uri=OJ: L:2008:330:0019:0020:EN:PDF. Retrieved on March 8, 2009. European Union, http://eur-lex.europa.eu/. Only European Union legislation printed in the paper edition of the *Official Journal of the European Union* is deemed authentic.

UN Assessment of Somali Piracy, November 2008

From November 10–21, 2008, the United Nations hosted a meeting by a group of leading international experts in Nairobi, Kenya, to gather the most current and accurate information available to help the international community "develop a coordinated response to the challenge of maritime piracy along the Somali coast." This assembled group included experienced Somali hands, naval and police officers, relief organizations, legal scholars, security specialists, etc., who offered considerable insights into the inner workings of this problem, most of which have subsequently proven to be quite reliable, if not all. A 92-page report was quickly compiled and submitted to the Security Council, from which some excerpts from its Chapter 3 are reproduced here below:

3. UNDERSTANDING PIRACY IN SOMALIA
Piracy in Somalia is deeply rooted in a number of socioeconomic factors, predominantly poverty, hunger, and civil insecurity of the

coastal population. Puntland is currently the epicenter of piracy. This is due, in no small part, to the fact that vessels can be identified and targeted much more easily as they travel through the Gulf of Aden.

3.1 Origins of Piracy in Somalia

Prior to 1990, piracy was not a major issue off the coast of Somalia, but like most coastal nations, there were irregular incidences of armed robbery against small fishing or leisure craft that fell prey to an armed group, or ships that foundered off the coast. A more structured form of piracy began in the mid-1990s, when some armed groups, claiming they were authorized coast guards charged with protecting Somalia's fishing resources, attacked vessels they claimed were fishing illegally in their territorial waters, and held them for ransom. This slowly expanded after 2000 to any vessel that sailed within, or close to Somali territorial waters. Both vessels and crews would be held hostage, and ransom demanded.

During 2005 an increase was noted in the number of attacks being attempted against vessels sailing in the Indian Ocean, off the coast of Somalia. By 2006, some of the pirate attacks were extending as far as 350 nautical miles off the coast of Somalia. During 2006 piracy escalated as more attempts were made to hijack ships, not only in the Indian Ocean, but also in the Gulf of Aden and the mouth of the Red Sea. The phenomenon grew through 2007 from the major pirate bases of Eyl, Hobyo, and Haradheere, concentrated along the east coast of Somalia. By 2008, this reached outlandish proportions, with ships being attacked seemingly at random and whenever the pirates decide. Consequently, marine travel off the northern coast of Somalia, known as Puntland, has become the most dangerous region in the world for pirate attacks.

3.1.1 Why Piracy in Somalia?

Compared to pirate operations in other parts of the world—namely the Java Sea, South China Sea, and off the coast of Nigeria—Somalia does not have the natural coastal terrain so required by pirates, namely numerous forested inlets and islands, where ships can be hidden from aerial and maritime surveillance. Somali pirates do not need this type of terrain because their piratical aims are very singular and straightforward, ransom for hostages only. They are not interested in stealing the cargo and/or reusing the ship for other purposes, where there is a need to have a secure location hidden from view, where a ship can be concealed while it is renamed and repainted. They are interested in ransom only.

When a ship is taken by Somali pirates, it and the crew are held for ransom. It is, in effect, a hostage situation. The ship is sailed to one of the bases where the pirates can be supplied with food, water, khat, weapons and ammunition, and other resources while the negotiations take place. This is all done very openly, with the ship visibly anchored off the Somali coast. The pirates are fully aware that they are relatively

secure from any rescue mission being launched directly against them
while on the ship. The only alternative remaining to guarantee a secure
and safe conclusion to the hostage situation is the payment of the
requested ransom.

One striking aspect of piracy along the Somali coast is that despite
differences of location and clan, the methodology used for the targeting,
attack and capture of ships, the detention of crews, the progress of
negotiation, the amounts of ransom demands, the methods of receiving
payments, and ultimately release of ship and hostages are all identical.
Some experts believe that these identical procedures come from a
coordination of the pirates's activities. Others believe that there is little
or no central coordination. These experts think that the basic
operational procedures were organically developed, either in Puntland
or in Central Region, and transferred to other groups along the coast. It
is also known that there is a fundamental operational directive or base
code of practice, among the pirates: That once a ship has been
ransomed and is released, that it cannot be further targeted by any
other group of pirates.

3.1.2 What Drives Piracy in Somalia?
There are many factors that drive piracy in Somalia. One should not be
surprised that piracy has taken root in Somalia, given the social
upheavals, human hardship, environmental degradation, and the
entrepreneurial spirit of the Somali. Piracy is flourishing in Somalia, as
it is a quick way for all involved to earn a large amount of money, way
beyond any other means of income generation. While the action of
piracy involves some risk, the benefits far outweigh that risk, a fact
indicated by the few arrests made, and less deaths and injury suffered
by pirates to date.

Poverty, lack of employment, environmental hardship, pitifully low
incomes, reduction of pastoralist and maritime resources due to
drought and illegal fishing, and a volatile security and political
situation all contribute to the rise and continuance of piracy in Somalia.
This situation will remain so until there is an effective and simultaneous
action taken against the pirate trade and an alternative means of income
support mechanism implemented to replace it; otherwise criminal
activity, in some shape or form, will continue to take priority as a means
of generating income among the armed militias of Somalia.

The pirates also firmly believe that they have every right and
entitlement to attack illegal fishing vessels operating in their territorial
waters, as their fishing resources are being pillaged daily by
international shipping vessels from Asia and Europe. The international
community is fully aware that this illegal activity has been going on for
nearly seventeen years, but has taken no action against it. The pirates
believe they are the only option to curtailing this injustice. Equally, the
pirates do admit that the initial idea of protecting their coastline has

been hijacked to the current situation, where any vulnerable vessel is a target. Targeting other ships is supposed to highlight the illegal shipping, but has now become such a huge international problem that the origins for the initial actions have been forgotten. However, they do admit that humanitarian aid and other supporting commercial vessels should not be targeted for piratical gain.

. . .

3.5 Pirate Methodology

The most active and renowned pirate bases are scattered along the Indian Ocean coast of Central Somalia and Puntland: Eyl, Hobyo, and Harardheere. These bases are well-equipped and strongly armed. It is currently beyond the capacity of the local authorities to carry out raids on these bases.

The methodology of the pirate attacks, from transport preparation, weapons preparation, target identification, and subsequent hostage negotiation, has improved with practice and reinvestment of funds from ransom payments.

Initially, pirate attacks were launched from beachheads in open 20-inch-long skiffs, with high freeboards and powered by 75–85 horsepower outboard motors whose range and safety was dictated by the state of the sea, amount of fuel on board, and engine power. The most highly regarded outboard motor along the east coast is the Yamaha 85 horsepower outboard motor. This allows a skiff to attain speeds of 30 knots in relatively calm seas with four people aboard. More recent reports indicate that these skiffs are now being powered by as much as two 150 horsepower-motors.

These skiffs move about looking for slow moving vulnerable commercial or fishing vessels, ideally traveling under 15 knots with a low freeboard. Once the vessel is targeted, the skiffs form a two- or three-pronged attack, depending upon the number of skiffs in the attack group. Attacking from a number of directions simultaneously, usually allows one of the skiffs to approach a vessel unnoticed, and enable a number of armed pirates to board the vessel. Once this is accomplished, the crew is easily captured and the remaining pirates come on board. The pirated vessel is then brought to one of the main bases of operation—Eyl, Hobyo, or Harardheere, depending upon the origin of the pirate's subclan—and negotiations begin for the release of the vessel.

In the late 1990s and early 2000, the number of hijacked vessels was very few and consisted of an equal representation of fishing vessels, commercial traders, or private yachts. When these relatively rare incidences occurred, they were viewed somewhat sensationally, and often involved the local support capability of the clan elders to assist in opening negotiations with the correct representatives of the identified pirates. In these early cases, the priority was the release of the crew, as the vessels and their contents were looted by the pirates as part of their *modus operandi*.

In mid-2000, a new breed of piracy was noted, one that started targeting and holding bigger commercial vessels for longer periods and demanding higher ransoms. With little to fear from local or international law, the trade mushroomed incrementally to the state it is today.

The step to this stage was founded on an interim period of targeting fishing vessels accused of fishing illegally in Somali territorial waters. The pirates called themselves "Somali coastguards," with such names as the Kismaayo Volunteer Coastguards and the Somalia Marines for Hobyo and Harardheere, and sanctioned their actions by stating they were protecting Somali fishing resources. When the rewards of these actions began to bear financial returns, attacks quickly ranged well beyond Somali territorial waters into the Indian Ocean looking for targets. With the extension of the operational area, their *modus operandi* also changed. No longer could beachhead launches give them the range they needed for deep-ocean operations. The pirates began to use "mother ships," larger ships or dhows already pirated that could move inconspicuously into the ocean, carrying pirates' weapons and skiffs. When a targeted ship was spotted, the skiffs were released close by and raced towards the targeted ship with pirates armed with automatic weapons and RPGs. These were used to threaten the crew into submission, either by waving their weapons or by firing volleys against the bridge, or in some cases, firing an RPG into the vessel. The pirated vessel was then taken to one of the land bases and held offshore during the negotiations.

In late 2007, the pirates realized that the rewards of captured vessels would increase, for less danger and trouble, if they targeted vessels exiting the chokepoint in the immediate region, principally the Gulf of Aden as ships exited the Red Sea out of the Suez Canal. This resulted in many more vessels being attacked, and increased hijacked vessels. This situation exists until the current time, even with the existence of the Combined Task Force warships and the arrival of a number of NATO and EU warships, and warships from other countries.

While the pirates still use the "mother ship" system, many observers now believe that some of the pirate groups combine AIS interception and satellite positioning systems to identify and track their intended target. Others also believe that the pirates are receiving information from "spotters," who are working in ports around the region and providing advanced knowledge on the routes and physical details of potential targeted vessels. Regardless of what system the pirates are using, they are still able to hijack ships within the tight operational confines of the Gulf of Aden, and amidst the increasing number of foreign warships.

3.6 Ransom

Ransom amounts demanded by the pirate groups over the past few years, have risen from the tens of thousands of US$ to hundreds of thousands. In 2008, the average ransom is estimated between $500,000–$2 million. Estimated income from piracy for 2008 is projected at between $18–30 million.

Ransom demands are now negotiated directly between the pirates on the seized vessel, and the shipowners or companies, using the ship's communication equipment. In most instances, ransoms are paid in cash and are delivered to the pirates aboard the seized ship. The cash is usually transported by a representative of the shipowner. Upon receipt of the money, the pirates wait until the money courier has departed before leaving the ship. To reduce the chance of identification, capture, and loss of the ransom, they will leave individually, travel separately, and divide the money amongst members of the group.

Reports of other payment methods indicate that ransoms are paid to a trusted third representative, at a regional location outside of Somalia. Upon receipt of the money, a call is placed to the pirates, and the ship and hostages released.

3.6.1 Dispersion of Ransom Incomes

At present, piracy has an air of respectability about it, with pirates much sought after due to their newfound wealth. At present, the revenues for ransoms are being diffused into various sectors of the communities, with a sizeable proportion being spent in Puntland. Garoowe, in Puntland, is one place that appears to be benefiting from this newfound income, with the construction of large homes, and increase in the price of marriage dowries, and more and more expensive vehicles appearing on the streets.

As a result of this spending, many ancillary businesses are reaping the rewards of increased income, thus improving their livelihood and standard of living. This spending is confined exclusively to Garoowe, but penetrates throughout the Puntland economy. With a projected income of nearly $30 million expected from piracy this year, the activity dwarfs the Puntland government income of $10 million dollars by three times.

No authority can compete with this easy and untaxed income. As long as a favorable size of the ransom money stays within Puntland, one can argue that the benefits of piracy is supporting a new and relatively vibrant economy, and presumably raising the living standards of a number of business interests, their families, and extended families. One of the concerns about this input of easy cash, is that it could be used for a more disruptive practice of affecting the outcome of upcoming elections in Puntland, where the money could be used to ensure that government representatives favorable to piracy activities, or not willing to interfere with their operations, remain in power to allow them to continue their activities undisturbed.

Source: UN Security Council, *Report of the Monitoring Group on Somalia pursuant to Security Council resolution 1811 (2008)*, 10 December 2008, S/2008/769. Retrieved from http://ods-dds-ny.un.org/doc/UNDOC/GEN/N08/604/73/PDF/N0860473.pdf?OpenElement. Retrieved on March 22, 2009. Reprinted with permission of the United Nations Publications Board.

UN Security Council Resolution 1846, Re: Piracy in Somalia

As more and more nations volunteered to participate in the ongoing anti-piracy efforts off the Horn of Africa, the Security Council continued issuing new resolutions in its support, gradually expanding the scope of these operations with the compliance and urging from the beleaguered Transitional Federal Government in Mogadishu. The latest in this string of UN Resolutions was adopted on December 2, 2008, and which reads in its totality:

The Security Council,

Recalling its previous resolutions concerning the situation in Somalia, especially resolutions 1814 (2008), 1816 (2008) and 1838 (2008),

Continuing to be gravely concerned by the threat that piracy and armed robbery at sea against vessels pose to the prompt, safe, and effective delivery of humanitarian aid to Somalia; to international navigation and the safety of commercial maritime routes; and to other vulnerable ships, including fishing activities in conformity with international law,

Reaffirming its respect for the sovereignty, territorial integrity, political independence, and unity of Somalia,

Further reaffirming that international law, as reflected in the United Nations Convention on the Law of the Sea of December 10, 1982 ("the Convention"), sets out the legal framework applicable to combating piracy and armed robbery at sea, as well as other ocean activities,

Taking into account the crisis situation in Somalia, and the lack of capacity of the Transitional Federal Government (TFG) to interdict pirates, or patrol and secure either the international sea lanes off the coast of Somalia or Somalia's territorial waters,

Taking note of the requests from the TFG for international assistance to counter piracy off its coasts, including the September 1, 2008 letter from the President of Somalia to the Secretary-General of the United Nations, expressing the appreciation of the TFG to the Security Council for its assistance, and expressing the TFG's willingness to consider working with other States and regional organizations to combat piracy and armed robbery at sea off the coast of Somalia; the November 20, 2008 letter conveying the request of the TFG that the provisions of resolution 1816 (2008) be renewed; and the November 20, request of the Permanent Representative of Somalia before the Security Council that the renewal be for an additional 12 months,

Further taking note of the letters from the TFG to the Secretary-General providing advance notification with respect to States cooperating with the TFG in the fight against piracy and armed robbery at sea off the coast of Somalia, and from other Member States to the Security Council to inform the Council of their actions, as requested in paragraphs 7 and 12 of resolution 1816 (2008), and encouraging those cooperating States, for which advance notification has been provided by the TFG to the Secretary-General, to continue their respective efforts,

Expressing again its determination to ensure the long-term security of World Food Program (WFP) maritime deliveries to Somalia,

Recalling that in its resolution 1838 (2008) it commended the contribution made by some States since November 2007 to protect (WFP) maritime convoys, and the establishment by the European Union of a coordination unit with the task of supporting the surveillance and protection activities carried out by some member States of the European Union off the coast of Somalia, as well as other international and national initiatives taken with a view to implementing resolutions 1814 (2008) and 1816 (2008),

Emphasizing that peace and stability within Somalia, the strengthening of State institutions, economic and social development, and respect for human rights and the rule of law are necessary to create the conditions for a full eradication of piracy and armed robbery at sea off the coast of Somalia,

Welcoming the signing of a peace and reconciliation Agreement ("the Djibouti Agreement") between the TFG and the Alliance for the Re-Liberation of Somalia on 19 August 2008, as well as their signing of a joint ceasefire agreement on October 26, 2008, noting that the Djibouti Agreement calls for the United

Nations to authorize and deploy an international stabilization force, and further noting the Secretary-General's report on Somalia of November 17, 2008, including his recommendations in this regard,

Commending the key role played by the African Union Mission to Somalia in facilitating delivery of humanitarian assistance to Somalia through the port of Mogadishu, and the contribution that African Union Mission to Somalia has made towards the goal of establishing lasting peace and stability in Somalia, and recognizing specifically the important contributions of the Governments of Uganda and Burundi to Somalia,

Welcoming the organization of a ministerial meeting of the Security Council in December 2008 to examine ways to improve international coordination in the fight against piracy and armed robbery off the coast of Somalia, and to ensure that the international community has the proper authorities and tools at its disposal to assist it in these efforts,

Determining that the incidents of piracy and armed robbery against vessels in the territorial waters of Somalia and the high seas off the coast of Somalia exacerbate the situation in Somalia, which continues to constitute a threat to international peace and security in the region,

Acting under Chapter VII of the Charter of the United Nations,

1. *Reiterates* that it condemns and deplores all acts of piracy and armed robbery against vessels in territorial waters and the high seas off the coast of Somalia;
2. *Expresses* its concern over the finding contained in the November 20, 2008 report of the Monitoring Group on Somalia, that escalating ransom payments are fuelling the growth of piracy off the coast of Somalia;
3. *Welcomes* the efforts of the International Maritime Organization (IMO) to update its guidance and recommendations to the shipping industry and to Governments for preventing and suppressing piracy and armed robbery at sea, and to provide this guidance as soon as practicable to all Member States and to the international shipping community operating off the coast of Somalia;
4. *Calls upon* States, in cooperation with the shipping industry, the insurance industry, and the IMO, to issue to ships entitled to fly their flag appropriate advice and guidance on avoidance, evasion, and defensive techniques and measures to take if under the threat of attack or attack when sailing in the waters off the coast of Somalia;

5. *Further calls upon* States and interested organizations, including the IMO, to provide technical assistance to Somalia and nearby coastal States upon their request to enhance the capacity of these States to ensure coastal and maritime security, including combating piracy and armed robbery at sea off the Somali and nearby coastlines;

6. *Welcomes* initiatives by Canada, Denmark, France, India, the Netherlands, the Russian Federation, Spain, the United Kingdom, the United States of America, and by regional and international organizations to counter piracy off the coast of Somalia pursuant to resolutions 1814 (2008), 1816 (2008), and 1838 (2008); the decision by the North Atlantic Treaty Organization (NATO) to counter piracy off the Somalia coast, including by escorting vessels of the WFP; and in particular the decision by the EU on November 10, 2008 to launch, for a period of 12 months from December 2008, a naval operation to protect WFP maritime convoys bringing humanitarian assistance to Somalia and other vulnerable ships, and to repress acts of piracy and armed robbery at sea off the coast of Somalia;

7. *Calls upon* States and regional organizations to coordinate, including by sharing information through bilateral channels or the United Nations, their efforts to deter acts of piracy and armed robbery at sea off the coast of Somalia in cooperation with each other, the IMO, the international shipping community, flag States, and the TFG;

8. *Requests* the Secretary-General to present to it a report, no later than three months after the adoption of this resolution, on ways to ensure the long-term security of international navigation off the coast of Somalia, including the long-term security of WFP maritime deliveries to Somalia, and a possible coordination and leadership role for the United Nations in this regard to rally Member States and regional organizations to counter piracy and armed robbery at sea off the coast of Somalia;

9. *Calls upon* States and regional organizations that have the capacity to do so, to take part actively in the fight against piracy and armed robbery at sea off the coast of Somalia, in particular, consistent with this resolution and relevant international law, by deploying naval vessels and military aircraft, and through seizure and disposition of boats, vessels, arms, and other related equipment used in the commission of piracy and armed robbery off the coast of Somalia, or for which there is reasonable ground for suspecting such use;

10. *Decides* that for a period of 12 months from the date of this resolution, States and regional organizations cooperating with the TFG in the fight against piracy and armed robbery at sea off the

coast of Somalia, for which advance notification has been provided by the TFG to the Secretary-General, may:

(a)   Enter into the territorial waters of Somalia for the purpose of repressing acts of piracy and armed robbery at sea, in a manner consistent with such action permitted on the high seas with respect to piracy under relevant international law; and

(b)   Use, within the territorial waters of Somalia, in a manner consistent with such action permitted on the high seas with respect to piracy under relevant international law, all necessary means to repress acts of piracy and armed robbery at sea;

11.   *Affirms* that the authorizations provided in this resolution apply only with respect to the situation in Somalia, and shall not affect the rights or obligations or responsibilities of Member States under international law, including any rights or obligations under the Convention, with respect to any other situation, and underscores in particular that this resolution shall not be considered as establishing customary international law; and affirms further that such authorizations have been provided only following the receipt of the 20 November letter conveying the consent of the TFG;

12.   *Affirms* that the measures imposed by paragraph 5 of resolution 733 (1992) and further elaborated upon by paragraphs 1 and 2 of resolution 1425 (2002) do not apply to supplies of technical assistance to Somalia solely for the purposes set out in paragraph 5 above, which have been exempted from those measures in accordance with the procedure set out in paragraphs 11 (b) and 12 of resolution 1772 (2007);

13.   *Requests* that cooperating States take appropriate steps to ensure that the activities they undertake pursuant to the authorization in paragraph 10, do not have the practical effect of denying or impairing the right of innocent passage to the ships of any third State;

14.   *Calls upon* all States, and in particular flag, port, and coastal States; States of the nationality of victims and perpetrators of piracy and armed robbery; and other States with relevant jurisdiction under international law and national legislation, to cooperate in determining jurisdiction, and in the investigation and prosecution of persons responsible for acts of piracy and armed robbery off the coast of Somalia, consistent with applicable international law including international human-rights law, and to render assistance by, among other actions, providing disposition and logistics assistance with respect to persons under their jurisdiction and control, such victims and witnesses and persons

detained as a result of operations conducted under this resolution;

15. *Notes* that the 1988 Convention for the Suppression of Unlawful Acts Against the Safety of Maritime Navigation ("SUA Convention") provides for parties to create criminal offences, establish jurisdiction, and accept delivery of persons responsible for or suspected of seizing or exercising control over a ship by force, or threat thereof, or any other form of intimidation; urges States parties to the SUA Convention to fully implement their obligations under said Convention and cooperate with the Secretary-General and the IMO to build judicial capacity for the successful prosecution of persons suspected of piracy and armed robbery at sea off the coast of Somalia;

16. *Requests* States and regional organizations cooperating with the TFG to inform the Security Council and the Secretary-General within nine months, of the progress of actions undertaken in the exercise of the authority provided in paragraph 10 above;

17. *Requests* the Secretary-General to report to the Security Council within 11 months of adoption of this resolution, on the implementation of this resolution and on the situation with respect to piracy and armed robbery in territorial waters and the high seas off the coast of Somalia;

18. *Requests* the Secretary-General of the IMO to brief the Council on the basis of cases brought to his attention by the agreement of all affected coastal States, and duly taking into account the existing bilateral and regional cooperative arrangements, on the situation with respect to piracy and armed robbery;

19. *Expresses* its intention to review the situation and consider, as appropriate, renewing the authority provided in paragraph 10 above for additional periods upon the request of the TFG;

20. *Decides* to remain seized of the matter.

Source: United Nations Security Council Resolution 1846 (2008), December 2, 2008. Retrieved from http://ods-dds-ny.un.org/doc/UNDOC/GEN/N08/630/29/PDF/N0863029.pdf?OpenElement. Retrieved on March 8, 2009.

U.S.-Sponsored UN Security Council Resolution 1851

During its final few months in office, the outgoing U.S. administration of Pres. George W. Bush—presumably with at least tacit understanding from the incoming President-elect, Barack Obama—led the drive toward adoption of yet another Security Council resolution on

December 16, 2008, which expanded the scope of potential coalition efforts by securing authorization for their use of land-based operations in the fight against piracy off the coast of Somalia. This document reads in its entirety:

The Security Council,

Recalling its previous resolutions concerning the situation in Somalia, especially resolutions 1814 (2008), 1816 (2008), 1838 (2008), 1844 (2008), and 1846 (2008),

Continuing to be gravely concerned by the dramatic increase in the incidents of piracy and armed robbery at sea off the coast of Somalia in the last six months, and by the threat that piracy and armed robbery at sea against vessels pose to the prompt, safe, and effective delivery of humanitarian aid to Somalia, and *noting* that pirate attacks off the coast of Somalia have become more sophisticated and daring, and have expanded in their geographic scope, notably evidenced by the hijacking of the M/V *Sirius Star* 500 nautical miles off the coast of Kenya and subsequent unsuccessful attempts well east of Tanzania,

Reaffirming its respect for the sovereignty, territorial integrity, political independence, and unity of Somalia, including Somalia's rights with respect to offshore natural resources, including fisheries, in accordance with international law,

Further reaffirming that international law, as reflected in the United Nations Convention on the Law of the Sea of December 10, 1982 (UNCLOS), sets out the legal framework applicable to combating piracy and armed robbery at sea, as well as other ocean activities,

Again taking into account the crisis situation in Somalia, and the lack of capacity of the Transitional Federal Government (TFG) to interdict, or upon interdiction to prosecute pirates, or to patrol and secure the waters off the coast of Somalia, including the international sea lanes and Somalia's territorial waters,

Noting the several requests from the TFG for international assistance to counter piracy off its coast, including the letter of 9 December 2008 from the President of Somalia requesting the international community to assist the TFG in taking all necessary measures to interdict those who use Somali territory and airspace to plan, facilitate or undertake acts of piracy and armed robbery at sea, and the September 1, 2008 letter from the President of Somalia to the Secretary-General of the UN expressing the appreciation of the TFG to the Security Council for its assistance and

212 Data and Documents

expressing the TFG's willingness to consider working with other States and regional organizations to combat piracy and armed robbery off the coast of Somalia,

Welcoming the launching of the EU operation Atalanta to combat piracy off the coast of Somalia and to protect vulnerable ships bound for Somalia, as well as the efforts by the North Atlantic Treaty Organization, and other States acting in a national capacity in cooperation with the TFG to suppress piracy off the coast of Somalia,

Also welcoming the recent initiatives of the Governments of Egypt, Kenya, and the Secretary-General's Special Representative for Somalia, and the United Nations Office on Drugs and Crime (UNODC) to achieve effective measures to remedy the causes, capabilities, and incidents of piracy and armed robbery off the coast of Somalia, and *emphasizing* the need for current and future counter-piracy operations to effectively coordinate their activities,

Noting with concern that the lack of capacity, domestic legislation, and clarity about how to dispose of pirates after their capture, has hindered more robust international action against the pirates off the coast of Somalia and in some cases led to pirates being released without facing justice, and *reiterating* that the 1988 Convention for the Suppression of Unlawful Acts Against the Safety of Maritime Navigation ("SUA Convention") provides for parties to create criminal offences, establish jurisdiction, and accept delivery of persons responsible for, or suspected of seizing or exercising control over a ship by force or threat thereof, or any other form of intimidation,

Welcoming the report of the Monitoring Group on Somalia of November 20, 2008 (S/2008/769), and *noting* the role piracy may play in financing embargo violations by armed groups,

Determining that the incidents of piracy and armed robbery at sea in the waters off the coast of Somalia exacerbate the situation in Somalia, which continues to constitute a threat to international peace and security in the region,

Acting under Chapter VII of the Charter of the United Nations,

1. *Reiterates* that it condemns and deplores all acts of piracy and armed robbery against vessels in waters off the coast of Somalia;
2. *Calls* upon States, regional, and international organizations that have the capacity to do so, to take part actively in the fight against piracy and armed robbery at sea off the coast of Somalia, in particular, consistent with this resolution, resolution 1846

(2008), and international law, by deploying naval vessels and military aircraft, and through seizure and disposition of boats, vessels, arms, and other related equipment used in the commission of piracy and armed robbery at sea off the coast of Somalia, or for which there are reasonable grounds for suspecting such use;

3. *Invites* all States and regional organizations fighting piracy off the coast of Somalia, to conclude special agreements or arrangements with countries willing to take custody of pirates, in order to embark law-enforcement officials ("ship-riders") from the latter countries, in particular countries in the region, to facilitate the investigation and prosecution of persons detained as a result of operations conducted under this resolution for acts of piracy and armed robbery at sea off the coast of Somalia, provided that the advance consent of the TFG is obtained for the exercise of third-state jurisdiction by ship-riders in Somali territorial waters, and that such agreements or arrangements do not prejudice the effective implementation of the SUA Convention;

4. *Encourages* all States and regional organizations fighting piracy and armed robbery at sea off the coast of Somalia, to establish an international cooperation mechanism to act as a common point of contact between and among states, regional, and international organizations on all aspects of combating piracy and armed robbery at sea off Somalia's coast; and *recalls* that future recommendations on ways to ensure the long-term security of international navigation off the coast of Somalia, including the long-term security of WFP maritime deliveries to Somalia, and a possible coordination and leadership role for the United Nations in this regard to rally Member States and regional organizations to counter piracy and armed robbery at sea off the coast of Somalia, are to be detailed in a report by the Secretary-General no later than three months after the adoption of resolution 1846;

5. *Further encourages* all states and regional organizations fighting piracy and armed robbery at sea off the coast of Somalia, to consider creating a center in the region to coordinate information relevant to piracy and armed robbery at sea off the coast of Somalia; to increase regional capacity with assistance of UNODC to arrange effective ship-rider agreements or arrangements consistent with UNCLOS; and to implement the SUA Convention, the United Nations Convention against Transnational Organized Crime, and other relevant instruments to which States in the region are party, in order to effectively investigate and prosecute piracy and armed robbery at sea offences;

6. In response to the letter from the TFG of December 9, 2008, *encourages* Member States to continue to cooperate with the TFG in the fight against piracy and armed robbery at sea; *notes* the primary role of the TFG in rooting out piracy and armed robbery at sea; and *decides* that for a period of 12 months from the date of adoption of resolution 1846, States and regional organizations cooperating in the fight against piracy and armed robbery at sea off the coast of Somalia, for which advance notification has been provided by the TFG to the Secretary-General, may undertake all necessary measures that are appropriate in Somalia, for the purpose of suppressing acts of piracy and armed robbery at sea, pursuant to the request of the TFG, provided, however, that any measures undertaken pursuant to the authority of this paragraph shall be undertaken consistent with applicable international humanitarian and human rights law;

7. *Calls on* Member States to assist the TFG, at its request and with notification to the Secretary-General, to strengthen its operational capacity to bring to justice those who are using Somali territory to plan, facilitate, or undertake criminal acts of piracy and armed robbery at sea, and *stresses* that any measures undertaken pursuant to this paragraph shall be consistent with applicable international human rights law;

8. *Welcomes* the communiqué issued by the International Conference on Piracy around Somalia held in Nairobi, Kenya, on December 11, 2008 and *encourages* Member States to work to enhance the capacity of relevant states in the region to combat piracy, including judicial capacity;

9. *Notes* with concern the findings contained in the 20 November 2008 report of the Monitoring Group on Somalia, that escalating ransom payments are fuelling the growth of piracy in waters off the coast of Somalia, and that the lack of enforcement of the arms embargo established by resolution 733 (1992) has permitted ready access to the arms and ammunition used by the pirates, and driven in part the phenomenal growth in piracy;

10. *Affirms* that the authorization provided in this resolution apply only with respect to the situation in Somalia and shall not affect the rights or obligations or responsibilities of Member States under international law, including any rights or obligations under UNCLOS, with respect to any other situation, and underscores in particular that this resolution shall not be considered as establishing customary international law, and *affirms further* that such authorizations have been provided only following the receipt of the December 9, 2008 letter conveying the consent of the TFG;

11. *Affirms* that the measures imposed by paragraph 5 of resolution 733 (1992) and further elaborated upon by paragraphs 1 and 2 or resolution 1425 (2002), shall not apply to weapons and military equipment destined for the sole use of Member States and regional organizations undertaking measures in accordance with paragraph 6 above;

12. *Urges* States in collaboration with the shipping and insurance industries, and the IMO to continue to develop avoidance, evasion, and defensive best practices and advisories to take when under attack or when sailing in waters off the coast of Somalia, and *further urges* States to make their citizens and vessels available for forensic investigation as appropriate, at the first port of call immediately following an act or attempted act of piracy or armed robbery at sea or release from captivity;

13. *Decides* to remain seized of the matter.

Source: United Nations Security Council Resolution 1851 (2008), 16 December 2008. Retrieved from http://ods-dds-ny.un.org/doc/UNDOC/GEN/N08/655/01/PDF/N0865501.pdf?OpenElement. Retrieved on March 22, 2009. Reprinted with permission from the United Nations Publication Board.

7

Directory of Organizations

Foreign navies can do nothing to stop piracy.

—Dahir Mohamed Hayeysi, a pirate gunman from Harardheere,
Somalia, April 2009

Naval Forces

Prior to the events of 9/11, the only foreign warships operating routinely in international waters near the Horn of Africa were detachments from the U.S. Fifth Fleet, under the overall strategic direction of U.S. Naval Forces Central Command, which is headquartered deep inside the Persian Gulf in Bahrain. However, after the terrorist attacks against New York City and Washington on September 11, 2001, warships from more than a dozen allied nations soon began rotating in and out of the Indian Ocean as well, to join the broad counteroffensive which was launched by the administration of President George W. Bush against terrorist groups and their backers through the Mideast and Asia, codenamed "Operation Enduring Freedom."

These coalition warships were organized into a separate United States Naval Forces Central Command (USNavCent) division by February 2002, intended to serve as an adjunct to the Fifth Fleet, and operating under the general designation of "Combined Maritime Forces." The coalition squadron known as Combined Task Force 150 helped support the newly-created U.S. Marine base being erected beside the international airport at Djibouti, which was to house a fast-strike unit codenamed "Combined Joint Task

Force-Horn of Africa," by conducting regional antiterrorist sweeps known as Maritime Security Operations in its adjacent waters.

Meanwhile, the U.S. Fifth Fleet was being built up into a huge force for the invasion of Iraq in March 2003, with the addition to its strength of five aircraft carriers, a half-dozen huge amphibious assault-ships, plus numerous other frontline warships. Soon after that invasion had succeeded, this large extra number of U.S. Navy battle-groups and major warships began to be drawn down out of the Arabian Sea and Indian Ocean, while lighter American and allied warships were moved in closer to occupied Iraq to protect its offshore oil installations, patrol its porous borders, and escort the convoys which would have to bring in the endless amounts of supplies required by the occupation forces. But as Iraq's internal security then began to spin out of control, a deterrent naval presence had to be sustained in this theater much longer than anticipated, to help maintain watch against interference and subversion from hostile neighboring states.

Consequently, when the separate issue of piracy began exploding out of Somalia a few years later, the U.S. Fifth Fleet still included numerous frontline warships as late as 2007–2008, which were deemed too large and elaborately armed to prove cost-effective in chasing down boatloads of teenage gunmen. Occasionally, some might be diverted for a limited time on an antipiracy sweep or rescue mission, while any would naturally steam to the assistance of any nearby merchantman under attack. However, the American container ship *Maersk Alabama* was to be jointly rescued in April 2009 by the 1,100-man, 41,500-ton amphibious assault-ship USS *Boxer*; the 270-man, 9,200-ton guided-missile destroyer USS *Bainbridge*; the 225-man, 4,100-ton guided-missile frigate USS *Halyburton*; plus a host of other high-priced resources—judged an excessively wasteful use of force by naval professional, when arrayed against only four young gunmen trapped aboard a bobbing lifeboat.

Moreover, some potentially useful smaller coalition warships from Combined Task Force 150 had not even authorized by their home governments to participate in any antipiracy campaigns whatsoever, indeed nothing beyond their original antiterrorist mandate, while Washington was increasingly reluctant to prolong its own commitment of heavy warships in the region for this entirely new purpose of hunting pirates. And given that it was the commercial traffic of Europe and Asia which were much more directly affected by this sudden upsurge in Somali piracy, it would instead be a variety of North Atlantic Treaty Organization, European Union, and multinational forces which were dispatched to combat piracy in the vital sea lanes of the Gulf of Aden and off the Horn of Africa, with the full approval and material backing from Washington.

To bolster these allied-led expeditions, the U.S. Navy agreed to reconstitute any coalition warships from its "Combined Maritime Forces" division which had been authorized by their home governments to participate in separate antipiracy operations, into a new USNavCent unit designated as Combined Task Force-151, which was intended to play a role in this new campaign under American command.

U.S. Navy and Coalition Partners

U.S. Naval Forces Central Command
(NAVCENT)
Manama, Bahrain
Tel: 011-973-1785-4027
e-Address: cusnc.navy.mil

The strategic headquarters for all American naval operations that are conducted in "the Red Sea, Arabian Sea, Gulf of Oman, parts of the Indian Ocean, as well as the coast of East Africa as far south as Kenya." Its commander directly controls the 10 U.S. Task Forces that comprise the U.S. Fifth Fleet, as well as a half-dozen Combined Task Forces, which form a separate division of USNavCent designated as "Combined Maritime Forces," and are made up of temporarily assigned coalition warships. The primary current mission of USNavCent is to defend and sustain the occupation of Iraq as well as to pursue extremist elements within the region; antipiracy sweeps and protection of commercial traffic are only secondary considerations among its manifold duties.

U.S. Fifth Fleet
(FIFTHFLT)
Manama, Bahrain
Tel: 011-973-1785-4000 (Naval Support Activity)
   011-973-1785-4027 (Public Affairs Office)

The actual U.S. naval warships deployed in this theater, whose command-staff are housed as part of USNavCent headquarters in Bahrain. The number of the U.S. Fifth Fleet's strength fluctuates, as vessels are rotated in and out for tours according to need, from the U.S. Pacific and Atlantic Fleets. In addition to the 10 U.S. Navy task forces currently comprising the Fifth Fleet, it also directs the activities of several attached coalition formations, such as:

- Combined Task Force 150, which patrols from the Strait of Hormuz, halfway across the Arabia Sea, south as far as the Seychelles, around the Horn of Africa and through the Gulf of Aden, up through the Bab-al-Mandeb Strait between Djibouti and Yemen, and into the Red Sea,
- Combined Task Force 151, a recently created squadron which patrols much this same area but is primarily focused on deterring and disrupting Somali pirate attacks against commercial shipping,
- Combined Task Force 152, which patrols the Persian Gulf from near its northern end, down as far as the Strait of Hormuz between Oman and Iran,
- Combined Task Force 158, which patrols the North Persian Gulf, to help protect Iraq's oil-terminals.

Given the huge expanse of ocean which constitutes the U.S. Fifth Fleet's theater-of-operations, its warships could only occasionally assist in antipiracy sweeps prior to January 2009, when the separate formation of its Combined Task Force 151 was created and specifically tasked with assisting in this duty.

Combined Maritime Forces
c/o U.S. Naval Forces
Central Command
Manama, Bahrain
Tel: 011-973-1785-4027

As mentioned above, this division was originally formed as part of regional U.S. naval strength in February 2002, from warships of more than a dozen allied nations that had begun arriving in the Indian Ocean to join in on the post-9/11 counteroffensive against terrorist groups, codenamed Operation "Enduring Freedom."

United into a squadron designated as Combined Task Force 150, with a few U.S. Navy warships also occasionally taking part, command of this separate formation was to be shared in turns: German Admiral Gottfried Hoch being appointed as Combined Task Force 150's first commander on May 5, 2002, to be succeeded a few months later by Spanish Rear Admiral Juan Moreno, etc.

Another similar allied unit formed as part of Operation "Enduring Freedom" and attached to USNavCent, would be Combined Task Force 152, comprised of regional navies and coast guard forces and established in March 2004 to "coordinate Theater Security Cooperation" in the international waters of the Arabian Gulf. Operations initially focused on local counterterrorism and security efforts, actively seeking to impede the use of those waters as a venue for a terrorist attack, or to transport hostile personnel, weapons, or other material along its coastlines. This formation consequently conducted Maritime Security Operations (MSO) in the territorial waters of all Gulf Cooperation Council nations, and has since expanded its mission to promote stability and maritime prosperity throughout the region. At the time of this writing, Combined Task Force 152 is commanded by Colonel Tareq Khalfan A. Al Zaabi of United Arab Emirates Navy Staff.

European and NATO Formations

As Somali pirates resumed their depredations after their usual summer-long hiatus for the monsoon season of 2008, striking ever farther out at sea early that autumn, with greater vigor than before, allied European nations began initiating their own independent antipiracy efforts—with Washington's full approval and support—so as to combat this growing menace to their oil-and commercial routes passing near the Horn of Africa, coordinating all efforts through the United Nations. Eventually, both the North Atlantic Treaty Organization (of which the United States is a leading member) and the European Union would dispatch separate expeditions into those troubled waters, uniting with already existing American, regional, and other multinational forces in a joint campaign to try to bring this problem under control.

NATO or North Atlantic Treaty Organization
c/o Allied Maritime
Component Command
Atlantic Building
Northwood Headquarters
Northwood, Middlesex
England HA6 3HP
Tel: +44 (0) 1923, 956763 (Public Affairs)
e-Address: manw.nato.int

This long-established alliance headquartered at Brussels, Belgium, created in April 1949 for collective defense during the aftermath of World War II and today comprised of the United States plus more than two-dozen other nations, was the first group to respond to a special request from the UN Secretary-General, to dispatch more warships into the Horn of Africa region, to temporarily supplement the few overworked naval vessels that were already escorting chartered merchantmen through those pirate-infested waters, delivering World Food Program humanitarian shipments into starving pockets of Somalia.

The NATO Council therefore agreed in late October 2008 to answer this plea, and before that month was out, the four warships of its Standing NATO Maritime Group 2 arrived off Somalia, to bolster the ongoing escort services under its operational codename of "Allied Provider." A second expedition was organized in March 2009, when Standing NATO Maritime Group 1 was also ordered to supplant the first deployment in that theater, and with even more robust mission orders to actively "deter, defend against, and disrupt pirate activities." This five-warship squadron included the 225-man, 4,100-ton guided-missile frigate USS *Halyburton*, which four days after this particular group had reached the Gulf of Aden on March 24, 2009, disrupted a pirate attack against the yacht *Grandezza*. SNMG-1 would continue patrolling in those waters for more than three more months, under the codename of Operation "Allied Protector."

NATO's third "contribution to international efforts to combat piracy off the Horn of Africa" came in August 2009, and proved even more ambitious. Codenamed Operation "Ocean Shield" and consisting of another five warships of a reconstituted NATO Maritime Group 2—including the 280-man, 8,900-ton American destroyer USS *Laboon*—it was not only tasked with chasing pirates, but furthermore the diplomatic mission of building up contacts and better relationships with regional governments so that they too might begin developing their own local counterpiracy measures.

Operation "Ocean Shield" has been authorized to continue until at least December 2012, with fresh squadrons arriving in succession to relieve one another, each performing four-month tours. In the spring of 2010, the NATO force deployed in the Gulf of Aden and off the Horn of Africa consisted of the 250-man, 5,300-ton British frigate HMS *Chatham* (flag); the 280-man, 8.900-ton American frigate USS *Cole*; the 220-man, 4,100-ton Turkish frigate

TCG *Gelibolu*; the 3,650-ton Greek frigate HS *Limnos*; and the 225-man, 3,100-ton Italian frigate ITS *Scirocco*. Typical actions included dispersal for an immediate helicopter reconnaissance of pirate bases along the Somali coast by *Scirocco*; a simultaneous rescue in the Gulf of Aden by *Gelibolu*—guided by a French surveillance-plane from the EU naval force—which steamed to the aid of the Danish chemical-carrier *Torm Ragmhild* as it was being chased by two pirate boats (plus the subsequent freeing of these pursuers' "mother ship," the hijacked dhow *Safina-al-Gavatri*); a sweep far out into the Indian Ocean by *Limnos*, which—piloted by Swedish and Luxembourgian patrol aircraft stationed in the Seychelles—snapped up 30 pirates and destroyed six attack boats between April 7–9, 2010; while to the east of the Gulf of Aden, *Chatham* doggedly shadowed the hijacked Indian dhow *Vishvakalyan* for three days, until it ran out of fuel and its pirate captors abandoned it to flee back into Somali waters.

Diplomatic efforts were equally as important, as on April 28, 2010, this NATO flagship hosted a visit by a delegation of eight representatives from in and around the pirate-controlled seaport of Eyl and its district, which included Suldan Said M. Garase, one of two traditional leaders for its Nugal region; a local chieftain and spiritual leader named Khalif Aw Ali; Abdi Hersi Alim, Governor for the Nugal region; as well as Mussé Osman Yusuf, the Mayor of Eyl's district.

EU NavFor or "European Union Naval Force"
Sandy Lane
Northwood, Middlesex
England HA6 3HP
Tel: +44 (0) 1923, 958611 (Media Center)
e-Address: www.eunavfor.eu

A joint task-force organized by a worried European Union, to patrol the troubled waters off the Horn of Africa in concert with other allied formations. The EU had already, with the establishment of EU NavCO in September 2008, created a coordination cell at its headquarters in Brussels, to receive input on this mushrooming problem from a broad cross section of the maritime community. Part of its buildup for combating piracy in that region, this office would soon evolve into the "Maritime Security Center-Horn of Africa" or MSC-HOA, an information hub for gathering and disseminating news on piratical activity in the Gulf of Aden, as well as tracking the movements of merchantmen transiting through its troubled waters, so as to provide better coordination with EU and other naval forces destined for that region.

Then at a general meeting in Brussels on November 10, 2008, its foreign ministers agreed to dispatch five to seven frigates, with a requisite number of support aircraft, within a month into the Horn of Africa region to protect merchant shipping from pirates, in addition to escorting WFP food relief shipments into Somalia. Codenamed "Operation Atalanta," this expedition represented an unprecedented step—the first independent naval campaign ever launched by what had formerly been only a financial, political, and cultural confederation.

The first six warships and three patrol aircraft, manned by a total of 1,200 men, began departing as of December 9, 2008 under the overall command of British Rear Admiral Phillip Jones. EU NavFor's first engagement occurred on Christmas Day 2008, when the 3,700-ton German frigate *Karlsruhe* received a distress call from the 65,000-ton Egyptian bulk carrier *Wadi-al-Arab*, as it was transiting through the Gulf of Aden. The German frigate promptly launched its helicopter, which drove off a pursuing pirate skiff with gunfire. An Egyptian seaman was subsequently treated for a pirate gunshot wound, while the suspected perpetrators were also detained, then released without their arms. More recent actions include:

- On the evening of April 30, 2010, a twin-engine Swedish patrol-aircraft out of the Seychelles spots a trio of suspect boats, roaming 450 nautical miles east of Somalia. Rear Admiral Jan Thörnquist, aboard his EU NavFor flagship— the 170-man, 3,800-ton HSwMS *Carlskrona*—directs the 750-man, 32,300-ton French amphibious assault-ship *Tonnerre* on an interception course, which sights this whaler and two skiffs by next morning, launching a helicopter to make a closer inspection. The 11 occupants are filmed frantically tossing their weaponry overboard, so that they are arrested on suspicion of piracy, their whaler being destroyed, and two skiffs hoisted onboard the carrier, along with their incriminating evidence.
- This same day of May 1, 2010, a helicopter from the 140-man, 3,600-ton French frigate *La Fayette* sights another pair of suspicious boats far out at sea, halfway

between Mogadishu and the Seychelles. This whaler and skiff attempt to flee, tossing weaponry overboard, until fired upon. The nine occupants are arrested on suspicion of piracy, the whaler destroyed, and the skiff retained as evidence.

- On the morning of May 4, 2010, while escorting a merchant convoy through the International Recommended Transit Corridor in the Gulf of Aden, a Super Auk-12 helicopter from a Japanese warship spots a suspicious skiff with seven men aboard, prowling 50 miles south of Al Mukalla in Yemen. After radioing EU NavFor, the 200-man, 3,360-ton Greek frigate HS *Elli* is sent to investigate. The skiff flees, tossing materials overboard, until fired upon; a boarding party eventually decides to release the now-unarmed skiff.

- On the morning of May 5, 2010, a Swedish patrol plane out of the Seychelles spots a trio of suspect pirate craft, roaming 400 nautical miles northwest of those islands. The French frigate *La Fayette* is directed on an interception course, and sights this whaler and two skiffs later that same afternoon. When one of the skiffs attempts to flee, its twin outboard-motors are destroyed by a burst of gunfire, and a total of twelve pirates are captured.

- Learning that the Russian-owned, Liberian-flagged tanker *Moscow University* has been boarded by pirates approximately 350 miles east of Suqutra Island, its 23 crewmen having retreated inside their fortified rudder compartment, the 300-man, 7,900-ton Russian destroyer *Marshal Shaposhnikov* races to the rescue. A EU NavFor aircraft soon arrives over the tanker and establishes radio-contact with its crew, while a German plane attached to the U.S.-led Combined Task Force 151 remains on standby, along with numerous other naval support-units. When *Shaposhnikov* sights the tanker on the morning of May 6, 2010, it launches a helicopter to reconnoiter, which is fired at by the pirates. Knowing the crew to be safe below decks, the Russian warship returns fire and a boarding party storms aboard, killing one pirate and capturing ten others, in freeing this vessel.

- On May 7, 2010, a Swedish patrol plane out of the Seychelles sights another trio of pirate craft, and the 130-man, 16,800-ton Dutch amphibious assault-ship *Johan de Witt* is sent to intercept. As it approaches this whaler and two skiffs by mid-afternoon, 11 pirates are observed tossing their weapons overboard, so that all are arrested.

Somali Coastal Forces

Since initiating regular antipiracy sweeps and convoy-escorts through the Gulf of Aden, European governments have also tried to cultivate partnerships with the fractured Somali governments along its southern shores. These efforts have achieved some degree of success in deflecting pirate raids out of the Gulf's narrow and vulnerable shipping lanes, for despite the sporadic sorties which are all that Somaliland's or Puntland's run-down naval strength can manage with only a handful of dilapidated patrol-boats, fear of a lengthy incarceration in one of their prisons has nonetheless driven many pirates to instead seek to hunt prey in the distant waters of the Indian Ocean.

Somaliland Coast Guard
Berbera, Somalia
e-Address: somalilandgov.com

Because of its strategic position directly overlooking the western reaches of the Gulf of Aden, the autonomous, divided, and ramshackle State of Somaliland (once a colony known as "British Somaliland") has been encouraged by various Western governments to maintain coast-guard activity in its territorial waters, in hopes of intercepting a few small pirate boats which might come sneaking along its extensive coastline, with the intent of veering steering out into the nearby international shipping lanes to snap up merchantmen.

In May 2010, the few-score men serving aboard the three tiny patrol-boats of the Somaliland Coast Guard were under the command of Vice Admiral Ahmed Ali Salah, headquartered in the shabby wreck-strewn harbor of Berbera. A system of informants sometimes gave warning of the transit of suspected pirate boats, while Western navies also deposited captives ashore to stand trial. Those convicted are incarcerated within Mandheera maximum-security prison, simmering about 30 miles out in the desert, south of the capital. The government of Somaliland is willing to sustain such efforts in hopes of having their breakaway State eventually recognized as an independent republic—"We do everything right," its exasperated President once told a Western reporter, "We even fight piracy!"—but most Western nations are still waiting for an African country to be the first to do so.

Puntland Coast Guard
("Ilaalinta Xeebaha Puntland")
Bossaso, Somalia
e-Mail Contact: info@puntlandgovt.com

Like Somaliland, the neighboring State of Puntland also has a vested interest in being seen to help the international community fight piracy and convict outside marauders, although its naval component is only a ramshackle unit with a colorfully checkered history. A couple of years after the separate "Puntland State of Somalia" had been established in 1998, a force of 70 militiamen—drawn from a careful cross section of all local clans—was organized in the year 2000 by the private British firm Hart Security Maritime Services, Ltd., to patrol close offshore in a single 65-foot trawler, acting against illegal fishing or toxic-waste dumping.

However, when a revolt erupted next year, these British advisers left and the President of Puntland was then overthrown by his predecessor, the ex-guerrilla chieftain Abdullahi Yusuf, who granted a new contract to reconstitute its coast guard—as well as administer offshore fishing licenses, a lucrative arrangement which entailed splitting any proceeds with the government—to a company headed by his supporters the Taars, a family of Somali exiles resettled in Toronto, Canada. They increased the Puntland Coast Guard's strength to more than 300 men aboard eight lightly armed oceangoing craft, yet when Yusuf was elected as national President and departed for Mogadishu late in 2004, a falling out ensued between the Taars and the new President of Puntland: Another exile returned from Canada, General Mohamud Musé Hersi.

Already beset by economic difficulties, the Taars were further embarrassed in March 2005 when three of their Coast Guardsmen—unpaid for almost three months—hijacked the Thai trawler *Sirichainava 12* and demanded $800,000 in ransom. An armed boarding party from the 167-man, 3,250-ton U.S. Coast Guard cutter *Munro*, backed by a Royal Navy attack helicopter, ended this standoff, with the three renegade Somali Coast Guardsmen being flown off to face trial in Bangkok, being sentenced to 10 years's imprisonment in Thailand as pirates.

Puntland's President Hersi consequently cancelled the remainder of the Taars's five-year contract to administer Coast Guard operations late in 2005, instead granting it to the Saudi company Al-Hababi. Some 250 new recruits were given basic training at Gardo, and this new force even made a two-day sortie from Bossaso in late April 2007, which netted nine trespassing trawlers, plus a pair of ships from Yemen and Egypt. However, the contract with Al-Hababi was subsequently cancelled in February 2008 and restored to the Taars by Hersi, after the Puntland Coast Guard had refused a direct Presidential order to free the hijacked tug *Svitzer Korsakov.*

Puntland Intelligence Service

This potentially useful unit was originally created in 2002 with financing from the U.S. government as part of Washington's global offensive against terror, intended to serve as a regional "intelligence and counter-terrorism agency" working in concert with American forces stationed in Djibouti. However, the Puntland Intelligence Service's headquarters in the city of Bossaso was blasted by two simultaneous suicide bomb attacks on October 29, 2008.

Darawiish

A paramilitary force, originally raised to be "primarily engaged in border security," and as such which might have been deployed against pirate boats circulating through Puntland's territorial waters out of central Somalia, along with their prizes. However, the Darawiish—several thousand strong—were soon converted in the lawless and fractious State to serve its government as an internal police force, and even engaged in combat against military forces from neighboring Somaliland during their frequent cross-border clashes.

Regional Coordinating Hubs

As the U.S. and Western navies began ramping up antipiracy patrols and escorted convoys in 2008, most especially through the pirate-infested waters of the Gulf of Aden, the dissemination of information to and from transiting commercial vessels became of primary importance for reducing and eventually defeating such criminality. Consequently, the European Union and United

Kingdom Maritime Trade Organization both set up purposely created communication centers, which operated in close concert with each other and the U.S. Navy's Marine Liaison Office in Bahrain.

Through a carefully coordinated system, sightings of suspected pirate craft by patrol aircraft, warships, or passing merchantmen could be gathered and instantly shared among all affected parties. Advisories could be issued, alternate routes proposed, danger zones avoided, all by on-line postings or radio communications. More distant approaching vessels could be redirected, even assembled into convoys, without slowing down the flow of traffic funneling into this chokepoint. And any merchantmen which did chance to be attacked, could contact either of these hubs by phone or e-mail even in the very act of being boarded, as they are kept manned 24 hours a day. This distress-signal would in turn be relayed to the nearest patrolling warship, so as to steam toward the rescue.

MARLO or "Marine Liaison Office"
U.S. Navy
P. O. Box 116
Manama, Bahrain
Tel: +973, 1785 3927
Cell: +973, 3944 2117
Fax: +973, 1785 3930
e-Address: Marlo.bahrain@me.navy.mil

The U.S. Navy's "Marine Liaison Office," located in Central Command's main headquarters in Manama, Bahrain. It helps coordinate exchanges of information between both the U.S. and coalition navies, as well as friendly regional coast-guard services.

MSC-HOA or "Maritime Security Centre (Horn of Africa)"
c/o EU NavFor
Sandy Lane
Northwood, Middlesex
ENGLAND HA6 3HP
Tel: +44 (0) 1923, 958545
Fax: +44 (0) 1923, 958520
e-Address: www.mschoa.org

An information hub established by European Union Naval Force Somali out of its West London headquarters, for gathering and disseminating news on piratical activities, as well as tracking movements of merchantmen through the troubled sea lanes of the Gulf of Aden.

UKMTO Dubai
Tel: +971 50 552, 3215
Fax: +971 4 306, 5710
e-Address: UKMTO@eim.ae

A British-run regional office, a subsidiary located in Dubai to serve as "the first point of contact" for merchant ships transiting through the Gulf of Aden or Horn of Africa region. The United Kingdom Maritime Trade Organization records details on courses and estimated times of arrival, publishes bulletins on-line with the latest intelligence, offers advice on the safety of routes, and maintains a round-the-clock listening post to receive distress calls or other radioed information from ships at sea, which can immediately be relayed to Maritime Security Center—Horn of Africa or other naval authorities. Every week, the UKMTO also issues a *Piracy Analysis and Warning Weekly (PAWW) Report*, apprising transiting mariners of expected dangers "in or near the Gulf of Aden and off the East coast of Somalia."

International Monitoring Agencies

Reports on the number and concentrations of piratical attacks world-wide, are marshaled and compiled several times a year by more remote institutions, to be used in a variety of ways. The U.S. Navy's Office of Naval Intelligence and the U.S. Department of Transportation's Maritime Administration use them to warn American mariners of danger-prone areas around the world. The United Nations' London-based International Maritime Organization monitors similar statistics for that multinational organization, while its Contact Group on Piracy off the Coast of Somalia assembles sporadically to report on the problem out of that specific troubled country. The International Maritime Bureau of the International Chambers of Commerce are concerned by piracy's particular effect on shipping and insurance rates, its Piracy

Reporting Center in Kuala Lumpur being the most often-quoted monitoring agency in this regard.

Civil Maritime Analysis Department
Office of Naval Intelligence
United States Navy
Washington, D.C.
Tel: 1-301-669-4905
Fax: 1-301-669-3247
e-Address: dpearl@nmic.navy.mil

Collates information from global sources and issues a weekly "Worldwide Threat to Shipping Report," which is posted for general consultation at the National Geospatial-Intelligence Agency's Maritime Safety Web site at nga.mil/portal/site/maritime.

Commercial Crime Services
c/o International Maritime Bureau
Cinnabar Wharf
26 Wapping High Street
London, England E1W 1NG
Tel: +44 (0)20, 7423 6960

The anti-crime division of the International Chamber of Commerce, which oversees three bureaus in total, two of which deal with Financial Investigation and Counterfeiting. The third, the International Maritime Bureau, is tasked with all other aspects for prevention of "trade fraud and malpractice," including acts of piracy.

Contact Group on Piracy Off the Coast of Somalia

A multilateral organization established by the United Nations to coordinate the antipiracy efforts of the various U.S., NATO, European Union, regional, and other naval forces patrolling the waters off the Horn of Africa. It has been criticized for not meeting regularly, and not including the two main groups that are most concerned in this problem: the owner-operators of the small coastal craft Maritime Security Center—Horn of Africa that make up the bulk of victims in the Gulf of Aden, and the Somalis themselves.

International Maritime Bureau
c/o International Chamber of Commerce
Cinnabar Wharf
26 Wapping High Street
London, England E1W 1NG
Tel: +44 (0)20, 7423 6960

A specialized division of the International Chamber of Commerce, the IMB was created in 1981 to fight all aspects of maritime crime and fraud.

International Maritime Organization
4, Albert Embankment
London, England SE1 7SR
Tel: +44 (0)20, 7735 7611
e-Address: www.imo.org

A United Nations's agency headquartered in London, originally created in 1959 to help regulate all aspects of safe international sea traffic. Among its numerous other activities today, the IMO coordinates international efforts to counter piratical acts.

Also maintains the "Maritime Knowledge Centre," whose online catalog can be accessed at MaritimeKnowledgeCentre@imo.org.

Maritime Administration
Office of Ship Operations, MAR-613
West Building
1200 New Jersey Avenue SE
Washington, D.C. 20590
Tel: 1-800-996-2723
Fax: 1-202-366-3954
e-Address: www.marad.dot.gov or opcentr1@marad.dot.gov

An agency of the U.S. Department of Transportation, created to facilitate all aspects of American waterborne transportation, in both domestic and international waters. Among many other duties, the Maritime Administration compiles and publishes reports on piratical acts around the globe, and issues advisories to forewarn American ship-masters and merchant seamen.

International Maritime Bureau Piracy Reporting Center
Kuala Lumpur, Malaysia
Tel: +60 3, 2031 0014
     +44 (0)20, 7423 6960 (main)
Fax: +60 3, 2078 5769
e-Address: piracy@icc-ccs.org

Often abbreviated as "IMB PRC," this office is maintained by the International Maritime Bureau (see above) out of London, England—itself a specialized division of the International Chamber of Commerce. The Piracy Reporting Center was created in October 1992 to record any and all piratical attacks occurring anywhere in the world, gathering up such data so as to provide warnings to seamen, shippers, and insurers, as well as to exert pressure on governments to eradicate such crimes. Its Web site offers weekly piracy alerts and a live map, listing actual and attempted pirate attacks by year from 2001 to the present, plus other information which can be accessed at www.icc-ccs.org/prc/piracyreport.php.

Somali Pirate Syndicates

Precise details on the numerous regional groups which have participated in past attacks, and are currently conducting forays off 1,000 miles of Somali coastline—as well as striking into the neighboring Gulf of Aden and far out into the Indian Ocean—is not only vague, but subject to frequent shifts or reinterpretations. Generally speaking, the most active and renowned pirate bases are scattered around three dilapidated seaports strung along the Indian Ocean coastline of central Somalia and southern Puntland: Eyl, Hobyo, and Haradheere. All are virtually inaccessible by overland roads out of the interior of the country, and their resident pirate syndicates are too influential and entrenched for local authorities to challenge them, if any should prove so inclined. Other reports suggest that there are three vague pirate agglomerations in Somalia: the "Northern Gang" based around Eyl; the "Central Gang" at Hobyo; and the "Southern Gang" around Harardheere, although none acknowledges these names.

A United Nations intelligence summary of May 2006, misleadingly identified four main pirate groups as operating at that time off the Somali coast:

1. The "National Volunteer Coast Guard" or NVCG, commanded by Garaad Mohamed, which is said to specialize in intercepting small boats and fishing vessels around Kismayu on the southern coast.
2. The "Marka Group," under the command of Sheikh Yusuf Mohamed Siad (also known as Yusuf Indha'adde), made up of several scattered and less-organized groups operating around the town of Marka.
3. Traditional Somali fishermen carrying gunmen out of Puntland, referred to generally as the 'Puntland Group."
4. The "Somali Marines," reputed to be the most powerful and sophisticated of the pirate groups with a military structure, a fleet admiral, vice admiral, head of financial operations, etc.

However, this information is garbled and repeats some common mistakes, such as:

"National Volunteer Coast Guard"

Eyl, Somalia

A misinterpretation of the Somali expression badaadinta badah, which literally means "saviors of the sea," although it is most often rendered in English-language translations as "coast guard." Because of its positive connotations, this expression is preferred by pirates and often used—in several variants by different pirate groups—to lend a veneer of legitimacy to their depredations at sea.

"Somali Marines"

Harardheere, Somalia

Fictitious nickname once given to the pirate organization created by Mohamed Abdi Hassan Hayir, more commonly known as "Afweyne." In 2003, this unemployed civil servant had sought to transform the random forays being launched by ad hoc bands against passing vessels offshore, into a profitable business venture. He gathered some seed money and hired successful pirates from Eyl to instruct his own followers at Harardheere. Afweyne's new organization would soon become characterized by its deliberate planning, focus of purpose, and logistical support.

The effectiveness of these new rovers began to garner international attention as of 2005. Next year, the UN Monitoring-Group would describe Afweyne's self-servingly titled Somali

Marines as "the most sophisticated of all Somali pirate groups" (Report S/2006/229). Not only could they operate at much greater distance offshore than other bands, they furthermore specialized in grand-scale "acts of piracy involving vessel seizure, kidnapping, and ransom demands," rather than petty robbery. The UN report also noted how during the capture and exploitation of the Indian vessel *Safina Al Bisarat*, "the Somali Marines demonstrated an effective level of competence and knowledge of dhow operations, and the maritime environment in which they operated" (ibid.).

However, as better intelligence was gathered on Afweyne's shadowy network, the term Somali Marines came to be dropped, although this loose-knit confederacy continues to operate around Harardheere today, partly under the direction of Afweyne's son. Major financiers of pirate enterprises remain shadowy, for obvious reasons, while government figures deny any knowledge of their activities—yet many are suspected of at least pocketing bribes derived from ransoms, if not outright complicity. The raiders themselves are usually teenage gunmen and poor fishermen, operating under the radioed directions of a veteran sub commander, who is often aboard a nearby mother ship or even stationed hundreds of miles away on land. Hijacked vessels are anchored openly offshore, and supplied for weeks on end by local merchants, who are paid once any ransoms are received.

Another UN report, compiled more than three years later in November 2008, offered more refined intelligence on this matter, Pirate groups revolve around clan and sub-clan lines, but are not exclusively so, with members from other clans accepted into the groups if they have a pakrticular skill that may be required, or they need extra numbers. Pirates also entice *bona fide* fishermen to forego using their skiffs at sea, and use them to assist the pirates, who will be paid far more than they can earn at fishing. There are also reports of fishermen being bullied into assisting the pirates, who generally have little or no knowledge of the sea. The most active groups involved in piracy include the following:

- Eyl: Isse Mahmuud and Leelkase of the Darood clan
- Garad: Omar Mahmuud of the Darood clan
- Hobyo: Habargedir (Saad, Ayr, Suleiman) of the Hawiye clan
- Harardheere: Habargedir (Ayr, Sarur, Suleiman) of the Hawiye clan
- Mogadishu: Habargedir (Ayr) of the Hawiye clan

At present, the epicenter of piracy is Puntland, where it is penetrating all levels of society, including government structures at both senior and junior level. A number of Puntland ministers are suspected of being involved in piracy and its attendant activities.

The pirates raise their manpower from the coastal localities of their bases, surrounding villages, and other clan members from the interior. Due to the lack of employment, there is no shortage of willing recruits for the business. Most of the operatives involved in piracy have very little education and would not find employment with any commercial operation or humanitarian-agency, except as an armed guard. From information received from a convicted pirate, a single armed pirate can earn anywhere from $6,000 to $10,000 from a $1 million ransom. This is approximately equivalent to a two-to-three-year salary for an armed guard at a humanitarian agency and much better than a local commercial enterprise would pay. The pirates also encourage fishermen to join their operations with the enticement of payments outlined above. By enticing fishermen to join their gangs, they get marine and boat-handling knowledge, and the use of their skiffs.

It is evident from the numbers of ships hijacked at any one time, that there is an almost endless supply of recruits available. These numbers do not include the support groups on land that support the pirates at sea, once they have pirated the vessel. These would include local traders supplying food, water, soft drinks, tea, qat, and whatever other necessities are required during a long drawn-out negotiation.

The pirates rely for logistical support upon the fishing communities where they live, or from which they are temporarily operating. These communities provide them with food, water, and shelter. Where on board food supplies prove inadequate for the crew and the pirates, provisions are supplied from ashore. Supplies of weapons and equipment (including ladders and grappling hooks) are judged to be easily obtainable, whilst the more sophisticated equipment, including satellite-phones and GPS navigation systems are likely to be the result of investing profits to increase capability.

Interesting, in terms of other "victims of Piracy," the pirates are strongly reliant on the traditionally lower-caste groups of fisherman to provide technical support to the operations. The pirates from nomadic, land-based clans cannot swim, and know very little about the ocean. Some are said to receive a basic salary only, and some are forced into the work.

While some members and businesses of the communities benefit from the acts of piracy, either intentionally or be default, other members of the communities speak out openly and directly against piracy. These include the religious leaders, who have condemned piracy and advised their communities not to support this action. They advise people not to be attracted by the wealth of the pirates, and have declared that any marriage to a pirate is regarded in their eyes as null and void, and therefore breaking strict Islamic law.

Source

Report S/2006/229 *of the U.N. Monitoring Group on Somalia, Submitted to the Security Council on May 4, 2006.* New York: United Nations Security Council, 2006.

8

Resources

If you ask around, everybody will tell you pirates are bad. But that's just in conversation . . .

—Haji Abdi Warsame, an elder from the coastal
Somali town of Eyl, October 2008

Because of a widespread and unflagging interest in the topic of piracy, a great many works are produced every year on this subject, from sensationalized mass-media accounts to more measured professional or scholarly studies. The following selections constitute a representative cross-sampling from among a far more plentiful body of materials, having been selected as carefully as possible, to avoid too much repetition of published works.

General Studies and Overviews

Bateman, Sam. "International Solutions to Problems of Maritime Security—Think Globally, Act Regionally!" *Maritime Studies* 139 (November–December 2004), pp. 9–17.

Pair of overview articles written by a retired Australian naval Commodore, who obtained a doctorate from the University of New South Wales, and specializes in maritime policy and regional security concerns.

———. "Piracy and the Challenge of Cooperative Security and Enforcement Policy." *Maritime Studies* 117 (March–April 2001), pp. 11–22.

Booth, Forrest, and Altenbrun, Larry. "Maritime and Port Security, Piracy, and Stowaways: Renewed Concerns over Old Problems." *University of San Francisco Maritime Law Journal* 15 (2002–03), pp. 1–47.

Scholarly article on modern international complications of policing various aspects of criminality at sea, amid heightened post-9/11 concerns.

Chalk, Peter. *The Maritime Dimension of International Security: Terrorism, Piracy, and Challenges for the United States.* Santa Monica, California: The Rand Corp., 2008. Found at www.rand.org.

A study prepared for the U.S. Air Force, assessing the potential threat from a "nexus" between modern pirates and terrorists, to launch a seaborne attack against the United States.

Ellen, Eric, editor. *Piracy at Sea.* Paris: International Chamber of Commerce for the International Maritime Bureau, March 1989.

One of the earliest overviews signaling a resurgence of criminality at sea, prepared by a former Chief Constable of the Port of London Police force.

Elliot, Robert. "Piracy on the High Seas." *Security Management* 51, Number 6 (June 2007), pp. 40–42.

Report indicating that while the number of pirate attacks worldwide has declined, their level of violence has risen, so that law-enforcement countermeasures must be maintained.

Farley, Mark C. "International and Regional Trends in Maritime Piracy, 1989–1993." Monterey, CA: Naval Postgraduate School, December 1993.

Unpublished thesis by a Lieutenant-Commander. in the U.S. Navy, toward a Master's degree in National Security Affairs; includes analysis of a database of 523 acts of piracy reported world-wide between January 1989 and September 1993.

Gottschalk, Jack A., and Flanagan, Brian P. *Jolly Roger with an Uzi: The Rise and Threat of Modern Piracy.* Annapolis: Naval Institute Press, 2000.

Wide-ranging book, covering historical eras and warning of the resurgence of criminality at sea off Indonesia, Brazil, Somalia, and in the South

China Sea, written by two lawyers familiar with modern piracy's consequences.

Heathcote, Peter. "An Explanation of the New Measures for Maritime Security Aboard Ships and in Port Facilities." *Maritime Studies* 137 (July–August 2004), pp. 13–21.

Article published in an international journal dedicated to modern marine issues, published by the Center for Maritime Research headquartered in Amsterdam.

Herrmann, Wilfried A. "Maritime Piracy and Anti-Piracy Measures, Part I: Piracy—Increasing Challenge with New Dimensions." *Naval Forces* 25 (February 2004), pp.18–25.

Wide-ranging article written by a German specialist in Asian studies.

International Maritime Bureau. *Piracy and Armed Robbery Against Ships, Annual Report: 1 January–31 December 2004.* Barking, Essex, England: International Chamber of Commerce Publishing, 2005.

One of a series of publications issued by this monitoring agency.

———. *Piracy and Armed Robbery Against Ships: Annual Report 2006.* Barking, England: International Chamber of Commerce Publishing, 2006.

See above.

———. *Piracy and Armed Robbery against Ships: Report for the Period January 1–December 31, 2008.* Barking, England: International Chamber of Commerce Publishing, 2009.

See above.

Jane's Overview 2008: Growth of Merchant Shipping. London: Jane's Information Group, 2008.

Brief annual report describing the state of world shipping by a British publisher who has long specialized in all aspects of naval issues.

Langewiesche, William. *The Outlaw Sea: A World of Freedom, Chaos, and Crime.* New York: Farrar, Straus & Giroux, 2004.

A sweeping overview by a well-traveled American journalist, describing the problems emerging from current maritime practices; only partly related to piracy.

Lehr, Peter, editor. *Violence at Sea: Piracy in the Age of Global Terrorism.* New York: Routledge, 2007.

An overview of modern piracy off the African coast, in the Arabian Sea, Bay of Bengal, Straits of Malacca, and South China Sea, with contributions from various specialists, all edited by an expert on Asian studies.

Ménard, Christian, chief editor and compiler. *Rapport d'information déposé en application de l'article 145 du Règlement par la Commission de la Défense nationale et des forces armies, sur la piraterie maritime.* Paris: l'Assemblée nationale, May 13, 2009.

A detailed and lengthy overview of the problems from modern piracy, presented by a Deputy to the French National Assembly.

Murphy, Martin N. *Contemporary Piracy and Maritime Terrorism: The Threat to International Security.* London: Adelphi Paper 338 for the International Institute for Strategic Studies, 2007.

A study assessing the potential of modern piracy to facilitate terrorist acts.

———. "Slow Alarm: The Response of the Marine Insurance Industry to the Threat of Piracy and Maritime Terrorism." *Maritime Studies* 148 (May–June 2006), pp. 1–14.

Parritt, Brian A. H. *Crime at Sea: A Practical Guide.* London: The Nautical Institute, 1996.

A manual intended for merchant Masters, written by a British Brigadier with a background in intelligence work.

———. *Security at Sea: Terrorism, Piracy, and Drugs—A Practical Guide.* London: Nautical Institute, 1991.

A manual intended for merchant Masters, written by a British Brigadier with a background in intelligence work.

———, editor. *Violence at Sea: A Review of Terrorism, Acts of War and Piracy, and Countermeasures to Prevent Terrorism.* Paris: International Chamber of Commerce Publishing, 1986.

Compilation of various papers presented in March 1986 at a workshop convened by the International Maritime Bureau at San Jose State University in California.

Reinhardt, Charles J. "Maritime Piracy: Sign of a Security Threat?" *Mercer on Transport & Logistics* 11, Number 1 (2005), pp. 16–19.

Brief statistical analysis of piratical incidents reported between 1995 and 2003 to the International Maritime Bureau, assessing their spread and potential threat.

Roach, J. Ashley. "Initiatives to Enhance Maritime Security at Sea." *Marine Policy* 28, Number 1 (2004), pp. 41–66.

General study of the many threats at sea—including hijacking, gunrunning, drug-smuggling, terrorists, migrant-smuggling, and armed robbery—which can be mitigated by multinational cooperation.

Romi-Levin, Rivka. *Piracy at Sea: Bibliography.* Haifa, Israel: Wydra Institute of Shipping and Aviation Research, July 2003.

Includes definitions of piracy; antipiracy measures for vessels; a 2003 International Maritime Organization report listing reported attacks by region; plus useful tables and diagrams, etc.

Talley, Wayne K. *Maritime Safety, Security, and Piracy.* London: Informa Law, 2008.

General overview of diverse aspects affecting the safety of ships and ports, written for the maritime industry.

Touret, Corinne. *La piraterie au vingtième siècle: Piraterie maritime et aérienne.* Paris: Librairie Générale de Droit et de Jurisprudence, 1992.

Study written by a French legal scholar, based upon her doctoral dissertation in obtaining a degree in Public Law.

Unsinger, Peter Charles. "Meeting a Commercial Need for Intelligence: The International Maritime Bureau." *International Journal of Intelligence and Counterintelligence* 12, Number 1 (March 1999), pp. 58–72.

Description of the monitoring bureau run by Eric Ellen, former Chief Constable of the Port of London Police force.

Villar, Roger. *Piracy Today: Robbery and Violence at Sea since 1980.* London: Conway Maritime Press, 1985.

Written by a Royal Navy Captain who was a decorated World War II veteran, and later helped found Jane's Information Services after retiring from the sea.

Walters, Stephen. "Contemporary Maritime Piracy." *Crime & Justice International* 23, Number 96 (January–February 2007), pp. 10–16.

Analyzes data on global pirate attacks in 2004 from the International Maritime Bureau's statistics, finding that most were by lone groups with low-tech weapons against anchored ships, the most violent incidents occurring in the Far East and Southeast Asia. Expresses concern, among other things, that future pirate attacks might shift into congested shipping lanes.

Background and History

Starting in the decade immediately following the conclusion of World War II, shipping industries all over the globe not only began a remarkable revival from their catastrophic losses during that struggle, they also entered into a period of unprecedented change and expansion. Sea lanes would become crowded with many more and much larger merchantmen, yet flying a myriad of unfamiliar flags and manned by greatly reduced crews of mixed nationalities, providing easy prey for tiny bands of armed pirates.

Maritime Transformation

The relatively small freighters and traders of the immediate post-World War II era, each manned by several-dozen Western seamen to operate its onboard winches, booms, etc., would soon become a thing of the past.

Greenman, David. "Freedom Freighters." *Ships Monthly* [UK], June 1976.

Brief but knowledgeable article about the basic Allied freighter designs prevalent during World War II, and which were subsequently sold off once peace was restored to form the backbone of the first postwar commercial fleets, both domestically and foreign.

Greenwald, Richard A.; Gibson, Andrew; and Donovan, Arthur. *The Abandoned Ocean: A History of United States Maritime Policy.* Columbia: University of South Carolina Press, 2000.

Detailed study of the abrupt decline of United States's merchant marine since the end of World War II, going from when U.S.-flagged vessels carried more than 55 percent of all global seaborne commerce in 1946, to a figure which today has been reduced to scarcely one percent.

La Pedraja, Rene de. *The Rise and Decline of U.S. Merchant Shipping in the Twentieth Century.* New York: Cengage Gale, 1992.

A comprehensive history of the rise and fall of the U.S. merchant shipping industry, from 1901 when financier J. P. Morgan's infamous International Mercantile Marine or IMM launched the nation into world trade.

Marx, Daniel, Jr. "The Merchant Ship Sales Act of 1946." *The Journal of Business of the University of Chicago* 21, Number 1 (January 1948), pp. 12–28.

A contemporary scholarly article describing in factual detail, the sale of America's wartime merchant fleet for postwar commercial use by any purchaser, many residing abroad.

Container Ships

One of the major developments driving the evolution into our modern commercial fleets, was the emergence and construction of ever-larger "container ships," capable of carrying enormous amounts of easily-transferable goods, with a minimum number of crewmen.

McKesson, Chris B. *Alternative Powering for Merchant Ships: Task 1 — Current and Forecast Powering Needs.* Long Beach: California State University "Center for the Commercial Deployment of Transportation Technologies," 2000.

A specialized study on the remarkable growth in size and range of container ships, most particularly in Pacific waters.

Mercogliano, Salvatore R. "The Container Revolution." *Sea History* 114 (Spring 2006), pp. 8–11.

Brief biographical study of the U.S. trucking magnate Malcolm P. McLean, who created the first successful containership enterprise, spawning a host of modern imitators all around the globe.

Supertankers

Just as with freighters, the small and heavily manned tankers of World War II-vintages also went through a dramatic technological transformation during the latter half of the twentieth century, being superseded by gigantic supertankers manned by tiny crews.

Shields, Jerry. *The Invisible Billionaire: Daniel Ludwig*. Boston: Houghton Mifflin, 1986.

A biography of the U.S. shipping magnate Daniel K. Ludwig, known as "the father of the supertanker."

Santa Maria Hijacking (1961)

An early example of the divergent and unresolved international perspectives on piracy in the immediate post-World War II era, was demonstrated during the hijacking of the Portuguese luxury liner Santa Maria *in late January 1961, by a small band of opponents of its repressive Salazar regime. Despite killing an officer and being pursued initially as pirates, world opinion soon shifted in favor of the hijackers, who were allowed to surrender in Brazil a few days later and claim political asylum.*

Antão, Nelson Moreira, and Tavares, Célia Gonçalves. "Henrique Galvão e o assalto ao *Santa Maria*: Percurso de uma dissidência do Estado Novo e suas repercussões internacionais." *Sapiens: História, Património e Arqueologia* [Portugal], December 2008, pp. 84–110. Http://www.revistasapiens.org/Biblioteca/numero0/henriquegalvao.pdf.

Excellent scholarly article, describing the political circumstances prevailing in Salazar's Portugal, which had led to this dramatic confrontation at sea.

Fenwick, Charles G. "Piracy in the Caribbean." *American Journal of International Law* 55, Number 4 (October 1961), pp. 426–428.

Brief legal opinion written by an U.S. scholar in the immediate aftermath of this hijacking, deeming it to have been a piratical act, despite popular opinions to the contrary, both at home and abroad.

Raby, David. "Transatlantic Intrigues: Humberto Delgado, Henrique Galvão, and the Portuguese Exiles in Brazil and Morocco,

1961–62." *Portuguese Journal of Social Science* 3, Number 3 (December 2004).

Modern account of this hijacking, as well as its aftermath among the exiled opponents of the Salazar regime.

Zeiger, Henry A. *The Seizing of the* Santa Maria. New York: Popular Library, 1961. Found at SolantAmity.com.

A contemporary book rushed into print the same year of the hijacking, drawn from numerous newspaper accounts, yet well-compiled and carefully written.

Achille Lauro Hijacking (1985)

Bohn, Michael K. *The* Achille Lauro *Hijacking: Lessons in the Politics and Prejudice of Terrorism.* Dulles, VA: Brassey's, 2004.

A recent study of this 20-year-old incident and its repercussions into modern times.

Cassesse, Antonio. *Terrorism, Politics, and Law: The* Achille Lauro *Affair.* Cambridge: Polity Press, 1989.

English translation of an Italian work, originally published two years earlier in Rome by Editori Riuniti.

Constantinople, George R. "Towards a New Definition of Piracy: The *Achille Lauro* Incident." *Virginia Journal of International Law* 26 (1986), pp. 723–753.

One of numerous opinion-pieces written by legal scholars in the aftermath to this hijacking, attempting to judge its impact on the international standards regarding piracy.

Halberstam, Malvina. "Terrorism on the High Seas: The *Achille Lauro*, Piracy, and the IMO Convention on Maritime Safety." *American Journal of International Law* 82 (1988), pp. 269–310.

See above.

Pancracio, Jean-Paul. "L'affaire de l'Achille Lauro et le droit international." *Annuaire français de droit international* 31 (1986), pp. 219–236.

See above.

Paust, Jordan J. "Extradition and United States Prosecution of the *Achille Lauro* Hostage-Takers: Navigating the Hazards." *Vanderbilt Journal of Transnational Law* 20 (1987), pp. 235–257.

Article by an American legal scholar, debating the various international charges and complaints leveled against the U.S. Navy's interception of an Egyptian airliner over the Mediterranean, while it was flying toward Tunisia with the Achille Lauro's *four escaping Palestinian hijackers.*

Ronzitti, Natalino, editor. *Maritime Terrorism and International Law.* Dordrecht, The Netherlands: Martinus Nijhoff, 1990.

A compilation of articles and papers by eight different legal scholars, dealing with the issues raised in the wake of the PLO hijacking of the Italian liner Achille Lauro.

Simon, Jeffrey D. *The Implications of the* Achille Lauro *Hijacking for the Maritime Community.* Santa Monica, CA: The Rand Corporation, 1986.

Brief professionally oriented study, issued in the immediate aftermath of the seizure of this Italian liner.

Flags of Convenience

Alderton, Tony, and Winchester, Nik J. "Regulation, Representation, and the Flag Market." *Journal for Maritime Research* [UK], September 2002.

An excellent historical study of the modern evolution of "open" ship registers in diverse nations, by a pair of professional observers.

Carlisle, Rodney. *Sovereignty for Sale: The Origin and Evolution of the Panamanian and Liberian Flags of Convenience.* Annapolis, MD: Naval Institute Press, 1981.

Study by a Canadian historian, detailing how the registry of American vessels under the flags of Panama since 1919 and Liberia since 1948, was driven by a corporate desire to economize on taxes and labor expenses.

———. "Second Registers: Maritime Nations Respond to Flags of Convenience, 1984–1998." *The Northern Mariner/Le marin du nord* [Canada] 19, Number 3 (2009), pp. 319–340.

Modern update on this issue.

Ferrell, Jessica K. "Controlling Flags of Convenience: One Measure to Stop Overfishing of Collapsing Fish Stocks." *Environmental Law* 35 (2005), pp. 323–390.

Lengthy scholarly argument addressing this issue, with the aim of controlling one single international maritime problem.

Stanley, William R. "Serving Aboard the World's Largest Flag of Convenience Fleet: Some Geographical Implications Concerning Crew's Nationality." *GeoJournal* [The Netherlands] 7, Number 3 (May 1983), pp. 261–269.

Statistical compilation and analysis by an U.S. professor of Geography, of the seamen from more than 100 different nations already serving worldwide at that time aboard the 2,500 merchantmen flying the Liberian flag.

Toweh, Alphonso. "Shipping's Flag of Convenience Pays Off for Liberia." *Business Day* [South Africa], March 3, 2008.

Brief newspaper article describing the economic benefits derived from this policy, by one of its earliest practitioners.

Treves, Tullio. "Flags of Convenience before the Law of the Sea Tribunal." *San Diego International Law Journal* 6 (2004), pp. 179–189.

Legal article written by a judge who served as a founding negotiator of the UN's Convention on the Law of the Sea, as well as a Professor at the University of Milan, and presides over the Tribunal of the Law of the Sea at Hamburg, Germany.

Winchester, Nik J., and Alderton, Tony. *Flag State Audit 2003.* Cardiff: Seafarers International Research Centre, 2003.

Statistical investigation of the global shipping industry and its use of "flags of convenience," by a professional maritime organization.

Wing, Maria J. "Rethinking the Easy Way Out: Flags of Convenience in the Post-September 11th Era." *Tulane Maritime Law Journal* 28 (2003), pp. 173–190.

Editorial piece, questioning the prevalent commercial practice of registering merchantmen in foreign countries, and the security concerns which might arise.

Proliferation of Light Arms

Boutwell, Jeffrey; Klare, Michael T.; and Reed, Laura W., editors. *Lethal Commerce: The Global Trade in Small Arms and Light Weapons.* Cambridge, Mass.: American Academy of Arts and Sciences, 1995.

A single volume containing articles by nine different contributors, who examine "one of the most important and least studied international security problems of the post-Cold War era: the proliferation of small arms and light weapons in trouble spots around the globe," *attempting to suggest some controls and remedies.*

Choong, William. "Today's WMD of Choice—the AK-47." *The Straits Times* [Singapore], December 25, 2008, and *AsiaOne News*, December 27, 2008. Retrieved on February 2, 2010.

Newspaper article repeating salient points from Larry Kahaner's book AK-47: The Weapon That Changed The Face of War.

Fleshman, Michael. "Small Arms in Africa: Counting the Cost of Gun Violence." *Africa Recovery [since renamed "Africa Renewal," United Nations]* 15, Number 4 (December 2001). Retrieved on February 2, 2010 from http://africa_recovery@un.org.

General, yet informative article on the deleterious spread of military light weaponry from African lawless war zones passing into the hands of civilians, especially among the young.

Haydon, Peter T., and Griffiths, Ann L., editors. *Maritime Security and Conflict Resolution at Sea in the Post-Cold War Era.* Halifax, Nova Scotia, Canada: Centre for Foreign Policy Studies at Dalhousie University, 1994.

Compilation of scholarly papers delivered at a conference, dealing with the changing nature of modern maritime threats, partially attributable to more potent weaponry.

Hympendahl, Klaus. *Pirates Aboard!: 40 Cases of Piracy Today and What Blue-water Cruisers Can Do About It.* Dobbs Ferry, NY: Sheridan House, 2003.

Compilation of firsthand accounts by various pleasure yachters, of having been boarded by armed gangs at various places around the globe, primarily during the period 1995–2001.

Killicoat, Phillip. *Weaponomics: The Global Market for Assault Rifles.* Washington, D.C.: World Bank Policy Research Working Paper 4202, Post-Conflict Transitions Working Paper No. 10, April 2007. http://econ.worldbank.org

One of many studies published on the spread of such military weaponry.

Nyuydine, Ngalim E. "Outdated Laws as Impetus for Illicit Proliferation of Small Arms and Light Weapons in Cameroon."

Subtitled "Paper Presented on the Occasion of an Informative Session on the Fight Against the Proliferation of Small Arms in Cameroon," *before a meeting at Yaoundé of the Cameroon Youth and Students Forum for Peace.*

Smith, Chris. "Light Weapons Proliferation: A Global Survey." *Jane's Intelligence Review* 11, Number 7 (July 1999), pp. 46–51.

A brief summary of this problem.

Steel, David G. "Piracy: Can the Order of the Oceans Be Safeguarded?" *Journal of the Royal United Service Institute* [UK] 141, Number 1 (1996), pp. 17–25.

Article by a British naval Commander, describing the resurgence of piratical acts around the world, and the need for international cooperation in order to effectively police territorial waters.

Wu, Bin, and Winchester, Nik J. "Crew Study of Seafarers: A Methodological Approach to the Global Labour Market for Seafarers." *Marine Policy* 29, Number 4 (2005), pp. 323–330.

One of the few studies revealing the extent of economizing measures being adopted by modern shippers, of hiring diverse nationalities to man their merchantmen.

International Law

Documents

1982 UN Convention on the Law of the Sea, Done at Montego Bay on December 10, 1982, Entered into Force on November 16, 1994. Available online at: http://www.un.org/Depts/los/convention_agreements/texts/unclos/unclos_e.pdf.

IMO Assembly Resolution A.922(22): Code of Practice for the Investigation of the Crimes of Piracy and Armed Robbery against Ships, November 29, 2001. Found at: http://www.imo.org/includes/blastDataOnly.asp/data_id%3D23528/A922(22).pdf.

IMO Maritime Safety Committee Circular 622, Revision 1: Recommendations to Governments for Preventing and Suppressing Acts of Piracy and Armed Robbery against Ships, June 16, 1999. Available online through links at http://www.imo.org.

IMO Maritime Safety Committee Circular 623, Revision 3: Guidance to Shipowners and Ship Operators, Shipmasters and Crews, on Preventing and Suppressing Acts of Piracy and Armed Robbery against Ships, May 29, 2002. Available online through links at http://www.imo.org.

General Works

Agyebeng, William K. "Theory in Search of Practice: The Right of Innocent Passage in the Territorial Sea." *Cornell International Law Journal* 39 (2006), pp. 371–399.

Balkin, Rosalie. "The International Maritime Organization and Maritime Security." *Tulane Maritime Law Journal* 30 (2006), pp. 1–34.

Barry, Ian Patrick. "The Right of Visit, Search, and Seizure of Foreign-Flagged Vessels on the High Seas, Pursuant to Customary International Law: A Defense of the Proliferation Security Initiative." *Hofstra Law Review* 33 (2004), pp. 299–330.

Becker, Michael A. "The Shifting Public Order of the Oceans: Freedom of Navigation and the Interdiction of Ships at Sea." *Harvard International Law Journal* 46 (2005), pp. 131–230.

Bornick, Brooke A. "Bounty Hunters and Pirates: Filling in the Gaps of the 1982 U.N. Convention on the Law of the Sea." *Florida Journal of International Law* 17 (2005), pp. 259–270.

Bryant, Dennis L. "Historical and Legal Aspects of Maritime Security." *University of San Francisco Maritime Law Journal* 17 (2004–05), pp. 1–27.

Dahlvang, Niclas. "Thieves, Robbers, & Terrorists: Piracy in the 21st Century." *Regent Journal of International Law* 4 (2006), pp. 17–45.

Diaz, Leticia, and Dubner, Barry Hart. "On the Problem of Utilizing Unilateral Action to Prevent Acts of Sea Piracy and Terrorism:

A Proactive Approach to the Evolution of International Law." *Syracuse Journal of International Law and Commerce* 32, Number 1 (2004), pp. 1–50.

Lengthy article studying the parameters of both modern piracy and terrorism, and suggesting that where regional countermeasures against either may have failed, unilateral action might be justified in order to avert a larger catastrophe.

Dubner, Barry H. *The Law of International Sea Piracy.* The Hague: Martinus Nijhoff, 1980.

———. "Piracy in Contemporary National and International Law." *California Western International Law Journal* 21, Number 1 (1990), pp. 139–149.

Ellen, Eric. "Contemporary Piracy." *California Western International Law Journal* 21, Number 1 (1989), pp. 123–128.

Garmon, Tina. "International Law of the Sea: Reconciling the Law of Piracy and Terrorism in the Wake of September 11th." *Tulane Maritime Law Journal* 27, Number 1 (Winter 2002), pp. 257–275.

Goodman, Th. H. "Leaving the Corsair's Name to Other Times: How to Enforce the Law of Sea Piracy in the 21st Century through Regional International Agreements." *Case Western Reserve Journal of International Law* 31, Number 1 (1999), pp. 139–168.

Goodwin, Joshua Michael. "Universal Jurisdiction and the Pirate: Time for an Old Couple to Part." *Vanderbilt Journal of Transnational Law* 39, Number 3 (May 2006), pp. 973–1012.

Gutoff, Jonathan M. "The Law of Piracy in Popular Culture." *Journal of Maritime Law & Commerce* 31, Number 4 (October 2000), pp. 643–648.

Lighthearted article contrasting the legal records of early pirates, with their depictions in modern fictional accounts.

Jesus, José Luis. "Protection of Foreign Ships against Piracy and Terrorism at Sea: Legal Aspects." *The International Journal of Marine and Coastal Law* 18, Number 3 (2003), pp. 363–400.

Lodge, Michael W. "Improving International Governance in the Deep Sea." *The International Journal of Marine and Coastal Law* 19 (2004), pp. 299–316.

Lodge, Michael W., and Frank Meere. "High Seas Governance: Meeting of the High Seas Task Force, Paris, March 9, 2005." *Maritime Studies* 141 (March–April 2005), pp. 1–15.

Mellor, Justin S. C. "Missing the Boat: the Legal and Practical Problems of the Prevention of Maritime Terrorism." *American University International Law Review* 18 (2002), pp. 341–397.

Menefee, Samuel P. "Anti-Piracy Law in the Year of the Ocean: Problems and Opportunity." *ILSA Journal of International and Comparative Law* 5 (1999), pp. 309–318.

———. "Foreign Naval Intervention in Cases of Piracy: Problems and Strategies. *The International Journal of Marine and Coastal Law* 14, Number 3 (1999), 358–361.

———. "'Yo Heave Ho!': Updating America's Piracy Laws." *California Western International Law Journal* 21 (1990), pp. 151–179.

Noone, Gregory P., et alia. "Prisoners of War in the 21st Century: Issues in Modern Warfare." *Naval Law Review* 50 (2004), pp. 1–69.

Noyes, John E. "An Introduction to the International Law of Piracy." *California Western International Law Journal* 21 (1990), pp. 105–121.

Paust, Jordan J. "Essays on Piracy." *California Western International Law Journal* 21, Number 1 (1989), pp. 105–122.

Pugh, Michael C. "Piracy and Armed Robbery at Sea: Problems and Remedies." *Low Intensity Conflict and Law Enforcement* 2, Number 1, 1993.

———, editor. *Maritime Security and Peacekeeping: A Framework for United Nations Operations.* Manchester, England: Manchester University Press, 1994.

Rubin, Alfred P. *The Law of Piracy.* New York: Transnational Publishers, 1998; first published by the Naval War College in Newport, RI, in 1988.

A historical work by a legal scholar, which covers the origins and evolution of the concept of piracy, as well as the subsequent enactment and application of statutes to counter this crime, up to the mid-twentieth century.

———. "Revising the Law of 'Piracy.'" *California Western International Law Journal* 21 (1990), pp. 129–137.

Stiles, Ethan C. "Reforming Current International Law to Combat Modern Sea Piracy." *Suffolk Transnational Law Review* 27, Number 2 (2004), pp. 299–326.

Tiribelli, Carlo. "Time to Update the 1988 Rome Convention for the Suppression of Unlawful Acts Against the Safety of Maritime Navigation." *Oregon Review of International Law* 8 (2006), pp. 133–155.

Westcott, Kathryn. "Pirates in the Dock." *BBC News* [UK], May 21, 2009.

News report describing the wish expressed by the Dutch Foreign Minister, Maxime Verhagen, that captured Somali pirates be tried somewhere else than The Netherlands—such as Kenya—revealing the difficulties and expense being faced by numerous Western countries seeking to prosecute such prisoners.

Southeast Asia

Ahmad, Hamzah, and Ogawa, Akira, eds. *Combating Piracy and Ship Robbery: Charting the Future in Asia-Pacific Waters.* Tokyo: The Okazaki Institute, 2001.

Compilation of thirteen papers delivered at a conference to address this growing problem in Asian waters.

Amirell, Stefan Eklöf. *Pirates in Paradise: A Modern History of Southeast Asia's Maritime Marauders.* Singapore: Institute of Southeast Asian Studies, 2006.

Excellent modern study by a Swedish scholar from the Centre for East and Southeast Asian Studies, at Lund University,

Barrios, Erik. "Casting a Wider Net: Addressing the Piracy Problem in Southeast Asia." *Boston College International and Comparative Law Review* 28 (2005), pp. 149–163.

Legal arguments addressing the problems of cross-border raids and multinational seaborne traffic in this region.

Bateman, Sam. "Safety and Security in the Malacca and Singapore Straits." *Maritime Studies* 148 (May–June 2006), pp. 20–23.

Brief overview of the efforts to contain the problem of piracy in these waters.

Beckman, Robert C. "Combating Piracy and Armed Robbery against Ships in Southeast Asia: The Way Forward." *Ocean Development and International Law* 33, Numbers 3–4 (July–December 2002), pp. 317–341.

Analyzes the dramatic increase in reported incidents of piracy and armed robbery against ships in the Malacca Straits and Indonesian waters during 1998–2000, proposing various solutions to address this growing problem.

Bradford, John F. "Japanese Anti-Piracy Initiatives in Southeast Asia: Policy Formulation and the Coastal State Responses."*Contemporary Southeast Asia* 26, Number 3 (December 2004), pp. 480–505.

Description of the measured assistance offered by the government of Japan, to support regional efforts defending commercial traffic transiting through Southeast Asian waters.

Burnett, John S. *Dangerous Waters: Modern Piracy and Terrorism on the High Seas.* New York: Dutton, 2002.

Account written by a former United Press International reporter, after he was robbed aboard his own small vessel while sailing alone through the South China Sea, and later traversed the Malacca Straits aboard a supertanker as part of his research into the growing problem of modern piracy.

Chalk, Peter. *Grey-Area Phenomena in Southeast Asia: Piracy, Drug Trafficking, and Political Terrorism.* Canberra: Strategic and Defence Studies Centre, Research School of Pacific and Asian Studies, Australian National University, 1997.

Early study of criminality in those waters by an Australian scholar, who also works for the RAND Corporation and lectures in America.

———. "Contemporary Maritime Piracy in Southeast Asia." *Studies in Conflict and Terrorism* 21, Number 2 (1998), pp. 87–112.

Paper by an Australian professor describing the nature of piratical attacks up to that time in the region, main countermeasures taken, and possible future multinational actions to suppress this criminality.

———. "Low-Intensity Conflict in Southeast Asia: Piracy, Drug Trafficking, and Political Terrorism." *Conflict Studies* 1, Number 1 (1998), pp. 1–36.

See above.

Davis, Gregory S. "Piracy in Southeast Asia: A Growing Threat to the United States' Vital Strategic and Commercial Interests." Quantico, VA: U.S. Marine Corps Command and Staff College, 2002.

Thesis which suggests that Southeast Asian links to both piracy and Islamic fundamentalism, might allow a terrorist group to use a hijacked ship for an attack on U.S. shores.

Eadie, Edward N. "Relevance of International Criminal Law to Piracy in Asian Waters." *Maritime Studies* 136 (May–June 2004), pp. 21–33.

———. "Definitions of Piracy, Particularly That of the International Maritime Bureau." *Maritime Studies* 119 (July–August 2001), pp. 10–16.

Eklöf, Stefan. *Pirates in Paradise: A Modern History of Southeast Asia's Maritime Marauders.* Copenhagen, Denmark: NIAS Press, 2006.

General history of Southeast Asian piracy over the past quarter-century, examining the historical, social, political, and economic factors that have contributed to the resurgence of piracy in that region.

Freeman, Donald B. *The Straits of Malacca: Gateway or Gauntlet?* Montreal: McGill-Queen's University Press, 2003.

Ho, Phil Joshua, and Raymond, Catherine Zara, editors. *The Best of Times, the Worst of Times: Maritime Security in the Asia-Pacific.* Singapore: World Scientific and the Institute of Defence and Strategic Studies, 2005.

A single volume bringing together the views of various international specialists, discussing current trends relating to maritime security as they apply to Asia.

International Maritime Organization. "Cooperation in the Straits of Malacca and Singapore." *Maritime Studies* 150 (September–October 2006), pp. 15–19.

Johnson, Derek, and Valencia, Mark J., editors. *Piracy in Southeast Asia: Status, Issues, and Responses.* Singapore: Institute of Southeast Asian Studies, 2005.

Excellent compilation of articles by eight different contributors, summarizing the evolution and state of piratical activity in Southeast Asia until that time, as well as some suggested avenues for joint international countermeasures.

Keyuan, Zou. "Enforcing the Law of Piracy in the South China Sea." *Journal of Maritime Law and Commerce* 3, Number 1 (2000), pp. 107–117.

———. "Piracy at Sea and China's Response." *Lloyd's Maritime and Commercial Law Quarterly* (2000), pp. 365–376.

Liss, Carolin. "The Role of Private Security Companies in Securing the Malacca Straits." *Maritime Studies* 157 (November–December 2007), pp. 14–22.

———. "Maritime Piracy in Southeast Asia." *Southeast Asian Affairs 2003* (Singapore: ISEAS, pp. 52–68).

Menefee, Samuel Pyeatt. "Modern Asian Maritime Crime." *Mains'l Haul* 36, Number 4 (Fall 2000), pp. 50–54.

Mo, John. "Options to Combat Maritime Piracy in Southeast Asia." *Ocean Development & International Law* 33 (2002), pp. 343–358.

Nguyen, Anh Viet. "What Are the Political and Strategic Interests of Major Regional Players in Addressing Piracy and the Risk of Maritime Terrorism?" *Maritime Studies* 146 (January–February 2006), pp. 12–19.

Ong-Webb, Graham Gerard, editor. *Piracy, Maritime Terrorism, and Securing the Malacca Straits.* Singapore: Institute of Southeast Asian Studies, 2006.

———. *"Ships Can Be Dangerous Too": Coupling Piracy and Maritime Terrorism in Southeast Asia's Maritime Security Framework.* Singapore: Institute of Southeast Asian Studies, 2004.

Peterson, M. J. "Naval Forces and the Control of Piracy in Southeast Asia." *Naval Forces* 6, Number 1 (1995), pp. 58–60.

Raymond, Catherine Zara. "Malacca Straits: A High-Risk Zone?" *Maritime Studies* 143 (July–August 2005), pp. 18–19.

Richardson, Michael. "Conference Report: The 5th Tri-Annual IMB Meeting on Piracy and Maritime Security, Kuala Lumpur, Malaysia, June 29 and 30, 2004." *Maritime Studies* 140 (January–February 2005), pp. 22–27.

————. "The Threats of Piracy and Maritime Terrorism in Southeast Asia." *Maritime Studies* 139 (November–December 2004), pp. 18–21.

Richardson, Michael, and Mukundan, P. *Political and Security Outlook 2004: Maritime Terrorism and Piracy.* Singapore: Institute of Southeast Asian Studies, 2004.

Rosenberg, David, and Chung, Christopher. "Maritime Security in the South China Sea: Coordinating Coastal and User-State Priorities." *Ocean Development and International Law* 39, Number 1 (2008), pp. 51–68.

Salleh, Iskandar Sazlan Mohd, and Yassin, Mat Taib. "Southeast Asian Maritime Security Cooperation: Malaysian Perspectives and Recent Developments." *Maritime Studies* 137 (July–August 2004), pp. 28–30.

Schuman, Michael. "How to Defeat Pirates: Success in the Strait of Malacca." *Time*, April 22, 2009.

Sheppard, Ben. "Maritime Security Measures." *Jane's Intelligence Review*, March 1, 2003.

Sittnick, Tammy M. "State Responsibility and Maritime Terrorism in the Strait of Malacca: Persuading Indonesia and Malaysia to Take Additional Steps to Secure the Strait." *Pacific Rim Law & Policy Journal* 14 (2005), pp. 743–769.

Stuart, Robert. *In Search of Pirates: A Modern-Day Odyssey in the South China Sea.* Edinburgh and London: Mainstream Publishing, 2002.

An early investigative report by a journalist who traveled through Indonesia, inspired by the rising number of piratical incidents being reported out of the South China Sea and Straits of Malacca.

Tanter, Richard. "The Challenges of Piracy in Southeast Asia and the Role of Australia." *Nautilus Institute: Austral Peace and Security Network [Australia]*, Austral Policy Forum Paper Number 07-19A, October 25, 2007. Found at austral@rmit.edu.au.

Edited summary of a longer version of a paper delivered by the scholar Carolin Liss at the "Australia and Asia: Issues of Global Security" conference, held at the University of Western Australia on August 17,

2007. An excellent summary of the future challenges in the fight against piracy in Southeast Asia.

————. "The Roots of Piracy in Southeast Asia." *Nautilus Institute: Austral Peace and Security Network [Australia]*, Austral Policy Forum Paper Number 07-18A, 22 October 2007. Found at austral @rmit.edu.au

Edited summary of a longer version of a paper delivered by the scholar Carolin Liss at the "Australia and Asia: Issues of Global Security" *conference, held at the University of Western Australia on 17 August 2007. An excellent overview of the origins of piracy in Southeast Asia.*

Teitler, Ger. "Piracy in Southeast Asia: A Historical Comparison." Amsterdam: *Maritime Studies* 1, Number 1 (2002), from the Centre for Maritime Research.

Ünlü, Nihan. "Protecting the Straits of Malacca and Singapore against Piracy and Terrorism." *The International Journal of Marine and Coastal Law* 21 (2006), pp. 539–549.

Vagg, John. "Rough Seas? Contemporary Piracy in South East Asia." *The British Journal of Criminology* 35, Number 1 (1995), pp. 63–80.

Vietnamese Boat People: Pirates's Vulnerable Prey. New York: U.S. Committee for Refugees, 1984.

Warren, James F. "A Tale of Two Centuries: The Globalisation of Maritime Raiding and Piracy in Southeast Asia at the End of the Eighteenth and Twentieth Centuries." *ARI Working Paper Series* 2 (2003).

Young, Adam J. *Contemporary Maritime Piracy in Southeast Asia: History, Causes, and Remedies.* Singapore: Institute of Southeast Asian Studies, 2007.

Young, Adam J, and Valencia, Mark J. "Conflation of Piracy and Terrorism in Southeast Asia: Rectitude and Utility." *Contemporary Southeast Asia* [Singapore] 25, Number 2 (August 2003), pp. 269–284.

Scholarly paper differentiating between the aims of modern pirates and terrorists, suggesting that a single counterapproach will not address both problems, but rather that solutions should be tailored to each particular situation.

Zubir, Mokhzani, and Basiron, Mohd Nizam. "The Strait of Malacca: The Rise of China, America's Intentions, and the Dilemma of the Littoral States." *Maritime Studies* 141 (March–April 2005), pp. 24–26.

Brief editorial on the complicated international perspectives regarding this vital commercial waterway.

Somalia and Horn of Africa

Abdinur, Mustafa Haji. "Life in Somalia's Pirate Army." *National Post* [Canada], April 30, 2009.

English translation of a French report originally published by Agence France-Presse, *offering insights into the* "code of conduct" *allegedly observed by pirates, according to various members.*

Ahmed, Mohamed. "Somali Sea Gangs Lure Investors at Pirate Lair." *Reuters*, December 1, 2009.

Report describing the "piracy" *exchange created at Harardheere, for locals to invest funds toward future forays, and receive shares from ship ransoms.*

Bahadur, Jay. " 'I'm Not a Pirate, I'm the Saviour of the Sea.' " *The Times Online* [UK], April 16, 2009.

Interview conducted by a Canadian reporter with a pirate chieftain from Eyl, Farah Hirsi "Boyah" Kulan, in the immediate aftermath to the Maersk Alabama incident.

———. "The Pirate King of Somalia." *Globe & Mail* [Canada], April 26, 2009.

Interview with another notorious pirate chieftain from Eyl, Garaad Mohamud Mohamed.

Baldauf, Scott. "Pirates, Inc.: Inside the Booming Somali Business." *Christian Science Monitor*, May 31, 2009.

A thoughtful report on piratical forays out of Somalia, as well as the financiers financing such forays by teenage gunmen, by a reporter who interviewed a half-dozen captured pirates in Berbera, Somaliland.

Best Management Practices to Deter Piracy in the Gulf of Aden and off the Coast of Somalia. London: Commercial Crime Services division of the International Chamber of Commerce, 2009.

A manual compiled from numerous recommendations offered by diverse firms and groups involved in maritime traffic in the Indian Ocean; originally issued in February 2009, followed by a revised edition in August 2009.

Bohaty, Rochelle F. H. "Chemical Vessels Under Siege." *Chemical & Engineering News* 86, Number 34 (August 25, 2008), pp. 27–28.

Article in the American Chemical Society's industrywide journal, describing the seizure and ransom of the Japanese chemical-tanker Golden Nori *that previous year, plus other threats by pirates against similar vessels.*

"Council Joint Action 2008/851/CFSP of November 10, 2008 on a European Union military operation to contribute to the deterrence, prevention, and repression of acts of piracy and armed robbery off the Somali coast." Brussels: *Official Journal of the European Union* 12.11.2008, pp. L 301/33 to 37.

The official European Union act organizing the dispatch of an expedition codenamed Operation "Atalanta," to combat piracy off Somalia.

Countering Piracy Off the Horn of Africa: Partnership & Action Plan. Washington, D.C.: National Security Council, December 2008.

An update of American policy regarding anti-piracy measures off Somalia, revised by the George W. Bush administration after the November 2008 election of Barack Obama, so as to incorporate more cooperation with allied nations in this struggle.

Fisher, Jonah. "Somali Pirate Patrol: Day Five." *BBC News* [UK], February 23, 2009.

Brief article by a British reporter, describing incidents during a patrol of the Gulf of Aden by the Royal Navy frigate HMS Northumberland, *as part of an EU task force protecting UN humanitarian shipments.*

Fitzgerald, Nina J., editor. *Somalia: Issues, History, and Bibliography.* New York: Nova Science, 2002.

Offers a brief version of this nation's troubled history, the challenges after its government's collapse, plus a selective bibliography.

"French Warship Captures Pirates." *BBC News*, April 15, 2009.

British press report on the capture of eleven Somali pirates involved in an attack against the American container ship Liberty Sun, *plus other incidents; compiled from various sources.*

Gerges, Makram A. "The Red Sea and Gulf of Aden Action Plan—Facing the Challenges of an Ocean Gateway." *Ocean & Coastal Management* 45 (2002), pp. 885–903.

Hansen, Stig Jarle. *Piracy in the Greater Gulf of Aden: Myths, Misconceptions, and Remedies*. Oslo: "Report 2009:29" of the Norwegian Institute for Urban and Regional Research, 2009.

An excellent recent study commissioned by Norway's Ministry of Defence, which combines numerous field interviews with former Somali pirates, as well as a thoughtful statistical analysis.

Hess, Robert L. *Italian Colonialism in Somalia*. Chicago: University of Chicago Press, 1966.

One of the few English-language scholarly studies on this subject, compiled from archival materials in Rome, with little input from Somali sources.

Howden, Daniel. "Gaddafi's Forty Years in Power Celebrated with a 'Gallery of Grotesques.'" *Belfast Telegraph* [Northern Ireland], September 2, 2009.

Among the dignitaries invited to this celebration was the notorious Somali pirate chieftain, Mohammed Abdi "Afweyne" Hassan.

Knaup, Horand. "Prelude to Piracy: The Poor Fishermen of Somalia." *Der Spiegel Online* [Germany], April 12, 2008.

English translation of a report on the plight of Somalia's fishing industry, providing recruits for piracy.

"Lawless Tradition of Piracy off the Coast of Somalia." *The Guardian* [UK], November 18, 2008.

Brief article, succinctly summarizing the evolution of criminality off Somalia.

Menkhaus, Ken John. *Somalia: State Collapse and the Threat of Terrorism*. Oxford and New York: Oxford University Press for the International Institute for Strategic Studies, 2004.

Brief description of the disintegration of Somali government and its consequences.

———. "Dangerous Waters." *Survival: Global Politics and Strategy* [UK] 51, Number 1 (February–March 2009), pp. 21–25.

Knowledgeable article on the current state of Somali piracy in the wake of the hijacking of the Saudi supertanker Sirius Star.

Middleton, Roger. *Piracy in Somalia: Threatening Global Trade, Feeding Local Wars*. London: Briefing Paper AFP BP 08/02 published by Chatham House, headquarters of the Royal Institute of International Affairs, October 2008.

Mojon, Jean-Marc. "Harardhere: The Cradle of Somali Piracy." *Middle East Online* [UK], October 29, 2009.

Report describing how Mohamed Abdi "Afweyne" Hassan Hayir had transformed this sleepy fishing village into a major pirate lair, where a pair of middle-aged British yachters were being held captive, among others.

National Security Council. *Countering Piracy Off the Horn of Africa: Partnership & Action Plan*. Washington, D.C.: The White House, December 2008.

Brief review of this problem, as well as a renewed attempt at finding an effective remedy—signaling a shift in policy, as it was issued during the waning days of the Bush administration.

Otterman, Sharon, and McDonald, Mark. "11 Pirates Seized by French Navy." *New York Times*, April 15, 2009.

Brief report describing the capture of eleven Somali pirates involved in an attack on the American container ship Liberty Sun *and other passing merchantmen, by the French warship* Nivôse.

"Peril on the High Seas." *The Economist: Premium Content Online* [UK], April 23, 2008.

Brief editorial observation on the palpable shift of depredations from "traditional piracy hot spots," such as the Malacca Strait and Indonesia, to the waters off Somalia.

Perl, Raphael. *Terrorist Attack on the USS Cole: Background and Issues for Congress.* Washington, D.C.: Congressional Research Service, RS20721, January 30, 2001.

Piracy Off the Somali Coast: Workshop Commissioned by the Special Representative of the Secretary-General of the United Nations to Somalia, Ambassador Ahmedou Ould-Abdallah. Nairobi, Kenya, November 2008.

Raffaele, Paul. "The Pirate Hunters." *Smithsonian Magazine* 38, Number 5 (August 2007), pp. 38–44.

An early article, as public interest began to swing over from the war on terror to the growing problem of a resurgent modern piracy. Gives a detailed account of the capture by the USS Winston S. Churchill *of ten Somali pirates, and their subsequent trial in Kenya.*

Report S/2005/625 of the U.N. Monitoring Group on Somalia, Submitted to the Security Council on October 4, 2005. New York: United Nations Security Council, 2005.

An overview of the many difficulties besetting Somalia, especially the importation of weaponry, in spite of an arms embargo; includes mentions of its burgeoning problem with piracy.

Report S/2006/229 of the U.N. Monitoring Group on Somalia, Submitted to the Security Council on May 4, 2006. New York: United Nations Security Council, 2006.

A study of the continuing difficulties in Somalia, including a growing number of piratical forays; offers some valuable intelligence on the proliferation of weaponry, and other insights on the organization of pirate groups.

Report S/2008/769 of the U.N. Monitoring Group on Somalia, Submitted to the Security Council on December 10, 2008. New York: United Nations Security Council, 2008.

Another in-depth study of the problems in Somalia, including significant acts of piracy.

Robinson, Simon, with Xan Rice. "In Peril on the Sea." *Time Magazine*, November 7, 2005.

Excellent report on the hijacking in late June 2005 of the U.N.-chartered aid-ship Semlow, *off the Somali coast.*

Schofield, Clive. "Horn of Africa Conflicts Threaten US Anti-Terrorism Efforts." *Jane's Intelligence Review*, June 2004.

———. "Plaguing the Waves: Rising Piracy Threat off the Horn of Africa." *Jane's Intelligence Review*, July 2007.

"Somali Piracy: 'We're Defending Our Waters.' " *Mail & Guardian Online [UK]*, October 14, 2008.

English translation of an Agence France-Presse interview with Abdi Garad and other Somali leaders, describing and even justifying piratical hijackings, plus their economic impact in that impoverished nation.

"Somali Warlord Threatens to Try Crew of UN Ship." *Associated Press*, August 24, 2005.

Description of how the pirate ringleader Afweyne used a local Somali official to threaten to try a captive crew for illegal fishing and chemical dumping, in order to sharpen his ransom demands.

Tripodi, Paolo. *The Colonial Legacy in Somalia.* New York: St. Martin's Press, 1999.

USS Cole Commission Report. Washington, D.C.: U.S. Department of Defense, 2001.

Results of the investigation of the suicide bombing of the American warship Cole, *while at anchor in the port of Aden in Yemen on October 12, 2000. Recommends a proactive as opposed to a defensive response to these sorts of acts of maritime terrorism.*

Waagacusub Independent Somali Journalists. "The Boss of Somali Pirates Sighted in Libya." *Waagacusub Media* [Sweden], August 29, 2009.

Refers to the attendance at the 40th anniversary celebrations of Muammar Gaddafi ascension to power, by the Somali pirate chieftain Mohamed Abdi Hassan Hayir, more commonly known as "Afweyne."

Nigeria

Although often listed as a current world hot spot for piracy, this large West African nation is actually beset by violent incidents in some of its rivers and coastal waters, not piratical acts on any of its outlying seas. Specifically, disenfranchised ethnic groups living within its oil-rich Niger Delta—deprived of the bulk of export profits, while subjected to many of the most onerous environmental hazards—have unilaterally begun targeting passing vessels, both foreign and domestic, in an effort to extort funds.

Egede, Edwin. "The Nigerian Territorial Waters Legislation and the 1982 Law of the Sea Convention." *The International Journal of Marine and Coastal Law* 19 (2004), pp. 151–176.

Fabi, Randy. "Piracy Off Nigeria Delays Oil Projects." *Reuters UK*, January 29, 2009.

Report describing how a "wave of piracy off Nigeria's southern coast, is delaying offshore energy projects in the world's eighth-biggest oil exporter."

Gambrell, Jon. "With Rusty Ammo, Nigeria Fights Piracy." *Mail & Guardian Online* [UK], March 31, 2010.

Republication of a SAPA report, describing the material limitations of the few Nigerian naval craft patrolling against pirates; this same story was also picked up by the Associated Press.

L'Huillery, Jacques. "Nigeria Becomes World Piracy Hot-Spot." *Mail & Guardian Online* [UK], May 20, 2008.

English translation of a French report originally published by Agence France-Presse, describing a recent upsurge in depredations in Nigerian waters, which its government was ill-prepared to challenge.

Ojukwu, Chudi Nelson. "Arrest and Detention of Ships and Other Property in Nigeria." *Tulane Maritime Law Journal* 28, Number 2 (Summer 2004), pp. 249–269.

Article by a legal writer, explaining the applications of admiralty law in Nigeria, especially as it affects foreign vessels.

Sirius Star Seizure (November 2008)

At present, only newspaper- and other similar mass-media accounts have been published about the interception of this huge Saudi super-tanker, whose multimillion dollar ransom is believed to have inspired many more Somali forays.

Cramb, Auslan. "Sailor Tells of the Moment Pirates Captured the *Sirius Star.*" *The Daily Telegraph* [UK], January 29, 2009, http://www.telegraph.co.uk.

Personal interview with 53-year-old James Grady, Second Officer of this vessel, after his safe return home to Johnstone, Scotland.

Jamieson, Alastair. "Briton Captured by Somali Pirates on *Sirius Star* Tells of Fears." *The Sunday Telegraph* [UK], January 25, 2009, http://www.telegraph.co.uk.

Interview with 45-year-old Peter French, who was serving as Chief Engineer aboard the supertanker when it was captured by Somali pirates.

Karon, Tony. "Battling the Somali Pirates: The Return of the Islamists." *Time Magazine*, November 25, 2008.

Article describing the short-lived intervention in the Sirius Star *affair by the militant Somali movement al-Shabaab, who threatened to act toward the release of this captive tanker, because they deemed any seizure of a Muslim-owned vessel as running contrary to Islamic law.*

Leach, Ben. "Somali Pirates Who Hijacked Supertanker *Sirius Star* 'Demand Ransom of $25 Million.' " *The Daily Telegraph* [UK], November 20, 2008, http://www.telegraph.co.uk.

Details of the negotiation regarding the ransom demand itself, as well as growing concern among Western observers as to the mushrooming problem of Somali pirate hijackings.

Roberts, Lesley. "Hostage's Secret Pictures of £2 Million Ransom Drop on Ship Hijacked by Pirates." *Sunday Mail* [UK], February 1, 2009, http://www.dailyrecord.co.uk.

Diary excerpts and pictures covertly taken by Second Officer James Grady, giving a vivid and progressive portrayal of his two-month captivity at the hands of these Somali pirates.

Wadhams, Nick. "As Somali Pirates Get Bolder, Policing Them Gets Tougher." *Time Magazine*, November 19, 2008.

Report filed by an American reporter stationed in Nairobi, Kenya, describing the piratical capture of the Saudi supertanker Sirius Star, *and the expected consequences from such a high-profile action.*

Maersk Alabama Incident (April 2009)

"A Pirate Comes to New York." *The World Newser: ABC World News' Daily Blog*, April 21, 2009.

Initial news report of the arrival of the captive Abduwali Abdukhadir Musé, lone surviving Somali pirate of the attack on the Maersk Alabama, *to face trial in lower Manhattan.*

Bone, James. "*Maersk Alabama* Crew Return to U.S. to Tell of Somali Pirate Ordeal." *The Times Online* [UK], April 18, 2009.

British newspaper account, summarizing the events surrounding the near-capture of this American container ship, as well as the killing of three of its four pirate atackers, and the release of Captain Phillips.

Casella, Robin. "Seekonk Sailor Recalls Experience at the Helm of *Maersk Alabama*." *Taunton Daily Gazette*, June 25, 2009.

Report compiled by the GateHouse News Service of a talk given before the Rotary Club at Raynham, Massachusetts, by Chief Mate Shane Murphy of the Maersk Alabama; *including some biographical facts about his early seafaring background.*

Curran, John. "Mutiny: Crew Blames Richard Phillips, *Maersk Alabama* Captain, For Ignoring Pirate Warnings." *Huffington Post Online*, December 2, 2009.

Account reporting on the lawsuit launched by four ex-crewmen, angry to learn that their ship had been steered into pirate-infested waters, despite advance warnings. Others defend Captain Phillips's actions.

Davis, Paul. "Chief Mate on Pirated Ship Sought Adventure and Found It Off Somalia." *The Providence Journal Online*, April 14, 2009.

Reflective report on the participation of Chief Mate Shane Murphy during the Maersk Alabama *hijacking, written during its immediate aftermath; includes biographical information.*

"Don't Give Up the Ship!: Quick Thinking and a Boatload of Know-how Saves the *Maersk Alabama*." *Marine Officer* (Summer 2009), 18 pp.

One of the best eyewitness accounts of the hijacking, compiled from surviving crewmen; published in Washington, D.C., in the official magazine of the Marine Engineers' Benevolent Association.

Houreld, Katharine. "*Maersk Alabama* Seized: Somali Pirates Overrun Danish Ship." *Huffington Post Online*, April 8, 2009.

An early report, including family reactions to the news that Captain Richard Phillips was being held hostage by Somali pirates.

Kahn, Joseph P. "Uncharted Waters." *Boston Globe Online*, August 29, 2009.

Report on Capt. Richard Phillips, compiled more than four months after having survived his captivity by pirates while in command of Maersk Alabama. *Includes some biographical details, as well as philosophical reflections on his unsought fame.*

Murphy, Shane, as told to Sean Flynn. " 'I'm Your Worst F**king Nightmare.' " *GQ Online*, November 18, 2009.

Dramatic and detailed eyewitness account of the piratical seizure of the American-flagged container ship Maersk Alabama, *as recounted several months later by its second-in-command.*

"Pirates Demand Ransom as U.S. Captain's Escape Bid Fails." *France 24 International News*, April 10, 2009.

English-language version of a French press report, filed after the second day of the Maersk Alabama *standoff. Quotes statements by principal leaders, including shore-based pirate chieftain Abdi Garad.*

"Pirates Issue New Threat Over US Hostage." *Sky News Online* [UK], April 11, 2009.

British press report, filed at the end of the third day of the Maersk Alabama *standoff; includes statements by principal figures, among them the pirate chieftain Abdi Garad.*

"U.S. Navy Closes Grip on Somali Pirates." *Agence France-Presse*, April 8, 2009.

English-language version of a French press report, filed early during the Maersk Alabama *standoff. Quotes statements by principal leaders, including shore-based pirate chieftain Abdi Garad.*

Watts, Alex. "Backlash Fear After U.S. Navy Shoots Pirates." *Sky News Online* [UK], April 13, 2009.

British press report, filed at the conclusion of the Maersk Alabama *ordeal, includes threatening statements made by the pirate chieftain Abdi Garad.*

Glossary

He insists that he is not a criminal, but that he knows what he is doing is wrong.

—a Western reporter, after interviewing the
pirate chieftain Boyah of Eyl, April 2009

AFP   Initials of the French news service "Agence France-Presse," whose reporters are often involved in covering piracy stories around the Horn of Africa.

African credit card   Jocular expression in some parts of Africa, including the pirate lair at Harardheere, to describe an AK-47 assault-rifle, as in the advertised sense of "don't leave home without it."

AIS   Acronym for "Automatic Identification System," a transmitter featured on most large merchantmen, which is often switched off by Masters during transit through any pirate-infested stretches of ocean, as it will reveal their ship's position, course, speed, etc., to any nearby predators.

badaadinta badah   A Somali term literally meaning "saviours of the sea," which is most often rendered into English-language translations as "coast guard." Because of its positive connotations, this expression is preferred by pirates and often used—in several variants by different pirate groups—to lend a veneer of legitimacy to their depredations at sea.

burcad badeed   Somali term literally meaning "ocean robber" or "sea bandit," often used in official government circles to describe and denigrate that nation's pirates, who prefer much more-favorable labels such as *badaadinta badah*.

CCS   Acronym for "Commercial Crime Services," a division of the International Chamber of Commerce, which is headquartered in London, England.

CGPCS   Acronym for the multilateral "Contact Group on Piracy off the Coast of Somalia," established by the United Nations to coordinate

273

anti-piracy efforts among the various American, NATO, European Union, regional, and other naval forces patrolling the waters off the Horn of Africa. It has been criticized for only meeting sporadically, and not including the two main groups that are focal to this problem: owner-operators of the small coastal-craft that make up the bulk of victims in the Gulf of Aden, and the Somalis themselves.

CTF   Naval acronym meaning "Combined Task Force."

dhow   An ancient Arabic ship-design, still often seen today in the Indian Ocean, as well as in the Arab Sea, Red Sea, and Mediterranean. Such vessels have a characteristically high-swept bow and are usually of only 150–350 tons burthen, sometimes with a single mast stepped aft. Employed for centuries as coastal traders, they have been victimized in recent times by Somali pirates to serve as their mother-ships, towing their captors' skiffs hundreds of miles farther out into the main sea-lanes, so as to unsuspectingly approach transiting merchantmen.

DWT   Maritime abbreviation for "Dead-Weight Tonnage."

EU   Initials for "European Union," a political and economic alliance comprised of most countries in Europe.

EUNavFor   Acronym for "European Union Naval Force," a joint squadron organized in December 2008 to patrol the troubled waters off the Horn of Africa, as a supplement to other allied formations.

haram   Arabic expression meaning "religiously forbidden," piracy being considered *haram* according to Islamic teachings.

hawala   Ancient Arabic money-transfer system, mentioned in Islamic legal texts as early as the eighth century, whereby a person pays a sum to a *hawaladar* in one place, who instructs a colleague at another locale to issue a like sum to another person. These transactions are done entirely on the honor system, no paperwork being involved, and has provided a useful function for centuries. One of its few modern drawbacks is that it allows large sums of illicitly-obtained funds, such as multimillion dollar pirate ransoms, to vanish without a trace among unknown recipients.

ICC   Initials representing the "International Chamber of Commerce."

ICU   Acronym for the "Islamic Courts Union," an umbrella group of Sharia courts who united under Sharif Sheikh Ahmed during the summer of 2006 to seize power at Mogadishu and much of southern Somalia. Their fundamentalist Islamic beliefs led them to ban piracy at such notorious ports as Hobyo and Harardheere, producing a noticeable decline in offshore depredations that autumn.

However, because some were conservative extremists and harbored al-Qaeda refugees, the ICU were defeated by an Ethiopian-led and American-backed intervention that same December 2006. A moderate wing thereupon went into exile in Eritrea and Djibouti, while more hard-line factions splintered into armed groups such as al-Shabaab and

Hizbul Islam, fighting on against the Ethiopian occupation. The moderate faction returned to office in a power-sharing arrangement in January 2009, only to then be attacked by its former two partners, as Somalia's civil strife continued unabated.

IMB Acronym for the International Chamber of Commerce's "International Maritime Bureau."

IMO Acronym for the United Nations's "International Maritime Organization."

intermodalism Name given to container traffic, the modern method of transporting goods within standardized metal containers that can be seamlessly conveyed on either ships, trains, or trucks, greatly accelerating deliveries through such speedier loading and offloading.

IRTC Acronym for the "International Recommended Transit Corridor," an area lying between 12° North, 58° East, and 10° South, where foreign navies suggest that merchantmen remain during their passages through the Gulf of Aden or around the Horn of Africa, so as to remain within range of aerial and naval patrols. Westbound vessels should tend toward its northern side, eastbound ships toward its southern side.

ISC Acronym for the "Information Sharing Center," an agency set up under the United Nations' ReCAAP agreement, for Asian nations beset by piracy to pool their intelligence.

ISPS Initials standing for "International Ship and Port Facility Security."

Joint Islamic Courts See "ICU."

JWC Acronym for the "Joint War Committee" of Lloyd's Market Association, the branch of that insurance brokerage which assesses the dangers posed by piracy and other threats in world sea lanes, affecting the insurance premiums which are to be charged for transiting merchantmen.

khat **or** *qat* Name of a mildly addictive East African plant, whose bright-green leaves are chewed as a stimulant, while also repressing hunger; a favorite of Somali pirates, it is sometimes known as well as *miraa*. When the fundamentalist Islamic Courts Union movement banned *khat* on November 17, 2006 for the entire month of Ramadan, riots ensued at Kismaayo and other ports.

Kill-and-Go See "Mopol."

knot Ancient measurement of sea-speed, equivalent to 6,080 feet or 1.15 miles, known as a "nautical mile" (see below). Consequently, a motorboat speeding at 20 knots, is traveling at 23 miles per hour.

LTTE Acronym for "Liberation Tigers of Tamil Eeelam," more commonly known as the "Tamil Tigers," the insurgent group fighting to create an independent state on the island of Sri Lanka. Their hijackings and attacks against offshore shipping, including numerous violent assaults on neutral or civilian vessels, were denounced as acts of piracy by the Sri Lankan authorities and foreign agencies, yet defended as legitimate tactics by the Tigers themselves and their overseas allies.

MARLO Acronym for "Marine Liaison Office," operated by U.S. Naval Forces Central Command in Bahrain as a conduit of information between the allied Combined Maritime Forces or CMF, and the commercial-shipping community sailing in the Gulf of Aden and Horn of Africa region.

MFV Common maritime acronym for a "motor fishing vessel."

MMEA Acronym for the "Malaysian Maritime Enforcement Agency," the equivalent of that nation's Coast Guard, established in November 2005.

MoPol Acronym for Nigeria's "Mobile Police," a force which has been deployed into the Niger Delta to protect tankers and oil-installations against repeated depredations by disgruntled local residents; also known as the "Kill-and-Go" police.

mother ship Any larger vessel that transports extra men, supplies, or equipment for smaller boats to use as their seaborne base of operations, such as the flagship or supply-ship for a fishing or a whaling fleet. In the context of piracy, though, it is largely applied to vessels captured near shore by Somali brigands in light skiffs, who then compel their captives to tow their light craft farther out to sea into the main sea lanes, and wait there aboard these innocuous-looking prizes to prey upon unsuspecting merchantmen.

MSCHOA Acronym for the "Maritime Security Centre—Horn of Africa," the planning and coordination headquarters for the European Union naval squadron or EU NAVFOR "Atalanta," which was deployed into the Gulf of Aden and off the coasts of Somalia in December 2008 on antipiracy patrols.

MSPA Acronym for the "Maritime Security Patrol Area," a movable traffic-lane through the Gulf of Aden created on August 22, 2008 to be patrolled by U.S. and allied warships or aircraft, so as to afford transiting merchantmen some measure of protection against Somali pirates, until more a long-term solution could be instituted. See also "IRTC" above.

MV Common maritime designation for a "motor vessel" or merchant freighter.

NATO Initials of the "North Atlantic Treaty Organization."

nautical mile A slightly longer distance than the measurement used on land, being equivalent to 1.15 miles ashore (see "knot" above").

NVCG Acronym for Somalia's self-proclaimed "National Volunteer Coast Guard," actually a pirate group.

ONI   Initials of the "Office of Naval Intelligence," a branch of the U.S. Navy based in Washington, D.C., whose Civil Maritime Analysis Department regularly collates and analyses information on piracy from global sources, and posts a weekly "Worldwide Threat to Shipping Report."

phantom ship   Nickname for any unregistered or falsely-named merchantman, usually a vessel hijacked by pirates, which is then repainted and given a new identity, so as to be used for further criminal purposes such as smuggling. A not-infrequent occurrence in the South China Sea during the late 1990s.

PRC   Initials of the "Piracy Reporting Center" maintained in Kuala Lumpur, Malaysia, by the International Maritime Bureau out of London, England, so that its designation is also oftentimes given as "IMB PRC."

qat   See *khat*.

ReCAAP   Acronym for the "Regional Cooperation Agreement on Combating Piracy and Armed Robbery against Ships," a treaty which was concluded between sixteen Asian countries by the United Nations' International Maritime Organization in November 2004, to help facilitate joint efforts toward stemming piratical assaults.

RPG   Acronym for "rocket-propelled grenade," a shoulder-fired infantry weapon favored by pirates, because of its ability to intimidate commercial vessels.

saami sare   Somali term for the ransoms extorted to release captive vessels.

satang   Indonesian name for the boarding poles used by Southeast Asian pirates to board merchantmen at sea, which are assembled aboard their boats as they draw near to their victims by tying shorter lengths of bamboo together with twine, then attaching a hook at one end; final measurement can attain 65 feet in length.

sea robbery   A legal term used to describe attacks upon commercial vessels in ports or national waters, as opposed to acts of piracy, which are perpetrated upon the high seas, beyond any government's jurisdiction. According to international law, such inshore attacks are not true acts of piracy, but rather criminal assaults on vessels or crews, just as armed robberies may occur against truck drivers moving about a port area, and so sea robbery should be dealt with by the local police.

ship-rider   Term for a law-enforcement official from a third country, who travels aboard a foreign naval vessel to help determine any possible criminal charges for subsequent prosecution on land, of any persons detained at sea on suspicion of committing piracy or armed robbery.

SNMG   Naval acronym for "Standing NATO Maritime Group," the multinational squadrons regularly assembled from among all NATO navies for joint exercises or patrols.

Supreme Islamic Courts Council   See "ICU."

Tamil Tigers   See "LTTE."

TEU   Commercial acronym for "Trailer Equivalent Units," the enclosed, stackable metal containers used to transport most goods at sea. Today's international standards call for containers that measure 20 feet, 40 feet, or 45 feet in length, with a uniform width of eight feet, although some variations do exist in certain countries. The standard height is usually a maximum of eight feet, six inches, although some "high-cube" containers can measure as much as nine feet, six inches tall.

TFG   Initials for Somalia's "Transitional Federal Government."

UKMTO   Acronym for the "United Kingdom Maritime Trade Organization" in Dubai, described as "the first point of contact" for merchant ships transiting through the Gulf of Aden or around the Horn of Africa region. The UKMTO serves as an "interface" between merchant Masters and the military, maintaining round-the-clock radio communication with ships at sea so as to relay any distress calls or other emergency information directly to MSCHOA and other naval commanders.

ULCC   Acronym for "ultra-large crude carrier," the biggest class of supertanker, behemoths of more than 300,000-ton displacements, who cannot even enter most harbors.

Union of Islamic Courts   See "ICU."

VLCC   Acronym for "very large crude-carrier," the second-biggest class of supertanker, usually in the 100,000–250,000-ton range.

water curtain   The simultaneous discharge of all fire-fighting equipment over the side of a large merchantman, which in the event of approaching pirates, is intended to surround the ship with heavy streams of water so as to deter their small boats from coming close enough alongside to attempt to board.

WFP   Initials of the United Nations's "World Food Program," often spelled in the English fashion as "Programme."

Index

About the Author

David F. Marley is a naval historian who has lived and traveled extensively in Latin America and Europe and currently resides in Canada. His published works include ABC-CLIO's *Pirates of the Americas*, *Wars of the Americas*, and *Historic Cities of the Americas*.